terra australis 43

Terra Australis reports the results of archaeological and related research within the south and east of Asia, though mainly Australia, New Guinea and island Melanesia — lands that remained terra australis incognita to generations of prehistorians. Its subject is the settlement of the diverse environments in this isolated quarter of the globe by peoples who have maintained their discrete and traditional ways of life into the recent recorded or remembered past and at times into the observable present.

List of volumes in Terra Australis

terra australis 43

Journeys into the Rainforest

Archaeology of Culture Change and Continuity
on the Evelyn Tableland, North Queensland

Åsa Ferrier

Australian
National
University

PRESS

ANU
PRESS

Published by ANU Press
The Australian National University
Acton ACT 2601 Australia
Email: anupress@anu.edu.au
Web: press.anu.edu.au

National Library of Australia Cataloguing-in-Publication entry

Creator:	Ferrier, Åsa, author.
Title	Journeys into the rainforest : archaeology of culture change and continuity on the Evelyn Tableland, Tropical North Queensland / Åsa Ferrier.
ISBN:	9781925022872 (paperback) 9781925022889 (ebook)
Series	Terra australis ; 43
Subjects:	Human settlements--Queensland--Evelyn Tableland--Antiquities. Rain forests--Queensland--Evelyn Tableland--Antiquities. Aboriginal Australians--Queensland--Evelyn Tableland--Social life and customs. Excavations (Archaeology)--Queensland--Evelyn Tableland. Evelyn Tableland (Qld)--Antiquities.
Dewey Number:	305.89915

Terra Australis Editorial Board: Sue O'Connor, Jack Golson, Simon Haberle, Sally Brockwell, Geoffrey Clark

Cover design and layout by ANU Press

Contents

List of Figures

List of Tables

Acknowledgements

This monograph is for the most part based on my PhD research. Firstly, I would like to thank my PhD supervisors Richard Cosgrove and Susan Lawrence for their guidance and patience during my years as a PhD student at La Trobe University, Melbourne, and for their ongoing support and friendships. I thank La Trobe University for granting me a postgraduate scholarship, staff and fellow archaeology students for support and encouragement, and Ming Wei, Rudy Frank, Josara de Lange, Richard Fullagar and Peter Saad for much needed technical assistance. AIATSIS (G05/7051) and ANSTO (07/034) provided me with research grants and staff at the John Oxley Library, Brisbane, California Academy of Sciences, San Francisco, CSIRO Atherton, and the Ravenshoe, Cairns and Eacham Historical Societies provided valuable research assistance for which I thank them. The research presented complements results from archaeological research carried out in the ARC-funded (DP0210363) *Toxic Harvest* project, directed by Richard Cosgrove and Judith Field. I thank them for giving me the opportunity to work on the Urumbal Pocket archaeological assemblage as a component of my PhD.

A project of this scale cannot be undertaken without the support of many people. I especially want to thank my family, Brad and Ned, for their love and patience and unwavering support. My son Ned inspires me to work that little bit harder when things get tough. His positive outlook on life, his love for learning and his sensible ways makes him wise beyond his years. I cannot thank my mother Ingrid enough for travelling from Sweden on numerous occasions when I needed her. Without her help, this book would not have been written. Thank you to Deanna and Ron Stager for their generosity and hospitality over many years. Thank you to Dale Owen and Toni Dunscombe for many hours of volunteering in the field and in the lab, the excavation teams, Jillian Garvey for her help during a few intensive pre-submission days, and to Jennie Eagle, Julie Butcher and Margaret Bufton for their support on the home front. I am grateful to Josara de Lange, Jon Luly, Peter Kershaw, Sean Ulm and David Frankel for providing constructive comments, and Duncan Ray and Ross Brown for valuable guidance and introductions in far north Queensland. The monograph was greatly improved from formal editorial advice provided by two anonymous reviewers, *Terra Australis* editorial committee members Sue O'Connor and Sally Brockwell and copyeditors Ursula Frederick and Katie Hayne.

My authority to write on traditional *Jirrbal* culture and society was granted to me by the late *Jirrbal* elders Maisie Barlow, Fred Barlow, Lizzie Wood and Lena Mitchell, as well as Elisabeth Cashmere. It was a privilege to work with them and record their stories, and to be able to fulfil their wish to share and preserve them for future generations of *Jirrbal* people. My principal informant Maisie Barlow passed away in 2013 at the age of 91. Maisie was a kind, forgiving, intelligent and generous person who invited me, her daughter from the south as she used to call me, into her traditional country and home. She called me *gungagarr*, kookaburra, because I always laughed a lot when we spent time together. I dedicate this monograph to the memory of my friend Maisie *Yarrkali* Barlow.

Åsa Ferrier, Melbourne 2015

1

Research Framework

Introduction

The archaeology of far north Queensland's rainforest region has up until recently received relatively scant attention from Australian archaeologists. This is hardly surprising as rainforests are difficult to work in as a result of high rainfall, difficult terrain and dense vegetation. This monograph is concerned with the archaeology of Aboriginal–European contact in a previously unexplored area of far north Queensland's rainforest region, investigating whether the application of a longitudinal (temporal) framework can produce useful new perspectives in the interpretation of the pre- and post-contact archaeological record. The contact and post-contact periods are a time when massive change and transformation took place for Aboriginal populations across the Australian continent and the only period in Aboriginal history for which documentary records exist. Research into contact archaeology, the recording and analysis of cross-cultural encounters in Australia, has expanded during the last two decades. The research presented here contributes to this growing interest.

This monograph presents interdisciplinary research that draws on archaeological evidence from three open Aboriginal occupation sites on the Evelyn Tableland, situated within the Wet Tropics World Heritage Area in tropical far north Queensland. All three archaeological sites investigated are considered 'traditional'; meaning here that they were used long-term, i.e. before Aboriginal–European contact took place in this area in the late nineteenth century, as well as in the post-contact period. Also presented is ethnohistorical information and oral history gathered during informal talks with Aboriginal elders and European descendants, assisting with interpretations of the pre- and post-contact archaeological records.

Study location and cultural setting

The research presented here is concerned with an area on the Evelyn Tableland, which is part of the larger Atherton-Evelyn Tableland region (referred to as the Tablelands in the text) (Fig. 1.1). At the time of European settlement, the Tablelands were predominantly occupied by *Dyirbal* people of three Aboriginal groups: the *Mamu*, *Ngadjon* and *Jirrbal* people, as well as the Tableland *Yidinjii* people in the north. The *Girramai*, *Gulngai* and *Djiru* Aboriginal people in the area southeast of the Evelyn Tableland are closely related to the *Jirrbal* people, with only slight differences in dialect separating the four groups (Dixon 1972). Before European arrival, *Girramai*, *Gulngai* and *Djiru* Aboriginal people lived predominantly on the coastal plains and utilised coastal resources. Some smaller groups also inhabited the rainforest region in and around the Tablelands as well as the coastal lowlands (Dixon 1972). Historical and linguistic evidence (Dixon 1972; Tindale 1974; M. Barlow, pers. comm., 2001) suggests that the rainforest and the archaeological sites investigated for this research project was home to the *Jirrbal* people at the time of Aboriginal–European contact (Fig 1.2). It has previously been suggested that the location of traditional *Jirrbal* territory, which includes areas of rainforest and open sclerophyll forest areas to the west of the rainforest region, was such that the *Jirrbal* people had access to resources from these two very different environments (Birtles 1997a, 1997b; Ferrier 1999; M. Barlow, pers. comm., 2004).

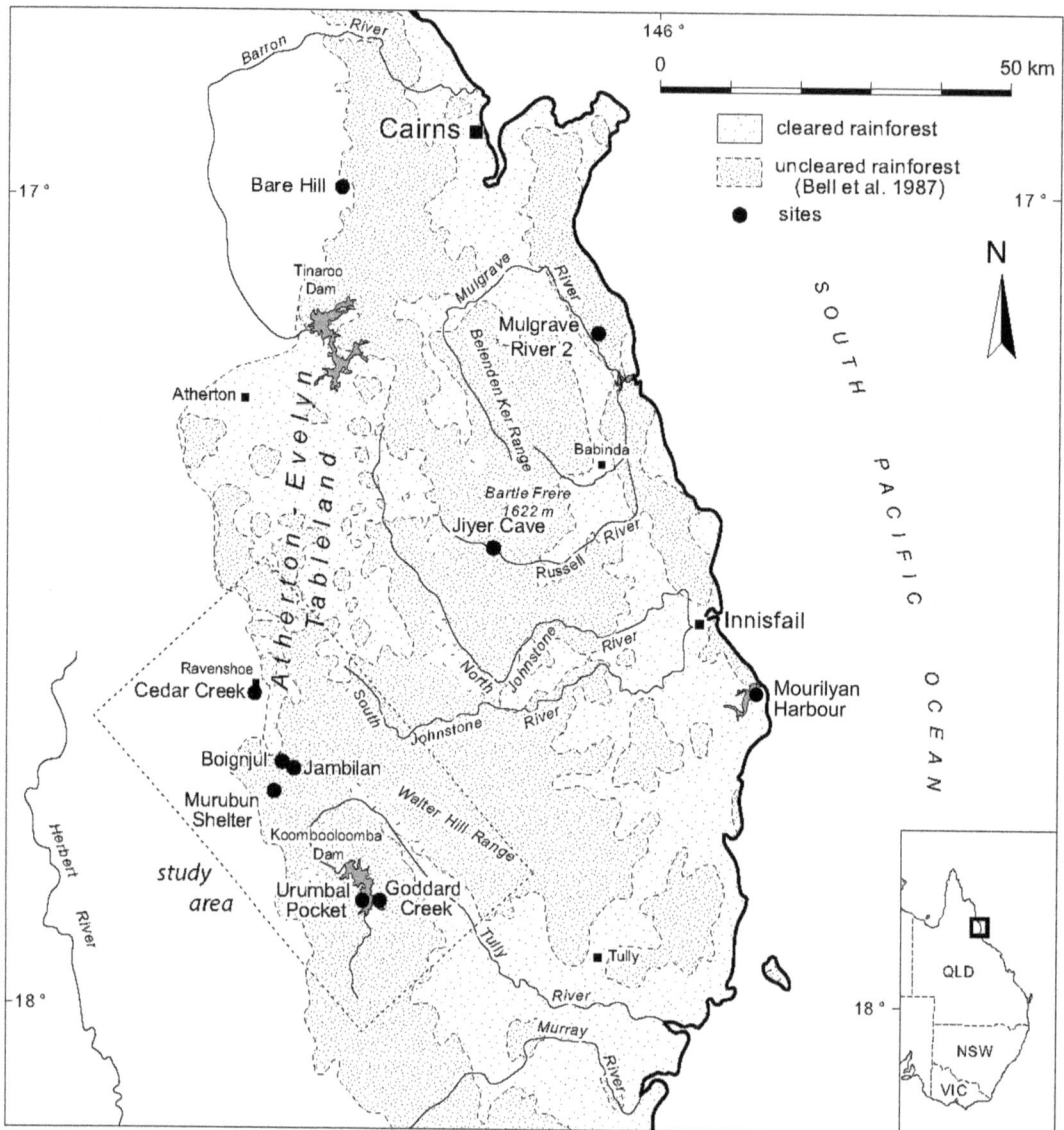

Figure 1.1 Map showing the location of the Atherton-Evelyn Tablelands in the rainforest region of far north Queensland, the study area in the southwest part of the Evelyn Tableland, and archaeological sites and other places mentioned in the text.

Source: Adapted from Cosgrove et al. 2007.

Ethnohistorical information (e.g. Ferrier 2002, 2006; Lumholtz 1889; Mjöberg 1918, 1923, 1925; Roth 1898, 1900, 1901–10), linguistic studies (Dixon 1972, 1991; Dixon and Koch 1995), archaeological studies (Cosgrove 1979, 1984, 1996, 2005; Cosgrove et al. 2007; Horsfall 1987, 1990, 1996) and studies on Aboriginal subsistence strategies (Ferrier and Cosgrove 2012; Harris 1978, 1987; Pedley 1992, 1993; Tuechler 2010; Tuechler et al. 2014) all provide important information on Aboriginal rainforest occupation and use of the Tablelands in the past. From this information, it appears that at the time of European contact, Aboriginal rainforest people exploited a diverse range of rainforest plant and animal species for subsistence as well as for the manufacture of artefacts, many of which are unique to the rainforest area. Some evidence suggests that campsites and rainforest tracks were regularly burnt to keep them clear of vegetation (Ritchie 1989:22; Tindale 1941:III). The existence of large eucalypt pockets within core rainforest also allowed for the establishment of semi-permanent campsites and large ceremonial gatherings to take place at certain times of the year (Mjöberg 1913, 1918).

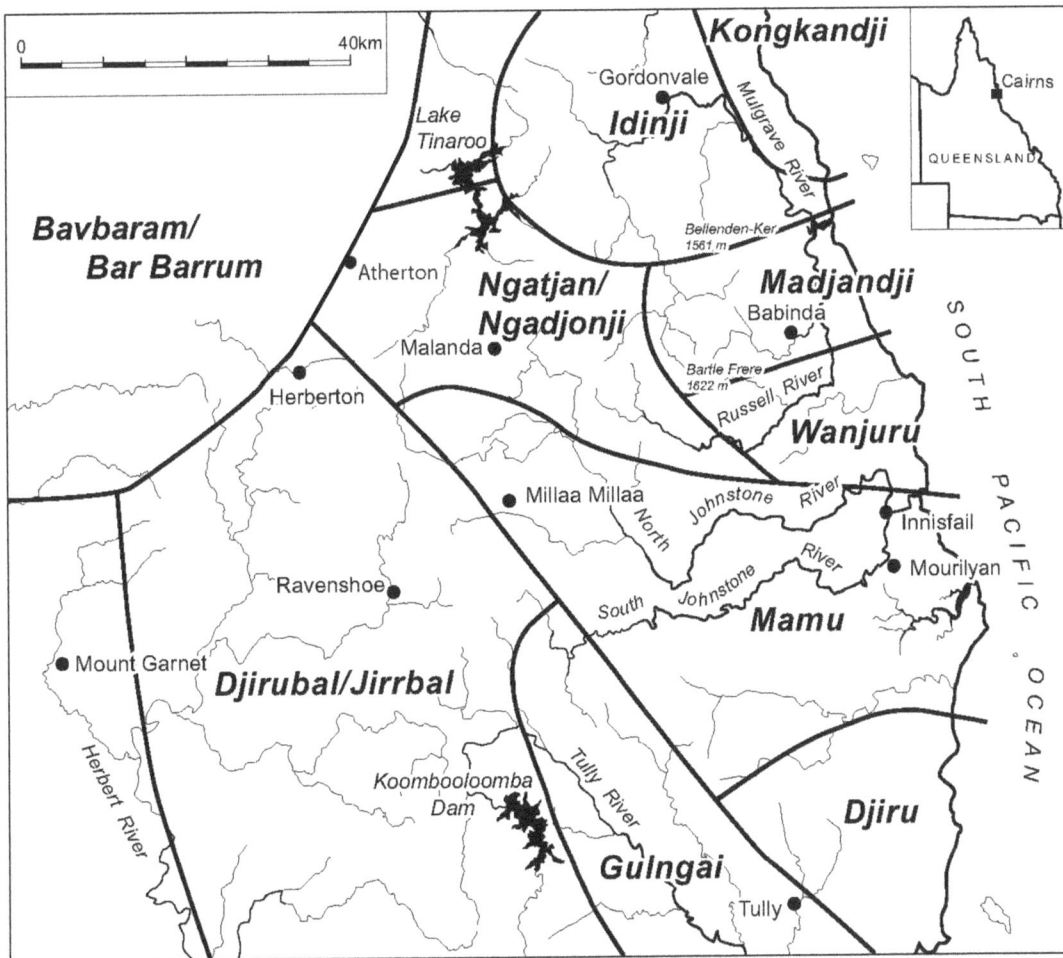

Figure 1.2 Rainforest tribes belonging to the *Dyirbal* Aboriginal language group discussed in the text and some of its neighbours. Tribal boundaries are estimates only.

Source: After Tindale 1974.

The development of contact archaeology in Australia

Early research into contact interactions

Up until the 1990s, research into Aboriginal and European contact interactions in Australia were predominantly the realm of historians. Reynolds' early influential works on frontier contact, framed around a European dominance–Aboriginal resistance model, depicted a violent frontier with Aboriginal people actively resisting European incursion (e.g. Reynolds 1972, 1990). Reynolds' work highlighted, for the first time, that in many instances Aboriginal people encountering Europeans were prepared to fight for land regarded as *terra nullius* by the colonising Europeans but which was existentially important to the Indigenous owners. As an outcome of Reynolds' work, many historical studies of contact interaction adopted the dominance–resistance model to specific situations and time periods (for example, Loos 1982; Morris 1989).

Regional studies

The focus in historical studies of contact gradually shifted away from the frontier to smaller regional studies, highlighting variability and complexity in Aboriginal responses to Europeans. For example, Attwood's (1989) research in Gippsland, Victoria, demonstrated that as a result of Aboriginal strategies of avoidance and indifference, only minor violent incidents occurred and Aboriginal people and Europeans managed to coexist. Williamson (2004:186) has suggested that the trend for early historical contact research to concentrate on particularistic studies—a trend persisting up until the late 1980s—may be seen as a feature of a disciplinary divide between archaeology and history. Finding a way to sensitively integrate archaeological data with documentary sources to write history continues to be a challenge in historical and contact archaeology generally.

Early studies in contact archaeology

One of the first contact archaeology studies in Australia was Allen's 1969 (2008) study of Port Essington, a historic site located on the Cobourg Peninsula, now in the Garig Gunak Barlu National Park, Northern Territory. In his exploration of this European military frontier settlement, he used both archaeological and historical data to investigate Aboriginal–European interactions as well as post-European Aboriginal behaviour at the site, with the aim of producing a history of Port Essington constructed from all of the available sources. Allen's research was groundbreaking within the context of Australian archaeology in many ways. It was the first PhD dissertation in Australian historical archaeology and the first to actively explore contact archaeology and the history of a particular place (Murray 2000:145; 2008:xi; Williamson 2004:184). Another early example of contact archaeology research and the use of diverse sources of information is McBryde's (1978) attempt to reconstruct cultural history in northeast New South Wales using ethnographic information. This study affirmed the value of literary sources in documenting culture at the very moment of change. Another early example is a study by McKnight (1976), in which the archaeology of contact between Macassan trepangers and Aboriginal people on the northern Australian coastline was documented. Early investigations into contact archaeology thus tended to focus on the earliest contact experience, and Allen's work aside, tended to model Aboriginal history as a single evolutionary process rudely halted by the arrival of Europeans. Overall, these archaeological studies are descriptive and particularistic rather than analytical with a focus on describing artefacts (see also Coutts et al. 1977; Rhodes 1986).

Proliferation of approaches to contact archaeology research

A proliferation of approaches to contact archaeology research has emerged over the last two decades, approaches that look beyond brief episodes of Aboriginal–European contact. Current research in contact archaeology is modelled upon a combination of innovative theory, new forms of data and alternative interpretations. Some of the sources that have been employed in more recent contact research include ethnographic collections (Ferrier 1999, 2002; Taçon et al. 2003), oral traditions (Clarke 1994, 2000), explorers' diaries and photographs (Birmingham 2000; Lydon 2002) as well as contact artefact assemblages (e.g. Carver 2005; Courtney and McNiven 1998; Harrison 2002; Wolski and Loy 1999). Archaeological research that uses concepts of continuity and change in constructing contact has also been employed in several rock art studies (e.g. Frederick 1999; May et al. 2010). Also influential in the development of contact archaeology is the development of Indigenous land rights and native title claims. This has resulted in a shift in emphasis away from prehistoric research, the results of which are difficult to use to demonstrate the continued links to traditionally owned lands as required in native title claims (e.g. Lilley 2000; Riches 2002). Consequently, a greater emphasis has been placed on research into the contact period and on the specific histories of Indigenous communities. However, it has been noted in assessments of the potential role of contact archaeology in native title determinations, that there is a lack of archaeological data and also issues surrounding what a contact material culture record look like (Fullagar and Head 1999, 2000; Harrison 2000, 2005; McDonald 2000; Veth 2000). In addition, the emphasis on Aboriginal pre-European traditions and continuity, and the ways they are interpreted in the Native Title Act, has demonstrated that to allow for Indigenous land rights in the future the Act needs to be changed to acknowledge that Indigenous communities have transformed both prior to and after European contact.

European-controlled sites and traditional sites

A review of Aboriginal–European contact archaeology research in Australia reveals that two main approaches have developed over the last two decades: integrated studies into culture contact at European-controlled sites, and studies that cover a long period of time and focus on culture change and continuity at traditional Aboriginal sites. Archaeological studies of Aboriginal–European interaction have mostly focused on European-controlled sites that contain Aboriginal artefacts and sites where Aboriginal occupation and Aboriginal–European interaction is historically documented. An early example is Birmingham's 1992 study at *Wybalenna*, an Aboriginal post-contact establishment on Flinders Island, Tasmania. Examples of other investigations at European-controlled sites include that of Brown et al. (2002) at the Ebenezer Mission cemetery, a study by Lydon (2002) of historical photographs from *Coranderrk* Aboriginal Station, and Paterson's study of Aboriginal–European culture contact at Strangways Springs Station in northern South Australia (2008). In a study by Porter (2003) of historical artefacts from Blackfellows Waterhole, a contact period site in western Victoria associated with historical documentation, it was demonstrated that the interpretation of the site was restricted by the ephemeral nature of the contact archaeological record. Porter's study highlights the generally ephemeral nature of contact archaeological records at European-controlled sites with documented Aboriginal occupation. The historic documentary record is often given precedence and, as a result, particular aspects of the colonial relationship are emphasised. Aspects of change in Aboriginal material culture as a result of European colonisation are also emphasised, whereas change and continuity in other aspects of Aboriginal culture are not often addressed. Archaeological investigations of the contact period that highlight changes and continuities in traditional Aboriginal material culture and society related to the process of Aboriginal–European contact are less common (Colley and Bickford 1995:13). However, analyses of Indigenous responses to contact situations that cover longer time periods than the actual moment of contact have been applied in culture contact studies locally (e.g. Clarke 1994, 2000; Colley 2000; Torrence and Clarke 2000:6) and internationally (e.g. Cusick 1998; Lightfoot 1995; Trigger 1983).

Investigating long-term Aboriginal history

Murray (1996a, 2000 and 2004) has suggested that contact archaeology has the potential to explore notions of 'shared histories' and investigate aspects of 'shared' experiences of colonialism in Australia. Several contact archaeology studies more interested in the long-term influences and effects of European settlement on Aboriginal people have moved away from the earliest contact period and instead focused on the entangled historical archaeology of both Aboriginal and European settlers (e.g. Clarke and Paterson 2003; Harrison and Williamson 2002; Torrence and Clark 2000). Murray's 'shared histories' model was applied by Harrison (2002) in contact archaeology studies in the southeast Kimberley and NSW regions. Harrison argued for two interrelated avenues of archaeological research in Australia as a powerful tool for understanding pre- and post-contact history: the 'shared' histories and archaeologies of post-AD 1788 Australia, and the relationship between these shared pasts and the long-term trajectories of Aboriginal Australia (Harrison 2002:38). This theme also emerged in a study by Head and Fullagar (1997) on the nature of the pastoral industry. Results from their research suggested that Aboriginal people in the northern Australian pastoral industry were able to maintain social obligations and attachments to particular places because of seasonal work activities in the tropics. Archaeological data, such as stone artefacts and ochre used for rock art, demonstrated continuities in the use of pre-contact sites into the post-contact period. These studies show the potential for investigations of long-term continuity and change in Aboriginal societies.

Another example of a long-term contact archaeology study is Colley's (2000) investigations into a rock shelter located in coastal NSW, which demonstrated that the archaeological record provides evidence for Indigenous people continuing to pursue key elements of their traditional lifestyle after European colonisation. Colley (2000:292) hypothesised, from the depth and nature of the deposits, a possible indication of change to a more intensive use of the rock-shelter following

European contact. In studies by Clarke (1994, 2000), trajectories of change and continuity in settlement and subsistence patterns on Groote Eylandt were investigated across a time period spanning the late Holocene to the present day. Clarke argued that recent archaeological sites can contribute to an overall understanding of the material correlates of short-term social change and that, at the level of landscape, they provide a powerful statement about the continuities, discontinuities and changes in hunter-gatherer land use practices within the social and historical context of encounters with outsiders (Clarke 2000:145). By constructing a regional case study, Clarke demonstrated change in settlement patterns during the period of Macassan–Aboriginal interactions on Groote Eylandt, as well as change and continuity in the archaeological record.

It has been suggested that one way to approach the writing of an Aboriginal history that encompasses the pre-contact, contact, and post-contact periods is through exploring the notion of trajectories defined as temporal sequences of transformations in culture systems (Clarke 1978; Williamson 1998 and 2004:191). Thus, rather than tracking a single evolutionary process halted by the arrival of Europeans, a sounder way of writing Aboriginal history may be to explore and trace 'cultural trajectories' and interpretive possibilities. This temporal approach to writing Aboriginal history allows for an integration of the archaeological and historical records and is applied in the research presented here.

Archaeology of the mid- to late Holocene period

Previous archaeological research in north Queensland's rainforest region suggests that a regional change took place in the mid- to late Holocene period, and it is in this time period that rainforest occupation and use appears to have become more permanent for the first time (Cosgrove et al. 2007; Ferrier and Cosgrove 2012; Horsfall 1987). A summary of Australian archaeological research related to this time period is presented to establish a baseline of archaeological knowledge for the research presented here. The start of the Holocene period has recently been formalised at 11,700 BP (Walker et al. 2009), however, the generally accepted meaning of the mid- to late Holocene period in Australian archaeological discourse is that it encompasses the last 5,000 years. The vast majority of archaeological sites recorded in Australia date to within this time period (Flood 1992:246; Williams 2013). This concentration has led a number of archaeologists to conclude that from around 5,000 years ago there was an increased intensity of Aboriginal occupation of the continent. It is around this time that the discard rates of archaeological materials within sites start to increase, intensities of regional land use increase, and previously little-used environments or resources become more systematically exploited (e.g. Barker 1991; Lourandos 1983, 1985; O'Connor 1992; Ross 1981).

Late Holocene intensification

Lourandos' influential work (1977, 1985, 1997; Lourandos and Ross 1994) challenged the early, static frameworks of Aboriginal history, which emphasised early cultural continuity and conservative exploitation of an apparently harsh environment. He promoted research on sites dated to the mid- to late Holocene period in order to detect and explain evidence of cultural change identified in material culture found in the archaeological record. In his explanations for change, Lourandos emphasised social factors and proposed an overall continent-wide process of socioeconomic intensification, predominantly based on evidence from southwest Victoria (Lourandos 1983, 1985). With this approach, Lourandos modelled trajectories on gross characteristics of the archaeological record and emphasised widespread cultural continuities within changing structures (Ulm 2004:191). In response, alternative frameworks were put forward to describe and analyse the processes affecting the nature of the archaeological record across the continent. These include site preservation factors, environmental change, population growth and the introduction of new technologies (e.g. Beaton 1985; Bird and Frankel 1991a; Frankel 1993; Hiscock 1986; Rowland 1999). Frankel (1991:147) argued that explanations of cultural change involving a single process of intensification puts limits on the characterisation of regional and local variability. Instead, changes within particular sites or regions should be viewed as largely independent, and archaeological evidence should be explained without reference to an overall continental scale model. Studies of archaeological databases (e.g. Bird and Frankel 1991b; Holdaway and Porch 1995) have also revealed a more complex picture than can be accommodated by a continental narrative, with the use of sites, places, landscapes and regions changing through time.

Research at a regional level

Ulm (2004:192) reflects on previous and current themes in the archaeology of mid- to late Holocene Australia and the constraints on understanding the archaeology of this period. He argues that in Lourandos' and others' use of generalised chronologies, and in the synthesis of evidence from distinctly different Holocene trajectories, unique regional patterns and trajectories are made insignificant as sites and regions are linked into a continental narrative. He discusses several detailed studies that emphasise long-term variability of behavioural responses to environmental change at the regional level across the continent: on the southeast Cape York Peninsula (David and Chant 1995), in the arid zone (Smith 1993; Veth 1995, 1996) and in southeast Queensland (Ulm and Hall 1996). These studies demonstrate that an examination of the basic assumptions underlying archaeological studies at the continental scale is important (e.g. Bird and Frankel 1991a; Hiscock and Attenbrow 1998; Holdaway et al. 2002). In a discussion of Holocene environmental variability, Rowland (1999) proposed that interpretations of cultural change should be reassessed in relation to improved knowledge of Holocene environmental change. Global climate oscillations occurred throughout the Holocene, but understandings of Holocene environmental variability have not yet been fully explored in the Australian archaeological context (Rowland 1999:11). The theme of exploring human–environment interactions and cultural change in response to environmental variability in the Holocene period has also been a focus of more recent research (e.g. Bourke et al. 2007; Brockwell et al. 2013; Haberle and David 2004). To further resolve the relative importance of climatic, environmental, and cultural changes on human activity and the archaeological record, high-resolution palaeoenvironmental sequences, studied in association with fine-resolution archaeological sequences, are clearly required.

The archaeological record of the last 5,000 years demonstrates that cultural changes were taking place in Aboriginal societies on the Australian continent. It appears that marginal areas like the rainforest region were occupied on a more permanent basis for the first time (Cosgrove et al. 2007; Ferrier and Cosgrove 2012), desert areas were periodically abandoned (Smith 1993; Veth 1995, 1996), people were possibly establishing semi-permanent camps in the western district of Victoria (seen archaeologically as mounds) and major technological changes took place (Cosgrove et al. 2007; Frankel 1991; Holdaway et al. 2002; Mulvaney and Kamminga 1999). These are developments, inventions and alterations that took place in dynamic Aboriginal societies, though not necessarily in a directional manner (Frankel 1991:148).

Research approach, objectives and methods

The research presented here is a study in contact archaeology. It investigates the potential of applying an analytical framework that takes a temporal and interdisciplinary approach to writing Aboriginal history in an area where no contact archaeology projects have been undertaken previously. The view is that without a pre-European (prehistoric) perspective, comparative analyses of culture change and continuity before, during, and after Aboriginal–European contact are inadequate. As already stated, at the core of contact archaeology there is a recognition of the value of information from sources other than material culture and a more critical and historical approach to the construction of archaeological knowledge. The research presented here therefore brings into play multiple perspectives and employs a variety of data sources. The specific methods and methodological issues faced in applying the proposed research approach to the analysis of different data sets are discussed in the individual data chapters. Analyses of archaeological evidence excavated from three traditional open sites facilitated the identification of the long-term cultural trajectories that this project focused on: material culture and technology, plant subsistence strategies and Aboriginal rainforest settlement patterns. The main objectives of the research are: (i) to present new archaeological evidence from three open sites located in north Queensland's rainforest region; (ii) to integrate the archaeological evidence with gathered historical (documentary and oral-historical) information, addressing both settler and Indigenous perspectives, which in turn allows agency to the Indigenous people whose land was intruded upon; and, (iii) to explore long-term change and continuity in the identified cultural trajectories.

Using a temporal framework requires an understanding of the different temporal scales applied to differing data sets, addressing the problem of how to sensibly integrate different sets of data such as fine-grained ethnographic observations and the longer-term structure of the archaeological record to investigate Aboriginal history. The data analyses presented recognise that both large-scale and short-term records have their own limitations and advantages; the pre-European archaeological record reflects longer temporal scales whereas the contact archaeological record reflects shorter-term events supplemented with historical information. To address this methodological problem, analyses of the relatively rich archaeological material from the Urumbal Pocket site examines Aboriginal rainforest use and occupation before European arrival in and around the traditional lands of the *Jirrbal* people on the Evelyn Tableland. Urumbal Pocket's long-term occupation history is used subsequently as a backdrop in the construction of occupation histories at two open sites (*Boignjul* and Cedar Creek) used by the *Jirrbal* people in the more recent past. Analyses of the archaeological and historical data sets demonstrate that careful application of ethnographic analogy can provide significant clues to past human behaviours and in gaining an understanding of long-term change and continuity in Aboriginal rainforest culture and society.

The data sources

Archaeological evidence

New archaeological evidence from three open sites provides small windows into the Aboriginal occupation of an area in the rainforest throughout the pre-contact and contact periods. The three sites investigated are Urumbal Pocket, *Boignjul* and Cedar Creek, all located within the traditional lands of the *Jirrbal* Aboriginal rainforest people. Analyses of the archaeological evidence excavated from these three sites facilitated the identification of the trajectories of culture change and continuity that form the focus of this investigation: (i) material culture and technology; (ii) plant subsistence strategies; and (iii) rainforest settlement patterns. The manner in which open sites may be identified archaeologically has been much debated (e.g. Binford 1980; Gould 1980; Kent 1987; Meehan and Jones 1988) and because open sites are prone to erosion through natural processes, an examination of these and other processes in each of the three archaeological sites allows for some assessment of site formation through time. An examination of Holocene environmental variability in the rainforest region allows for change and continuity interpreted from the archaeological record to be considered in relation to Holocene environmental change.

Historical information

A relatively rich body of ethnographic information from the rainforest region exists. In addition, the ethnohistorical record details some aspects of interactions between early European settlers and the local Aboriginal rainforest people. Two primary documentary sources used herein, Coyyan (1915, 1918) and Mjöberg (1913a), are both directly linked to the *Jirrbal* people through the first-hand observations made by these authors. A series of newspaper columns written by prospector Michael

O'Leary under the pseudonym of *Coyyan* (Coyyan 1915, 1918) provide information on Aboriginal rainforest use in the early phase of Aboriginal–European contact of the 1880s as well as insights into pre-European Aboriginal lifestyles in the study area. The O'Leary material has not been analysed or used in any detail previously.

A second primary source of historical information is the previously unanalysed diaries and related publications of Swedish scientist Eric Mjöberg, who spent several months travelling in the rainforest region in 1913[1]. After 75 years in obscurity, Mjöberg's diaries have recently been located in the California Academy of Sciences archives (C. Hallgren, pers. comm., 2005). The diaries provide information on the Aboriginal use of the rainforests in the study area and on Aboriginal–European interactions in the transitional contact period (Mjöberg 1913a, 1913b, 1914, 1918, 1925). Mjöberg viewed the Australian 'natives' as a dying race that had to be studied and captured in words and photographs before European influences resulted in their inevitable extinction, an attitude far from unusual at that time (see, for example, May 2010). It led, however, to important documentation of Aboriginal rainforest culture and society in the study area that provides some important information on change and continuity in the post-contact period (Ferrier 1999, 2002, 2006). These two sources provide a documentary history, which is used in this study to assist interpretations of the archaeology of contact in the rainforests of the Evelyn Tableland.

Oral traditions and living memory

Aboriginal perspectives of recent open campsites and their childhood memories of life in the rainforest provide another line of evidence that is integrated into the analysis. The inclusion of historical information from Indigenous and non-Indigenous people with associations to the study area gives the study a 'human' perspective that is denied in investigations confined to the archaeological or documentary record alone. The principal informant in the study is *Jirrbal* elder Maisie *Yarrcali* Barlow. Maisie was born in the early 1920s, and later in life she resumed the storytelling tradition (and other rainforest traditions) which had been interrupted by European settlement (Barlow 2001). The acknowledgement and understanding of an Aboriginal history in the area before contact, and the documenting of Aboriginal people as individuals participating and adapting to rapid changes in the contact period are important to the *Jirrbal* community. Oral information about this particular time period will not be available forever and the research presented here contributes to the recording and preservation of some of that knowledge. Maisie's stories reflect aspects of a lifestyle that arose from traditional rainforest occupation, and from traditions told to her by her grandmother when she was a young girl, as well as from her own observations and experiences in the post-contact period. Informal interviews were carried out with Maisie Barlow at her home and at all three archaeological sites investigated. She also assisted with translating historical information provided by Lizzie Wood, who lived at Cedar Creek as a young child in the 1910s. During a cultural mapping project carried out in the study area in the early 1990s (Duke and Collins 1994), Aboriginal sites were recorded and classified according to their past use and function, and map references to site locations were given. Many elders were still alive and participated in the project. The report was made available for the purpose of this study by permission from the *Jirrbal* elders and the report's authors. Valuable information on the study area's logging history was provided by retired timber cutter Reg Lockyer, who was born in the 1930s and grew up near Ravenshoe. He is amongst generations of timber cutters who logged rainforests up until the time it was declared part of the Wet Tropics World Heritage Area in 1986 and has a thorough understanding of the rainforests around Ravenshoe and the upper Tully River where he has lived and worked for most of his life.

---

1   The pages of these diaries are unnumbered and therefore quotes from this source do not include pagination.

2

Study Region: Environmental, Historical and Cultural Background

Introduction

This chapter presents background information regarding (i) the understanding of the environmental context, (ii) the distinct Aboriginal rainforest culture recorded at the time of European contact, (iii) the outcomes of Aboriginal interactions and negotiations with Europeans over the decades that followed first contact and (iv) the archaeological evidence, to the study area. The first section describes the environmental setting of the rainforest region, and demonstrates that a great level of biodiversity exists in this region. Information from palaeoecological research in the region is summarised to facilitate an appreciation of the climatic and environmental variability of the late Pleistocene and Holocene periods that has impact on human occupation in the region. This is followed by a summary of early European history of the study area and a description of the cultural setting of the study, including a discussion on some of the long-term outcomes of European settlement on Aboriginal people. The chapter concludes with a summary of previous archaeological research conducted in the rainforest region.

Environmental setting

The Wet Tropics Bioregion of northeast Queensland covers approximately 12,000 square km. It incorporates approximately the area between Rossville and Cardwell in the east and the Atherton-Evelyn Tablelands to the west (Fig. 2.1). The Tablelands are separated from the coastal plains by a mountain range that includes the highest mountain in Queensland, Mt Bartle Frere, at 1,622 m above sea level. The study area is located on the Evelyn Tableland in the southwest corner of the Tablelands (Fig 2.1). To the north and west, the Tablelands are enclosed by the low ridges of the Lamb and Great Dividing Ranges respectively. To the southeast the land is broken up by the drainage systems of the Russell and North Johnstone Rivers, which drain into the Pacific Ocean. To the east it falls into the headwaters of the Mulgrave River, which separates the Tablelands from the Bellenden Ker Range. The Tablelands range in elevation from 500–1,200 m, and are located approximately 32 km overland from the present coastline (Birtles 1997a:172). The western side of the Tablelands is drier and cloaked by open woodland, with eucalypt woodlands dominating. Today the regional landscape is rural, characterised by pasture interspersed with remnant rainforest patches and clearings dominated by sclerophyll species.

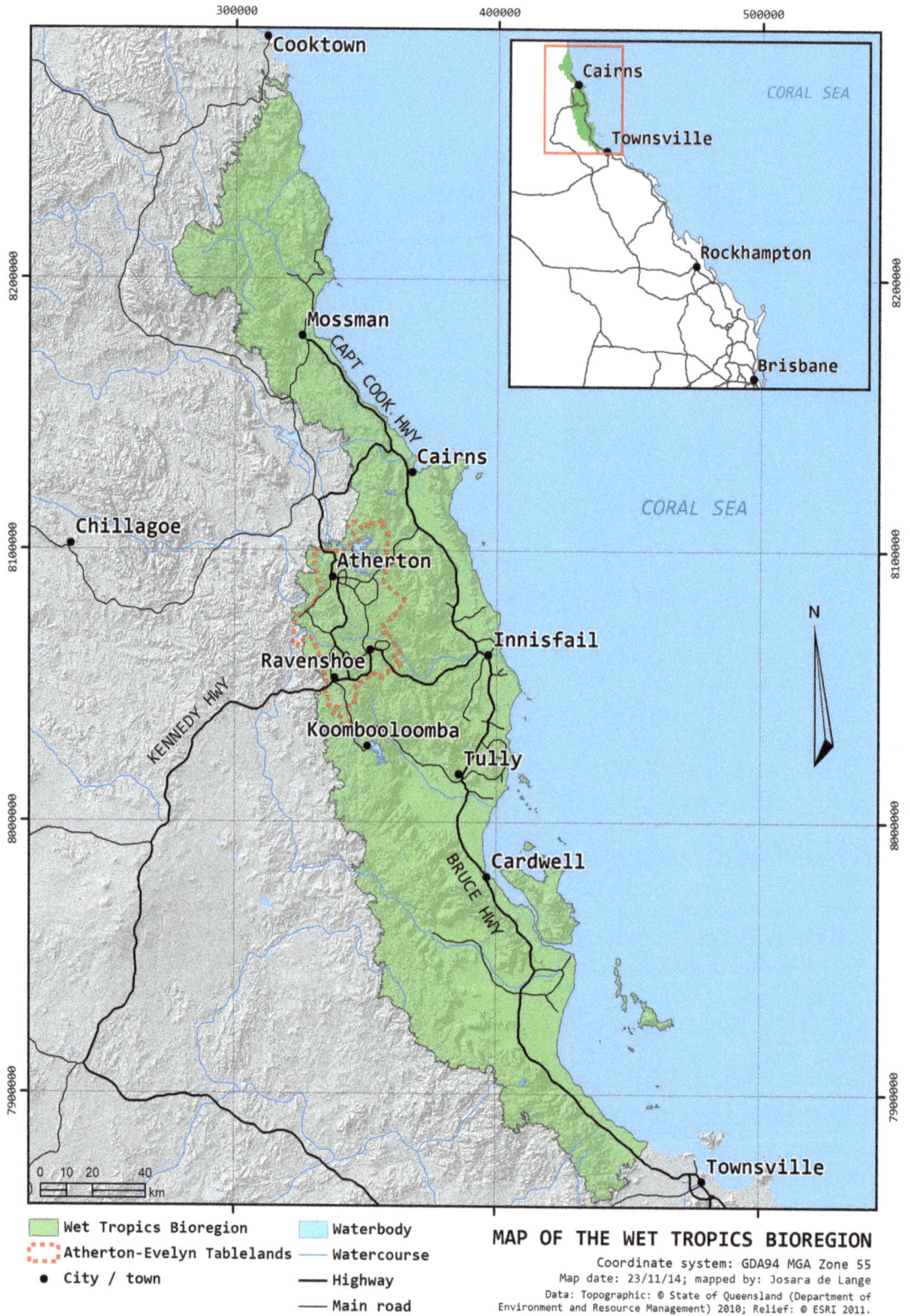

Figure 2.1 The Wet Tropics Bioregion and surrounds in northeast Queensland showing the location of the Atherton Tablelands.

Source: Produced by J. de Lange.

The great biodiversity of the area and the identification of plants of great evolutionary significance (among other factors) resulted in a World Heritage nomination in 1986, and listing as a World Heritage Area in 1988. The World Heritage Area covers around 9,200 square km. Almost all of it is rainforest, representing about 90% of the rainforest in north Queensland, and 40% of the rainforest remaining on the continent (Wet Tropics 2012). In November 2012, the Wet Tropics World Heritage Area's Indigenous heritage values were included as part of the existing Wet Tropics of Queensland National Heritage Listing. The listing recognises that 'Rainforest Aboriginal heritage is unique to the Wet Tropics and is a remarkable and continuous Indigenous connection with a tropical rainforest environment' (Wet Tropics Management Authority n.d.).

The Wet Tropics Bioregion contains the largest continuous expanse of tropical rainforest in Australia (Hopkins et al. 1993:360). The composition of rainforests across the region varies depending on altitude, aspect, rainfall and soils, with some rainforest species crossing the boundary into neighbouring open, *Eucalyptus*-dominated forests. With a combination of topographic diversity, soil variations and local climatic complexity, the region supports a mosaic of forest types (Hilbert et al. 2007:105). Before European colonisation, most of the area was covered in dense rainforest, intermittently broken up by patches of sclerophyll forest often referred to as 'pockets' by early explorers and settlers. Some of the pockets are a result of localised impoverished environmental conditions, including exposure to southeast winds, poorer soils and lower rainfall (Harris 1978), however, many are on basaltic soils where rainforest would be expected to grow. It has been postulated (Harris 1978) that these eucalypt/grass-dominated pockets were maintained by Aboriginal people, using fire and weeding to keep them clear of invading rainforest species. It is evident from historical documents that Aboriginal people used the pockets as favoured campsites, as well as ceremonial, and hunting grounds at the time of European contact (Birtles 1997a; Harris 1978; Mjöberg 1913a, 1918). Quickly realising the desirability of such open spaces within the rainforest as camping grounds and for grazing horses (Birtles 1997a:172), the Europeans took advantage of the clearings, and towns like Atherton (Prior's Pocket) and Yungaburra (Allumbah Pocket) were established on traditional Aboriginal campsites.

The rainforest in the region is characterised by:

> the prominence of robust woody lianas, vascular epiphytes, mostly entire leaf margins, many compound leaves of mesophyll size or larger, with drip tips and pulvini, and by a complex flora of both phanerogams and cryptogams. Some of the trees are deciduous (Webb 1959:552).

Tracey and Webb (1975) and Tracey (1982) have developed a detailed structural classification for rainforest and related vegetation types in the Wet Tropics. Thirteen sub-formations of rainforest, as well as 10 types of rainforest with emergent sclerophylls, have been identified. Rainforests in the eastern and southeastern parts of the Tablelands are described as 'Complex mesophyll vine forest' (CMVF or Type 1 a-c rainforests, i.e. true tropical rainforests):

1a. Canopy uneven (20–40 m) and occasionally with scattered emergents (45 m). Many and obscure layers, most crowns occupy less of 1/3 in height, trunks mostly 60–120 cm in diameter with plank buttresses common. Woody lianas, vascular epiphytes, tree palms and wide-leaved fleshy herbs common. Mostly evergreen and mesophyll with many notophylls. Present in very wet to wet lowlands and foothills, very wet and cloudy uplands and as gallery forests in river valleys in moist and dry lowlands. On basalts, basic volcanics and mixed colluvium and riverine alluvium.

1b. Originally in very wet to wet uplands on eastern and southeastern edge of Atherton Tableland but now only well represented at Lake Barrine and Lake Eacham. Trees taller than in 1a (35–55 m) and canopy more uneven. On basalts and basalt-derived pyroclastics.

1c. Local on very wet to wet lowlands and river valleys, canopy 36–42 metres on alluvial deposits (Tracey and Webb 1975; Tracey 1982).

In the western and northern areas of the Tablelands, complex notophyll vine forests (CNVF or Type 5 rainforests, i.e. lower montane or subtropical rainforests) characterise the vegetation:

5. Canopy uneven (20–45 m) with many tree layers, crowns often reaching half way down stems. Trunk sizes are uneven; plank buttresses, robust woody lianes, epiphytes, aroids and gingers are common. Now very restricted on cloudy wet highlands and on moist to dry lowlands, foothills and uplands but before European clearing more common toward the rainfall limit of rainforest, for example on the Atherton Tablelands north and west of Malanda. On basalts (Tracey and Webb 1975; Tracey 1982).

The vegetation of the tropical rainforest region of far northeast Queensland is thus complex and varied, with more than 2,000 tree, shrub and vine species already identified, excluding categories such as herbs, mosses, ferns and orchids. Moreover, the identification of new species continues (Beasley 2006:80).

Because of its geomorphic and climatic settings, the humid tropical rainforest region is characterised by steep gradients in rainfall and temperature. Rainfall is seasonal, with most rain falling during the wet summer season between January and April. Mean rainfall generally exceeds 1,300 mm per annum and annual mean temperatures vary, from more than 25°C on the coastal lowlands to less than 17°C on the highest mountain peaks (Nix 1991).

Past environments

A number of palaeoecological investigations on the Atherton Tableland has resulted in a palaeoecology that is very well understood, at least in an Australian context. Understanding vegetation and climate change through time assists in efforts to interpret human adaptive responses as reflected in archaeological deposits. Analyses of pollen from cores extracted from crater lakes and swamps have provided a detailed history of rainforest dynamics and rainforest–woodland interactions in the late Pleistocene and Holocene periods. At Lynch's Crater on the Atherton Tableland, palynological and sedimentary evidence indicate the replacement of moist Araucarian forests by pyrophytic woodlands dominated by *Eucalyptus* species during the late Pleistocene (Haberle 2005; Kershaw 1986, 1994:408; Moss and Kershaw 2000; Turney et al. 2001). Sedimentological study of terrace deposits on the upper Tully River in the study area suggests slope instability in the terminal Pleistocene, probably due to reduced vegetation cover and fluctuating precipitation. Associated charcoal in layers approximately 10,000 years old points to drier conditions and a more active fire regime in the study area at this time (Cosgrove et al. 2007:154; Nott et al. 2001). Based on charcoal fragments collected from rainforest zones across the region, it has been suggested that *Eucalyptus* woodlands occupied substantial areas of the present rainforest between 27,000 BP and 3500 BP (Hopkins et al. 1993), with *Eucalyptus* woodlands reaching their maximum geographical extent in the period between 13,000 and 8000 BP (Hopkins et al. 1993:357).

The role of past human use of fire on the distribution and composition of tropical rainforests has been a topic of debate since Kershaw identified a charcoal peak associated with rainforest attrition in the pollen record from Lynch's Crater, commencing at 38,000 BP (Kershaw 1976, 1986), and more recently re-dated to 45,000 BP (Turney et al. 2001). It has been suggested that the increase in charcoal evidence reflects the arrival of humans on the landscape ca. 40,000 years ago, however, no archaeological sites investigated in the rainforest region have been dated to the Pleistocene period. Changes detected in rainforest vegetation across the Wet Tropics Bioregion from ocean core ODP-820 in the adjacent Coral Sea further suggest that a regional increase in sea-surface temperature may have influenced regional vegetation changes through its effect on rainfall, with people probably involved in more recent changes (Moss and Kershaw 2000, 2007). Analyses of high-resolution pollen records from Lake Euramoo, also on the Atherton Tableland (Haberle 2005), show that in the period from 16,000 BP until 8500 BP the area was covered by wet sclerophyll forest, with some rainforest patches. The period between 8500 BP and 5000 BP saw a dramatic expansion of complex rainforest. From around 5000 BP a change to drier rainforests suggested that climatic conditions were drier than at present with ENSO (El Niño Southern Oscillation) activity increasing after 3000 BP and a continuation of dry rainforest expansion (Haberle 2005).

It thus appears that rainforest distribution on the Tablelands has been quite variable through time and that fire has played a role in its varied composition and dynamics (Hiscock and Kershaw 1992). Pollen evidence also suggests that rainforest was patchily distributed until around 8300 BP, and that the spread of rainforest across the Tablelands took up to 2,000 years. Prior to this, the Tablelands were dominated by open sclerophyll woodlands. Hilbert postulates that deep river gullies and high mountains acted as refugia for patches of rainforest, which survived there during the Last Glacial Maximum (Hilbert et al. 2007:104). It has been argued that the Holocene climatic and environmental variability demonstrated in pollen cores from the rainforest region provides a partial explanation for the 'intensification' of land use and changes in cultural practices by Aboriginal people in northern Australia (Cosgrove et al. 2007; Ferrier and Cosgrove 2012; Lourandos and David 1998; Tibby and Haberle 2007). Future results from high-resolution palaeoecological studies in the rainforest region are expected to refine the late Pleistocene and Holocene climatic and environmental records, leading to a better understanding of past Aboriginal land use and management and impacts on rainforest biodiversity.

Post-Aboriginal–European contact environments

Tracey (1982) estimated that more than 40% of the original area of rainforest on the Tablelands at the time of contact in the late nineteenth century had been cleared, mainly for cane farming and cattle grazing. Extensive rainforest areas exist today on the hills and mountains, however, only fragments remain on the lowlands, Tablelands and adjacent slopes (Tracey 1982:1). Dense rainforest is also found on steep ridges along the major rivers, around Lake Eacham and Lake Barrine and other historical scenic reserves, as well as in relatively inaccessible areas. The remoteness and unsuitability of these areas for cultivation has contributed to the persistence of rainforest in a modified landscape, however, most of these forests were logged to some extent in the past (Frawley 1990).

European settlement in the study area had its beginnings in gold and tin mining and timber cutting, with explorer and prospector reports paying specific attention to large stands of red cedar (*Toona ciliatis*) or 'red gold' as it was popularly called. Expansions in mining, agriculture and pastoralism to the south and west of the rainforest region led the settled colony to expand northwards to include the Tablelands (Ritchie 1989:114). In 1876, James Venture Mulligan made his way to the rainforested Atherton Tableland and reported on magnificent specimens of 'monstrous' red cedars and kauri pines (Birtles 1997a:200). Prior to this, the Bloomfield, Daintree, Johnstone and Tully valleys had already been raided by loggers for the red cedar used to construct Cooktown and for export south (Birtles 1997a:200). In an attempt to conserve Queensland's surviving cedar stands, the Under-Secretary for Lands, W.A. Tully, appealed to the Legislative Assembly in 1881:

> We are exhausting the stock of some of the most valuable timber trees more quickly than it can be replaced by the natural growth of young ones, and this is going on all around us. In some districts the cedar has disappeared, and the young trees, before they have attained maturity, are cut down without scruple (Tully 1881:145).

Tully's report proved unpopular and was dismissed and ignored, and in the same year of his report, cedar-cutters arrived in the rainforests on the Atherton Tableland. Historical documents (e.g. Mjöberg 1918) suggest rainforest clearing accelerated from the beginning of the twentieth century; timber gathering and subsequent land clearing by early settlers, intensive agriculture and mining were all responsible for the deterioration of the rainforests (Ritchie 1989:12). The first European settlers on the Evelyn Tableland were similarly lured by the red cedar and also by kauri (*Agathis* spp.) trees (R. Lockyer, pers. comm., 2005).

European history

The first European exploration party to traverse the coastal rainforests was led by Edmund Kennedy in 1848. After a highly successful 'performance' on Sir Thomas Mitchell's 1846 explorations, Kennedy was appointed to lead an ambitious but ultimately disastrous expedition to Cape York. After a series of unfortunate and unpredictable events, with the rainforest being a major obstacle, 10 party members died, including Kennedy, who was speared and killed on Cape York (Beale 1977). Kennedy's fate was widely published and is believed to have discouraged European settlement for many years (Ritchie 1989:61).

European arrival on the Atherton Tableland

The documented history of European settlement on the Atherton Tableland can be traced back to the 1870s. Gold prospector James Venture Mulligan travelled along the perimeter of the rainforest west of the Tablelands (Mulligan 1877) on Aboriginal paths, accompanied by Aboriginal guides (Mulligan 1876, 1885a, 1885b, 1885c). The success of Mulligan in navigating the region can be attributed largely to the use of Aboriginal guides; a strategy that was copied by subsequent exploration parties and eventually facilitated the logging of the rainforest after red cedar was discovered. The mining settlement at Herberton was established in 1880 (Fig 2.1). By 1882, the government opened up almost 50,000 hectares on the Atherton Tableland for settlement, encompassing areas of rainforest and open eucalypt forest (Ritchie 1989). The original wagon roads connecting Cairns and the coastal settlements with Herberton traversed the rainforest via large, open *Eucalyptus*-dominated pockets. By taking advantage of those clearings, small townships soon began to be established on the Atherton Tableland. Prior's Pocket, a cedar-getters camp, became the chosen site for the new township of Atherton (named after John Atherton, the first European to take up land in the district) and by 1897, Atherton's population was almost 400 (Toohey 2001:33). By 1910 the railway connecting Cairns to Herberton via Atherton was extended, with a branch that ran through a number of small towns such as Tolga, Yungaburra, Peeramon, Kureen and on to Malanda (Toohey 2001:87). At each stop a pub was built from red cedar logs and wood from other rainforest trees.

The clearing of the rainforest, initially in the form of limited cutting of specific rainforest timbers and later in the form of more extensive logging for agricultural and grazing purposes, resulted in the forced removal and dislocation of Aboriginal people from their traditional hunting and gathering grounds. Early phases of European settlement of the Atherton Tableland (and elsewhere in the rainforest) were impeded by tension and conflict between the newcomers and the Aboriginal people (discussed in more detail in Chapter 3). Added to this, the obstacles of the rainforest environment and the tropical climate also delayed European settlement. The pace of change increased in the early twentieth century as clearing of the scrub for agriculture was made viable by better transport and conflicts with the Aboriginal people were resolved.

First Europeans on the Evelyn Tableland

The first European settlement on the Evelyn Tableland dates to the early 1880s (Smith 2001:v). Evelyn Station was originally owned by government member and gold miner Frank Stubley. The station, located in sclerophyll forest near the edge of the rainforest, included a large tract of land in traditional *Jirrbal* country, the eastern section largely being covered in dense rainforest. Stubley lost Evelyn Station and left the area in 1887 when the land was resumed by the bank and sub-divided into a number of large blocks (Smith 2001:2). More than a decade lapsed before mining giant John Moffatt of Irvinebank acquired the title to a section of land on Evelyn Station in 1898, having been informed that large stands of cedar trees grew on the station. The Mazlin brothers had discovered red cedar trees growing adjacent to two creeks back in 1881, which gave the small settlement its first name—Cedar Creek. The logging of red cedar on both North and South Cedar Creek began at the turn of the twentieth century (Smith 2001:3). Sometime later, the township at Cedar Creek was renamed Ravenshoe (Fig. 2.1) after a town in Northumberland, England, where a branch of the family of one of the early settlers had originated (Smith 2001:3). In 1907, Ravenshoe and surrounds were surveyed and divided into 300 blocks. A large contingent of ex-miners and other townspeople from Charters Towers, further inland, applied for the selections and brought their families across from the west (Culloty 1992; North Cedar Creek Settlers Group 1908), while others came from Irvinebank (Fig. 2.1). One of these men was Bill Rogers, John Moffatt's head groom, whom he awarded a gift of land for a lifetime's service (Toohey 2001:65). The land, a large eucalypt pocket on the edge of the rainforest, was at the time the setting of an Aboriginal campsite and a ceremonial ground, and the surrounding landscape the hunting and gathering grounds of the *Jirrbal* peoples.

Cultural setting

Aboriginal group boundaries used in this research are defined on the basis of oral traditions, linguistics and political geography. According to these sources, the name *Dyirbal* is generally given to the Aboriginal language grouping for the southern part of this rainforest region. Linguistic evidence suggests that at least six main groups belonged to the *Dyirbal* language group at contact, all descendants from a single ancestor group (Dixon 1972; Pedley 1992:1; Tindale 1974). Access to land was regulated in terms of access across boundaries, which also defined the extent of a group's territory. Group territories and boundaries within the *Dyirbal* language group are presently under review, and group territories and language group names as illustrated in Figure 1.2 in Chapter 1 should be considered as estimates only.

The *Jirrbal* people of Cedar Creek and the upper Tully River

According to oral traditions (Barlow 2001) and linguistic analyses (Dixon 1972), the study area (Fig. 1.1) was, in pre-European times, the traditional land of the *Jirrbal* Aboriginal people. Traditional *Jirrbal* land lies at the western edge of the rainforest region, including both rainforest and more open *Eucalyptus*-dominated areas (Barlow 2001; Tindale 1974). At the turn of the twentieth century, the European population in the study area was relatively small, and large areas of rainforest to the south and east were still untouched by logging and European settlement.

Jirrbal traditions (Barlow 2001) suggest that people used to live in groups comprising of six to eight families spread across the district. Each group maintained their own camp, which was usually located at the fringe of the rainforest (M. Barlow, pers. comm., 2004; L. Wood, pers. comm., 2004). According to *Jirrbal* elders Maisie Barlow and Lizzie Wood, families from one such location, Cedar Creek (Fig. 1.1), would walk down to the Tully Falls on the Tully River to fish for eels and to prepare for the annual inter-group gathering on the coastal lowlands, which took place during the cooler winter months (M. Barlow, pers. comm., 2004; L. Wood, pers. comm., 2004). *Jirrbal* people from Cedar Creek, along with other Tableland people, would walk along the mountain ridges down to the lowlands for such events. In turn, the Cedar Creek people would host coastal and Tableland groups at their own ceremonial ground during the wet season. Historical information demonstrates that *Jirrbal* people were using their traditional campsite and ceremonial ground at Cedar Creek in 1913 (Mjöberg 1918). This traditional campsite is most likely the Aboriginal campsite Eric Mjöberg visited in 1913, which he referred to as 'Cedar Creek' (Duke and Collins 1994; Mjöberg 1913a; Mjöberg 1918; M. Barlow, pers. comm., 2004; V. van der Vliet, pers. comm., 2006).

Contact period campsites

Documentary research in libraries and archives was undertaken in efforts to locate historical information on Aboriginal rainforest culture and, more specifically, information on *Jirrbal* culture and society. The intention was to identify campsites that *Jirrbal* people remembered visiting or living in during their childhoods (pre-1940s) that might have potential for archaeological investigation.

Data collected previously by Duke and Collins (1994) and Bird (1999), and in interviews with *Jirrbal* elders and senior Ravenshoe residents, was also consulted. Oral history interviews were carried out and during these informal interviews with *Jirrbal* elders Maisie Barlow and Lizzie Wood, contact period sites, site locations and *Jirrbal* history were discussed. During the discussions it became clear that, to the *Jirrbal* people of Cedar Creek, European settlement on traditional lands resulted in an abrupt interruption to Aboriginal rainforest settlement and use. The township of Ravenshoe has grown substantially since the late 1940s. European houses and roads have been built where traditional Aboriginal campsites used to be along Cedar Creek, and a golf course was constructed in the 1920s in the adjacent eucalypt pocket (M. Barlow, pers. comm., 2005; V. van der Vliet, pers. comm., 2007).

'Town camps'

No mission station was established on the Tablelands, with the result that many *Jirrbal* people were instead removed from their traditional lands and relocated to the *Yarrabah* mission south of Cairns, approximately 140 kilometres from Ravenshoe. Others were removed to stations outside of the rainforest region, or forced to live in allocated fringe camps or on reserves near European settlements. Many people were sent to Palm Island as punishment for crimes against European property, and never returned (M. Barlow, pers. comm., 2004). The first place the remaining *Jirrbal* families moved to after having been forced to abandon their traditional campsites along Cedar Creek (M. Barlow, pers. comm., 2004; L. Wood, pers. comm., 2004) was Old Bellamy's farm (referred to as Edward's farm in 2004), located on the outskirts of Ravenshoe. This event most likely took place sometime in the early 1920s and Old Bellamy's farm is where Maisie Barlow was born in 1922. In 1928–29, an influenza epidemic killed almost half the *Jirrbal* people living in Ravenshoe. Many of the survivors, including those at Bellamy's farm, were relocated to a place referred to as 'The Little Millstream Reserve' (Duke and Collins 1994:63). The settlement is remembered amongst *Jirrbal* elders and townspeople and was permanently occupied until the late 1940s. The settlement had a number of improvised European-style cottages made from tin:

> They erected little tin sheds down there on the Millstream in the 1930s and they [*Jirrbal* people] lived there. They would walk across South Cedar Creek on a little bridge, across the golf course and come into town. They [Europeans] burnt the village down later, got the bulldozer and pushed the houses over and got rid of it all. There are graves down there, many of the old people died living there (V. van der Vliet, pers. comm., 2006).

No evidence of the settlement on the Millstream River remains (personal observation). The graves of many local *Jirrbal* people remain unmarked at the location, which is presently used as a caravan rest stop. The *Jirrbal* settlement on Old Bellamy's farm, along with many other Aboriginal contact period campsites near Ravenshoe, is located on private land. It was the elders' wish not to trouble the European residents in Ravenshoe by trying to gain access to private land in the context of this research project. As a result, the focus of the archaeological investigations shifted to contact period sites located within the Wet Tropics World Heritage Area and in forestry zones outside of Ravenshoe.

'An end to traditional life ways'

The characteristic rainforest ceremonies (discussed in Chapter 3), which had survived European contact, were reported by the *Cairns Post* to have been banned in Ravenshoe and other areas in the mid-1940s. This decision was taken by authorities who claimed that glass and metal objects attached to spears and other weapons made the ceremonies too dangerous (Toohey 2001:156). A desire to prevent large groups of Aboriginal people congregating in one place is probably closer to the truth. Later in the post-contact period, many Aboriginal children were taken away from their families and placed in homes as domestic helpers, and young Aboriginal men and women were hired in various types of employment, often far from their traditional lands in the rainforest (M. Barlow, pers. comm., 2004; L. Wood, pers. comm., 2004).

Memories recalled by *Jirrbal* elders and senior residents in Ravenshoe attest to an end of 'traditional' Aboriginal life in the mid-1940s. This process probably started in the 1930s when Aboriginal children were sent out to work on cattle stations away from the rainforest region, breaking the oral tradition of Aboriginal elders passing on traditional knowledge to their grandchildren:

> When the children got sent away to work, I was around 12 or 13 [making it mid-1930s], our grandparents could no longer teach us the traditions like they used to do. My grandmother taught me about rainforest food and the role of women, but then we were sent away to work. It stopped when the children left (M. Barlow, pers. comm., 2004).

Despite a history of upheaval and dislocation of *Jirrbal* people from their traditional land, as opportunities arose, many *Jirrbal* people returned to Ravenshoe and other places in traditional *Jirrbal* country. It is these strong ancestral links to traditional land that have allowed for the survival of *Jirrbal* oral traditions.

Previous archaeological research

Indications of the presence of people in northeast Queensland's rainforest region in antiquity were reported early in the twentieth century. Unusual stone artefacts were recorded in newspaper articles and journals, most of them found by farmers clearing land for agriculture (e.g. Colliver and Woolston 1966; Cosgrove 1979). Surface stone artefact finds are the most commonly recorded archaeological site type in the rainforest region (Horsfall 1996). Thousands of edge-ground axes, *ooyurkas* (t-shaped stone implements), incised slate grinding stones and other stone implements have been recovered from cane fields on the coastal lowlands and on the Tablelands. Some farmers have accumulated impressive stone artefact collections this way (Cosgrove 1984, 1996; W. Jonsson, pers. comm., 2006; R. Stager, pers. comm., 2000).

Speculations on the nature and duration of Aboriginal occupation of the rainforest region date to Birdsell's and Tindale's 1938–39 Harvard-Adelaide Expedition (Tindale and Birdsell 1941). Birdsell suggested that these rainforests had been occupied continuously for some 30,000 years. However, palaeoecological studies have shown that the extent of rainforest decreased significantly in the late Pleistocene, and only returned around 8,000 years ago. As a result, the Birdsell model is now only of historical importance.

Bare Hill

The first archaeological excavation in the rainforest region was carried out by Richard Wright at Bare Hill (Fig. 1.1), a granite rock shelter in sclerophyll forest, close to the western margins of the rainforests near Mareeba on the Atherton Tableland (Wright 1971). No dates have been published from the Bare Hill site (Horsfall 1996:176; R. Wright, pers. comm., 2007). The excavations revealed a few flaked stone implements, interpreted to be tools, and large quantities of unmodified quartz flakes. Pieces of worked shell, bone and charcoal were also recovered. Wright concluded that people using the shelter in the past had limited access to tractable stone material and imported marine shells for flaking (Wright 1971:139). Bones from rainforest animals were recovered and argued as evidence for Aboriginal people exploiting the rainforest for food.

Herbert and Burdekin Rivers project

An archaeological research project was carried out by Helen Brayshaw in the Herbert-Burdekin district, located in the southern extremity of the Wet Tropics Bioregion (Fig. 2.1) (Brayshaw 1990). In *Well Beaten Paths*, Brayshaw presents the results of an ethnographic and archaeological study, providing detailed descriptions of ethnographic collections from the Herbert-Burdekin area, summaries of ethnohistorical sources and the results from four archaeological excavations. A wide range of faunal and cultural remains were recovered, although bird and plant remains were completely absent, apparently as a result of unfavourable conditions of preservation (Brayshaw 1990:195). Human bones were recovered in two of the rock shelters investigated. Brayshaw (1990:195) concluded that the varying composition of the remains excavated indicates that these sites were used selectively and perhaps for particular social activities. All four sites are dated to within the last 2,000 years.

Jiyer Cave and Mulgrave River 2

In the early 1980s, John Campbell began excavations at *Jiyer* Cave, located in dense rainforest on the Russell River (Fig. 1.1) (Campbell 1982). Nicky Horsfall continued the excavations at *Jiyer* Cave and results from her archaeological investigations show increases in human occupation intensity, subsistence specialisation and increased site occupation through time, with the earliest evidence for human occupation appearing around 5,000 years ago (Horsfall 1987, 1996). Quartz is the dominant stone raw material. Plant remains, in the form of carbonised nutshell fragments of both toxic and non-toxic varieties, were also identified. The period of most intensive cultural activity started around 2500 BP, peaking in the last 1,000 to 1,500 years (Horsfall 1996:180–181). Horsfall (1987) also conducted a small excavation at Mulgrave River 2 (Fig. 1.1), an open rainforest site. Here, quartz was again the most common raw material, and plant remains were also recovered.

Horsfall's results raised questions about rainforest occupation on a regional scale (Cosgrove 1996). However, further investigations into the antiquity of the *Jiyer* Cave archaeological deposits, and rainforest occupation in general, supported previous findings with no evidence of earlier human occupation detected (Cosgrove and Raymont 2002). Stone artefacts made on quartz, basalt and crystal quartz were the dominant raw materials represented and the organic remains included fish bones, unidentified nut shell fragments and pieces of egg shell from the scrub turkey (*Aletura lathami*). In addition, European-manufactured artefacts were also recovered consisting of 18 pieces of glass, some of which have been flaked, one piece of clay pipe and one metal fragment. These artefacts suggest that *Jiyer* Cave continued to be used by Aboriginal people in the contact period. Archaeological excavations at the Mulgrave River 2 open site and the Mourilyan Harbour midden site (Fig. 1.1) (Cosgrove and Field 2004), both located in coastal lowland, returned chronologies similar to *Jiyer* Cave. None of the sites exceeds an antiquity of 5000 BP and the evidence suggests a late period of intensive cultural activity, especially the last 1,000 to 1,500 years.

Russell River and North Johnstone River surveys

The next phase of investigations took place in the late 1990s, when Cosgrove and a team of students and traditional owners carried out archaeological surveys in remote rainforest locations on the Atherton Tableland. Open sites and rock shelters were recorded on the Russell River (Cosgrove 1997) and the North Johnstone River (Cosgrove 1999) (Fig. 1.1) Stone artefacts and fragments of marine shell (*Polymesoda coaxans*) were located on the surface of unexcavated rock shelters on the North Johnstone River. Artefacts of European-manufactured raw materials, some of which could be dated to the late nineteenth century based on manufacturing style (Cosgrove 1999) were also located. One hypothesis that presents itself is that the presence of historical artefacts in traditional sites located in remote rainforest locations may indicate that more secluded rainforest areas continued to be used by Aboriginal people in the early contact period, perhaps as a way of avoiding contact with Europeans.

Archaeological research on the Evelyn Tableland

Archaeological research in the rainforest region between 2002 and 2005 (Cosgrove et al. 2007) expanded the understanding of the archaeological record, especially on the Evelyn Tableland. In addition to exploring the possibility of rainforest occupation before 5000 BP, Cosgrove and Field (2004) also aimed to understand, through archaeological investigations, the role played by toxic plant foods in the development and establishment of permanent Aboriginal rainforest occupation. During the course of the project, surveys and excavations were conducted. On an exposed band of soil around Koombooloomba Dam on the upper Tully River located approximately 40 km south of Ravenshoe (Fig. 1.1), 131 new artefact locations were recorded, including 31 artefacts scatters, 66 hatchets and 34 broken axes (Cosgrove et al. 2007). Also noted were fragments of worked glass as well as fragments of incised slate grinding stones (*morahs*) and top stones (*moogis*), both thought to have been used in the context of plant food processing (R. Cosgrove, pers. comm., 2005). Three archaeological sites were excavated in this area (Fig 1.1). Two sites, Urumbal Pocket and Goddard Creek, are located at Koombooloomba Dam and are both periodically exposed during low water levels. The third site, *Murubun*, is a large granite overhang located in sclerophyll forest bordering rainforests to the northwest of Koombooloomba Dam. It was first identified by Horsfall (1988) in a cultural heritage survey. Quartz is the predominant stone raw material at all three sites, but small amounts of slate, rhyolite and fine-grained materials are also present. The presence of these materials suggests contact with people living in areas to the west of the rainforest region, where acid volcanics dominate the regional geology (Henderson and Stephenson 1980) or, alternatively, a periodic use of two different environments by the same group of people. Fragmentary plant remains were also consistently present at these sites and more than 20,000 pieces of carbonised nutshell from a variety of toxic and non-toxic rainforest plants were recovered from the excavations (Cosgrove et al. 2007:160–161). The chronology from these three sites consistently show low level rainforest occupation before 2000 BP, after which occupation became more intensive and probably permanent (Cosgrove et al. 2007).

Summary

Our current understanding of pre-European Aboriginal rainforest occupation is relatively fragmentary. The research presented here draws on multiple lines of evidence to enhance our understanding of long-term Aboriginal rainforest occupation, including, for the first time, the early contact period. Archaeological sites investigated across the rainforest region show evidence of occupation from about 5000 BP with an indication of intensive cultural activity in the late Holocene, especially in the last 1,000 to 1,500 years. Oral traditions and historical documents suggest that the *Jirrbal* people were amongst the last Aboriginal people in the rainforest region to come into direct contact with Europeans. The archaeological record demonstrates that some remote traditional sites continued to be used after the time of European settlement, which allowed aspects of traditional rainforest use to survive into the recent past.

3

The Documentary Evidence

Introduction

This chapter presents an analysis of ethnographic information available from the study area with the aim of assisting archaeological interpretation. Chapter 2 established that the *Jirrbal* people from the Cedar Creek, upper Tully River area, were amongst the last rainforest groups on the Tablelands to come into permanent contact with Europeans. The documentary evidence from the Tablelands is presented first, followed by analyses of two documentary sources that are directly linked to the study area: the early observations by Michael O'Leary on the upper Tully River; and Eric Mjöberg's documents, including his 1913 diary notes from the Cedar Creek campsite.

Ethnohistorical information

The earliest European accounts from the rainforest region are mostly fleeting descriptions of European encounters with Aboriginal people, written by government-employed explorers and prospectors. They provide descriptions of characteristic material culture items observed in Aboriginal campsites, as well as the detection of substantial tracks and large clearings in the rainforest. The dates, nature of observations and the locations of the primary explorers and commentators in the northeast Queensland rainforest region are shown in Table 3.1.

Table 3.1 Tablelands rainforest explorers, dates and locations.

Explorer	Date of exploration	Nature of observation	Area of observation
Edmund Kennedy	1848	Transitory. First inland European expedition to Cape York	Traversed the Cardwell Range probably crossing the upper Tully River at Urumbal Pocket
James Mulligan	1877	Transitory/gold prospecting	Atherton Tableland
Michael O'Leary	1880s	Transitory/gold prospecting	Culpa goldfield on the upper Tully River
Christie Palmerston	1882 (2 April – 2 Aug)	Transitory/in government employ seeking railway route	From a location on the coast across to the Atherton Tableland
	1882 (31 Oct – 12 Nov, 21 Dec – 30 Dec)	Transitory/in government employ seeking railway route	Return trip from Geraldton (Innisfail) to Herberton, following the North Johnstone River and Beatrice River
	1884–1885 (21 Dec – 27 Jan)	Transitory/gold prospecting	From Herberton to the Barron Falls, covering areas around the Atherton Tablelands, Beatrice River and the North Johnstone River
	1886 (12 July – 9 Nov)	Transitory/gold prospecting	Three journeys along the Russell River and its tributaries
Carl Lumholtz	1882–1883	Established scientific exploration of rainforest flora, fauna and traditional Aboriginal society	Started at lower Herbert River on the coast, moving north and northwest following the Herbert River

Explorer	Date of exploration	Nature of observation	Area of observation
Archibald Meston	1889	Transitory/scientific flora and fauna expedition	Travelled in the Bellenden Ker Range and Mt Bartle Frere area, moving along Russell River and Mulgrave River
Walter E. Roth	1898–1900	Transitory/in government employ as Northern Protector of Aborigines and documenting traditional Aboriginal culture	Recorded in areas adjacent to Atherton and along the lower Tully River
Eric Mjöberg	1913	Established scientific exploration of rainforest fauna, flora and 'remnants' of traditional Aboriginal society	Areas on the Atherton-Evelyn Tablelands, upper Tully River, Russell River and upper North Johnstone River, Cedar Creek and Evelyn. Visited Yarrabah mission

Source: After Ferrier 1999.

Material culture collections

Material culture collections from the rainforest region consist mainly of characteristic traditional organic items that have been documented in the ethnographic rainforest literature, and will not be repeated in any great detail here (however, see for example Bottoms 1999; Brayshaw 1990; Colliver and Woolston 1980; Ferrier 1999, 2002, 2006; Pedley 1992; Roth 1898, 1901–10). Material culture items in rainforest collections generally include a variety of artefacts such as wooden shields, spears, spear-throwers, throwing clubs and boomerangs, and a variety of baskets, bark blankets and other items. Historical documents demonstrate that Aboriginal rainforest people used the lawyer cane (*Calamus* spp.) in the manufacture of many traditional organic artefacts related to subsistence strategies including baskets for sieving toxic nuts and climbing ropes used to collect food from treetops. Fish, eel, and wallaby nets were also made from lawyer cane fibres. In addition, substantial weather proof huts were built from the cane's vines and leaves, enabling Tableland rainforest groups to live a more sedentary life during the wet season (Duke and Collins 1994; Mjöberg 1918:365–366; Roth 1901–10).

1849: The Kennedy expedition

The first inland European expedition to Cape York was led by Edmund Kennedy. Edgar Beale's biography on Kennedy, titled *Kennedy of Cape York* (1977), provides information based on Kennedy's 1849 diary entries, which, amongst other things, provide some insight into the pre-European rainforest environment. Kennedy described large areas of thick and impenetrable lawyer cane, which had to be hacked through, on a steep range separating the coastal lowlands from the drier and open woodlands west of the rainforest region. He wrote that the landscape was a patchwork made up of open forest pockets and dense rainforest. At times, Kennedy's party followed Aboriginal tracks that criss-crossed through the rainforest, however, they were mostly avoided. This is because he considered that attacks by the 'natives' were more likely to occur out in the open (Beale 1977:176). The fate of the expedition was well publicised (*The Moreton Bay Courier* 1849:4). Ten party members died, including Kennedy, who was speared and killed. It has been suggested that the ill-fated expedition may have restricted European settlement of the far north for many years (Ritchie 1989:61).

1870s–80s: Gold prospecting and scientific explorations

The first European township in the region, Cardwell (Fig. 2.1), was established in 1864 on the coastal lowlands. European settlement across the rainforest region occurred in the decades following the arrival of *Waybala* (*Jirrbal* word for European people and settlement) on the coast, and gradually expanded to include rainforests and sclerophyll forest areas located at the western edge of the rainforest region. Some of the earliest written accounts from the Atherton Tableland are from prospectors who travelled to the area in search of various metals and minerals. The discovery of gold on the Palmer River to the north in 1873, and in the early 1880s on the Russell River to the east, brought thousands of prospectors to the Atherton Tableland.

In 1876, gold prospector James Mulligan described, for the first time, large clusters of huts located in open eucalypt pockets on the northwestern fringe of the rainforest on the Atherton Tableland, which he referred to as 'townships'. At each campsite many wide and open tracks met, some of which his party followed for many kilometres, skirting around the edge of the rainforest:

> There are roads off the main track to each of their townships, which consist of well-thatched gunyahs [huts], big enough to hold five or six people. We counted eleven townships since we came to the edge of the scrub (Mulligan 1877:401).

Mulligan conducted several prospecting expeditions together with fellow prospector-explorer Christie Palmerston who, in 1882, was commissioned by the Queensland government to search for a railway route, connecting the coast with Herberton (Fig. 2.1) located on the Wild River (Savage 1989:17). During his subsequent gold prospecting explorations along the Russell River and on the South and North Johnstone Rivers (Fig. 2.1), Palmerston (1883, 1885–87, 1888) records some details of Aboriginal use of the rainforest in his diaries. Although transitory in nature, dates, landmarks, distances, and detailed observations characterise these diaries. For example, they depict the nature of the vegetation and Aboriginal paths connecting cleared campsites within dense rainforest (Savage 1989). In spite of Palmerston's unsympathetic behaviour towards the Aboriginal people he met in his sojourns, his observations are important in attempts to piece together a picture of pre-European Aboriginal rainforest culture and settlement. On the North Johnstone River, Palmerston described what he referred to as a pocket:

> A pocket – that is a piece of open country about a quarter of an acre in size, circular shaped, used by the aborigines [sic] for war dances and fighting. They take particular care to keep the place free from jungle, which would creep over in a few seasons if allowed. There were several gunyahs [huts] around its margins (Palmerston 1885–86:232).

Palmerston continued by describing cleared paths linking these pockets throughout the rainforest:

> There were many large paths leading from the pockets in many directions. A fair sized aborigines' [sic] pathway crosses the mountain and we followed it along the summit, when it led us straight into an aborigines' camp … we emerged upon another scrupulously cleaned pocket, equal in size to the one left this morning, only its covering paths are much larger. It has a floor like appearance. We steeply ascended a table-land's [sic] summit, where we picked up a lot of fresh nigger [sic] tracks, which led us into another large open encampment by sunset (Palmerston 1885–86:232–233).

Government geologist Robert Logan Jack, whilst documenting the geology of the Russell River in 1888, recorded clearings in the rainforest in the upper Russell River area:

> A few cleared spots in the jungle that were used for corroboree of the tribe and for meetings of neighbouring tribes. These bora-grounds are probably of great antiquity as no tradition of their origin can be gathered from the natives. The clearing of an acre of jungle with stone implements (aided perhaps by fire in the very rare dry seasons) must have been the work of a very long time (Jack 1888:3).

These early historical accounts from the Tablelands clearly demonstrate that at the time of European arrival in the rainforest, this landscape was managed by Aboriginal people. It appears that the large open pathways, open eucalypt and grassy pockets, as well as smaller rainforest clearings described by Mulligan, Palmerston and others, were integral to Aboriginal ways of life and tenure in the rainforest.

Figure 3.1 Campsite image from the rainforest region with Aboriginal huts in an open pocket dominated by *Eucalyptus* spp. trees.

Source: Archibald Meston, Mulgrave River, northern Queensland, 1905. South Australian Museum Archives.

Archibald Meston

In 1889, journalist and explorer Archibald Meston undertook and led the first botanical and zoological collecting expedition to the Atherton Tableland. During the expedition, Meston made special efforts to find out Aboriginal names for natural features of the landscape (Ritchie 1989:51). Meston's 1889 report provides some detail on Aboriginal subsistence practices and the location of Aboriginal campsites he encountered in the rainforest (Fig. 3.1). His first-hand observations of material culture items relating to toxic food processing were the first descriptions in writing. Furthermore, Meston's observations demonstrate that the rainforest region provided a resource base that allowed Aboriginal people on the Atherton Tableland to establish seasonal camps which he referred to as 'wet weather camps' (Meston 1889:8):

> Their [rainforest Aborigines] food is chiefly vegetarian, varied occasionally by the flesh of the wallaby, the tree-climbing kangaroo, fish, birds, eggs and three or four varieties of opossums. The koa nut, and other large nuts not yet botanically named, are the chief articles of diet. Some of the nuts and roots they eat are poisonous in their raw state, and these are pounded up and placed in dilly bags in running water for a couple of days to have the poisonous principle washed out. Of edible nuts of various kinds they have an unlimited supply. In pursuit of tree climbing animals, they take a vine and run up the tallest trees. Their main camps are always built on some healthy dry situation, beside or very near a running stream. These main 'wet weather camps' is where they remain during the wet season, and store large supplies of nuts. We saw no camps higher than 2000 feet and very rarely any above 1000 feet. The nuts they chiefly live on are only found on the flats and in the valleys (Meston 1889:8).

During this period of early rainforest explorations, Herbert Spencer's social Darwinism characterised culture research. His theory positioned white people as a superior race, a theory which sparked and legitimised the expansion of colonies and establishment of mission stations, including Australia. Therefore, the early scientifically produced evidence from the rainforest region was aimed at capturing pre-European Aboriginal rainforest culture and society before its imminent disappearance (Lumholtz 1889; Mjöberg 1913, 1918; Roth 1898, 1900–10).

Carl Lumholtz

The earliest scientific study of this kind is Lumholtz's early 1880s account of his time on the Herbert River, located in the southern extremity of the rainforest region (Fig. 2.1). He and others worked in a period when ideas of biological and cultural development dominated:

I am interested in gaining knowledge about the Australian Aborigines, since they are considered to be the lowest race on earth. I believe the Aborigines are a doomed people … the most degraded and hopeless of all savage races (Lumholtz 1889:375).

In *Amongst Cannibals* (1889), Lumholtz depicts himself as the white explorer who achieves the trust of the local Aboriginal people with the power of a gun, tobacco, and friendliness (Lumholtz 1889:117). Lumholtz's accounts on the lifestyles of the Aboriginal rainforest people he met suggests that many pre-European aspects of Aboriginal rainforest culture had survived European settlement in the Herbert River area. The local Aboriginal people were still carrying out traditional hunting and gathering practices such as burning large grassy pockets to flush out kangaroos, producing and using many traditional organic rainforest implements, and participating in ceremonial activities. He also documented the use of woollen government blankets amongst the Aboriginal people he met on the Herbert River (Lumholtz 1889:287). He was informed by Europeans that the local Aboriginal people had recently been allowed to come to Herbert Vale Station and that they were becoming fond of wearing the garments and ornaments of white people and of smoking tobacco (Lumholtz 1889:82). Lumholtz wrote about some of the cruelties towards Aboriginal people in the area, referring to stories told to him by settlers and squatters who were shooting 'cattle killers' living on their runs. He also recognised the damage that was being done by the Native Police force:

> That inhuman institution has also been an important factor in the destruction of the natives. They have not only slain a large number, but also contributed largely to their demoralisation (Lumholtz 1889:374).

Whilst acknowledging the devastating effects European settlement was having on the Aboriginal population, Lumholtz firmly believed that Aboriginal people were inevitably destined for extinction. This theory legitimised events that took place in north Queensland, and elsewhere in Australia, and also helped shape government policy.

1890s: Photographers in the rainforest

Towards the end of the nineteenth century, studio photographers from Cairns, Townsville and Brisbane were active in the rainforest region. They travelled to the Atherton Tableland via a new train line connecting Cairns with Atherton, to photograph 'traditional' Aboriginal people and artefacts, European logging activities and the rainforest environment. Some of the photographs were made into postcards (G. Genex, pers. comm., 2006). A visual history of Aboriginal rainforest culture is offered in the photographs from this period (see Figs. 3.2–3.4).

Figure 3.2 Construction of a hut in a cleared area at the edge of the rainforest on the Atherton Tableland.

Source: Courtesy John Oxley Library: Atkinson collection. Photograph also appears in Mjöberg's 1918 travel account, 1918:182.

Figure 3.3 Aboriginal walking track through rainforest.
Source: Courtesy John Oxley Library, Brisbane.

Figure 3.4 Aboriginal men in traditional ceremonial costume with their shields, swords, and spears.

The photograph appears in Mjöberg's travel account *Amongst Stone Age People in the Queensland Wilderness* (1918), entitled 'A secret meeting in a remote rainforest location, a so called "yabba-yabba". Here decisions are made by the chief, along with his closest associates, the old and wise within the tribe, on the most important questions.'

Source: Mjöberg 1918:388.

Despite the staging of people and artefacts in many of the photographs, they illustrate the traditional painted wooden shields cut out of buttress roots from fig trees that were used together with long one-handed hardwood swords and spears during the corroborees (Figs. 3.4–3.5). These material culture items are unique to the rainforest region, as well as the use of cockatoo feathers in body decoration seen in Figure 3.4 (Coyyan 1918, part V); M. Barlow, pers. comm., 2004).

In addition to the characteristic organic rainforest weapons, two domestic items also distinguish rainforest groups from other Aboriginal groups (Fig. 3.5). These are a bark basket used to carry water and other liquids, and lawyer cane baskets, used to carry fruits, nuts and other portable items (including babies) (Mjöberg 1918:240), they are also used in the processing of toxic nuts.

Figure 3.5 Aboriginal family group on the Atherton Tableland with painted shields, spears and a hardwood sword, as well as two characteristic domestic rainforest items, a water-carrying bark basket (left) and a bicornual lawyer cane basket (right), 1890s.

Source: Atkinson collection, courtesy Cairns Historical Society, Cairns.

Transformations on the Tablelands

Aboriginal resistance from the rainforest

The history of Aboriginal resistance to European settlement on the Tablelands was investigated by Loos (1982). He found that from the early 1880s, as Europeans began to arrive and settle in the Tablelands area, Aboriginal rainforest people were driven away from their traditional hunting and gathering grounds by the Native Mounted Police force. However, the use of the Native Mounted Police force on the Tablelands was more or less abandoned a few years later, partly because Native Troopers and a Sub-Inspector Nichols had killed at least four Aboriginal people at Irvinebank in 1884. Nichols was discharged but the incident appeared in the *Herberton Advertiser* and the word 'massacre' was used for the first time in the Queensland Parliament (Genever 2006:6). However, the main reason for the abandonment of the Native Police force was the rainforest environment, where horses could not be used and the advantage of rifles over spears was limited. The effectiveness of the Native Police force, and the devastating results that had been seen in other parts of southern and central Queensland was greatly diminished and the force was abandoned by the Queensland Government as a result (Loos 1982:103).

Loos' research into newspaper articles and police reports from the 1880s show that during the early resistance period relatively secure refugia were to be found for Aboriginal people in traditional rainforest campsites. However, because of their confinement to rainforest campsites and the loss of access to traditional hunting and gathering grounds, people were starving. As a means of securing food, raids were conducted on European houses, cattle were speared, and food, crops, and other items were stolen from European camps and settlements (Loos 1982:110). In a report from Atherton Police Station, dated 25 November 1888, Constable Hansen described a 19-day search for Aboriginal camps through rainforest near the township of Atherton (Loos 1982:109). He found rainforest camps containing bushels of corn plus a variety of European items, including steel axes and tomahawks. Before the end of December, Hansen had brought several Aboriginal people to Atherton from such rainforest camps, who informed him of their hunger. In response, many of the European settlers requested that the Queensland Government provide Aboriginal rainforest people with food rations as a measure to stop Aboriginal resistance and attacks on European homes and stock (*Herberton Advertiser* 1888, 1889; Loos 1982:109). Aboriginal resistance from the rainforest was more or less extinguished by the implementation of a new government policy in 1889 that recognised food shortage as the main reason behind Aboriginal attacks on Europeans (Loos 1982). By the turn of the twentieth century, Aboriginal rainforest people were living in fringe camps near European towns. They were supplied with food rations and in some areas, to some extent, allowed to supplement their European food rations with traditional foods (M. Barlow, pers. comm., 2004; L. Wood, pers. comm., 2004).

The 1897 Protection Act

Walter E. Roth was the first Protector appointed in north Queensland. The appointment of Protectors of Aborigines in Queensland was part of a government initiative to keep the peace between European settlers and Aboriginal people. Presented at the time as a charitable and humane measure, the 1897 *Aboriginals Protection and Restriction of the Sale of Opium Act* controlled the fate of Aboriginal people across Queensland. Its practical outcome was oppressive, further restricting the freedom of Aboriginal people. As the new policy paved the way for the establishment of Aboriginal reserves and missions, Aboriginal people were relocated by the newly designated 'Protectors' (Evans et al. 1988).

As previously discussed, the Native Police force had been the main government instrument for the administration of Aboriginal people. With the implementation of the Protection Act of 1897, this policy was abandoned and the troopers were dispersed. Bushman Michael O'Leary reflected on the serious consequences this had for the Aboriginal people living in remote rainforest locations:

At that time most of the troopers were disbanded and allowed to roam at large. They visited the outside parts and induced the young females to accompany them to where they could trade in spirits, or charcoal opium. This sudden disbanding of the troopers had the effect of wiping out a lot of those scrub blacks in a very short space of time. Once those cast-off troopers were allowed a free leg they rose to the occasion and the consequence was that the different tribes vanished with astonishing rapidity (Coyyan 1918, part VIII:2).

Soon after the implementation of the 1897 Protection Act, official police records reported trouble on the Atherton Tablelands by Aboriginal people moving up from the coastal lowland areas. Their reports were most likely referring to dispersed Aboriginal troopers on the coast coming up to the Tablelands:

7.7.1898. Higgins [Const. 596] to Sub-Inspector of Police Cairns. The blacks come from the coast up the Murray and Tully Rivers on to the Tableland and is very troublesome (Police Department, 1898: A/38047).

It appears that the Protection Act did little to protect traditional rainforest people still living on the Tablelands. In 1910, Tom Mitchell was appointed as the first official Protector of Aborigines in Ravenshoe, an office usually held by the local police officer, missionaries, or civil servants. A mission station was never established at Ravenshoe and, since the nearest police station at the time was in Herberton, the postmaster of Ravenshoe was appointed to take on this position (Toohey 2001:65). Also officially appointed was the 'King' of the *Jirrbal* people, who was required to travel to Herberton once a year to receive an annual gift from the authorities to distribute to his people. This included blankets, tomahawks, plugs of tobacco and pipes. On these occasions, he was expected to wear his breastplate of office. 'King' or 'brass plates' were presented to perceived chiefs or leaders of a tribe, or to faithful servants who helped in some way to ease the white peoples' progress in Australia (Troy 1993). The plates were presented to Aboriginal people from the earliest time of European settlement through to the first decades of the twentieth century (Troy 1993). The first such appointee in Ravenshoe was given the name King George after King George V in England who acceded to the throne in 1910 (Toohey 2001:66) (Fig. 3.6).

Figure 3.6 King George of Ravenshoe receiving the annual handout of blankets from the Protector of Aborigines, circa 1910.

Source: The photograph is displayed in the Ravenshoe cultural centre (also see Reynolds 1972, front cover).

In 1913, Eric Mjöberg had an encounter with King George of Ravenshoe, who accompanied him into the rainforest to collect insects. Mjöberg commented that: 'The king speaks relatively good English and are [sic] assisting the Europeans in various ways' (Mjöberg 1913a). The European appointment of Aboriginal Kings was also commented on by O'Leary:

> Well, it may appear all right, but it is a bit of blissful ignorance, that is, as far as those scrub blacks are, or were, concerned. They had no king or even chief man. Old age played an important part among them: even both sexes were respected when hoary frost made its appearance. Still, it was only respect for old age for no one among those blacks was elevated to a pedestal (Coyyan 1918, part V:2).

Thus, the Queensland Government was partly usurping traditional Aboriginal power structures to maintain control and regulation by elevating certain older Aboriginal people to the status of king or chief of a tribe. The distribution of European gifts such as blankets and tomahawks was most likely an attempt to keep peace with Aboriginal people and avoid further raids on European farms and settlements. The overall outcome of the Protection Act for the Aboriginal rainforest people on the Tablelands was that Aboriginal culture and society underwent further transformations to accommodate new government policy.

Ethnohistorical evidence from the Evelyn Tableland

The remainder of this chapter presents analyses of two ethnohistorical sources that can be directly linked to the Evelyn Tableland: the early writings of Michael O'Leary and Eric Mjöberg's documents from 1913.

Michael O'Leary

Prospector Michael O'Leary was one of the first Europeans to arrive in the upper Tully River area in the early 1880s. He employed local Aboriginal men and boys in his pursuit of an alluvial gold resource (Toohey 2001:68–69). The mining did not produce a large amount of gold and by 1905, the small-scale gold rush was over. During his years prospecting in the rainforests of the Evelyn Tableland, O'Leary wrote a bush diary which he later published as extracts in local newspapers, under the name *Coyyan*, the local Aboriginal word for white quartz (D. Donoghue, pers. comm., 2008). O'Leary never explained why he wrote under the name *Coyyan*. Perhaps Aboriginal men gave him the name because he was a white man, or perhaps he got the name as a result of prospecting for gold and asking about where to find white quartz sources. O'Leary communicated with the local Aboriginal people in their language:

> For the person who wants to learn their language thoroughly, the young boys are the best to learn from, as they are generally slow of speech, and sound the accents clearly (Coyyan 1915:1).

His main work, 10 newspaper columns titled 'The Aboriginals' (Coyyan 1918, parts I–X), discuss many aspects of Aboriginal rainforest culture, much of it based on first-hand observations of the lifestyles of the upper Tully River Aboriginal people in the late 1800s. He concluded with the statement:

> I make no apology for this crude attempt to give the reader some knowledge of those people who once were, but are no more, that is, as far as their ancient habits and customs are concerned. What I have penned about them is not from hearsay, it is from actual experience while living among those people. The wages system and the regulated hours of labor [sic] held no charms for me, so therefore I chose the rough but independent and free life of the metal hunter. Naturally, this mode of life threw us in daily contact with those people [Aboriginal people]. Again, I do not wish to impress the reader that I am a real live authority on the subject, for most bushmen can relate some curious traits that they have witnessed at different times. I have omitted many instances that might have amused the reader, but for the present this humble effort will be sufficient. COYYAN (Finis.) (Coyyan 1918, part X:2).

O'Leary's writings show bitterness towards government officials and their attitudes towards Aboriginal people. He was clearly upset about the Protection Act and the work of the missionaries, perhaps reasons behind his decision to publish his diary. In one instance, he is openly critical of the Queensland Government and Roth's work as Protector of the Aborigines. Angry about the effects Europeans and government policies were having on the Aboriginal rainforest people he wrote:

> They [Aboriginal people] began to see things in a different light. They gradually began to learn the white man's ways. The old men of the tribe lost their control of the younger male members. The excitement of discovery led many of them further a field [sic]. Fear, of course, now keeps the slaves in their place (Coyyan 1918, part V:3).

From his writings, it appears that O'Leary wanted to inform the newspaper readers about traditional Aboriginal rainforest culture and society and historical background. Perhaps it was an attempt to make the readers aware of some of the reasons why things had changed in traditional Aboriginal society since European arrival. Whatever his motives, the columns hold new and significant information on pre-European Aboriginal rainforest culture and society in the study area.

Eric Mjöberg

Around three decades after O'Leary's gold prospecting days on the upper Tully River, Swedish scientist Eric Mjöberg undertook an expedition to the rainforest region and other places in Queensland (Ferrier 2006). A short background to Eric Mjöberg is presented below, which includes a consideration of his motives for carrying out ethnographic research and his academic and professional achievements.

Eric Mjöberg was born in 1882 in Sweden. He was employed by the Swedish Museum of Natural History between 1903 and 1912 whilst undertaking his university studies. He received his PhD in entomology in 1910. Mjöberg's life ambition was to explore and conduct scientific research in the tropics. Between 1903 and 1910, the Stockholm Natural History Museum's professor, entomologist and explorer Yngve Sjöstedt, introduced Mjöberg to the scientific world of exploring. The European tradition of foreign expeditions and explorations that began in the eighteenth century still flourished at the turn of the twentieth century and Mjöberg was attracted to the idea of exploring exotic tropical places (Ferrier 2006). Financed by scholarships, Mjöberg organised and lead an expedition to the Kimberley region of Western Australia in 1910 with a group of other scientists, including ethnographer Yngve Laurell (Kronestedt 1989:60). Laurell's collection of ethnographic items and recording of Aboriginal society and culture appears to have influenced Mjöberg, because his subsequent expeditions to the tropics involved ethnographic as well as scientific research agendas. Results from the Kimberley trip were published in various journals and in a popular travel account titled *Amongst Wild Animals and People in Australia* (1915, 2012). On Mjöberg's return from Australia in early 1912, Sjöstedt, an influential member of the Traveller's Club in Stockholm, introduced Mjöberg to its members and, as a result, he became a member of the club (Fig. 3.7).

Figure 3.7 Members of the Traveller's Club, Stockholm, Sweden, circa 1912. Mjöberg is seated second from the right.

Source: Courtesy California Academy of Sciences Archives: Mjöberg Collection.

The purpose of this exclusive club was to 'stimulate friendships between men who have travelled and explored at least two continents outside of Europe' (Traveller's Club 1912: iii). Mjöberg's membership resulted in him receiving a grant from the club. Later that year he set out on a second expedition to Australia, this time to Queensland. The location was inspired by a brief visit to Queensland's southern rainforests in 1911, during his first Australia expedition (Mjöberg 1918). This time he travelled alone with scientific biological research agendas and ethnographic research agendas. This included collecting mammal, insect and botanical specimens on behalf of the Swedish Museum of Natural History (Ferrier 2006). The aim of the expedition was to collect specimens from the southern and northern parts of Queensland and to compare and contrast the two ecological zones (Mjöberg 1918:52). The scientific results from the two expeditions to Australia (1910–11 and 1912–13) were published over a number of years in a compilation titled *Results of Dr E Mjöberg's Swedish Scientific Expeditions to Australia 1910–1913*. The ethnographic results were published in scientific journals (e.g. Mjöberg 1925) and in a travel account titled *Amongst Stone Age People in Queensland's Wilderness* (1918).

Mjöberg spent 1917 and 1918 in the USA on a lecture tour presenting his results at various institutions. Feeling restricted and unsatisfied with his life in Sweden after returning from the USA, he decided to take up a position as director of a zoological research station in Deli, on Sumatra. Later, Mjöberg accepted a position as director at the Sarawak museum in Borneo and undertook a year-long expedition to Mount Tibang followed by a return journey to Sweden in 1926. Between 1927 and 1929 he undertook three journeys to India, mainly collecting ethnographic items that he sold to museums and at auctions. By 1931, he was seriously ill and confined to a life in bed. He died in Stockholm in 1938 at the age of 56 (Ferrier 2006; Svenskt Biografiskt Lexikon 1984:538–541).

Analysis of Eric Mjöberg's diaries

Mjöberg's original diaries, photographs and other written material from the two Australia expeditions were located in the archives of the California Academy of Sciences (CAS) in San Francisco in 2001 (C. Hallgren, pers. comm., 2005). For unknown reasons, the collection was confiscated by American customs as Mjöberg was about to leave the USA, presumably at the end of his lecture tour in 1918. It was subsequently sold at auction and donated in 1932 to CAS. Research on the collection by the author has shown that Mjöberg wrote at least three diaries during his north Queensland expedition (1913a). Diary 1 documents his arrival in Cairns in early January 1913, the organisation of his fieldwork on the Tablelands and the first two months of collecting faunal specimens and insects in the rainforest. Diary 2 (dated 24/3/1913–4/9/1913) documents his time on the Evelyn Tableland, time spent at Yarrabah mission, and a trip to Chillagoe located in the dry area west of the rainforest region. Diary 3 documents an expedition to Laura and the Coleman River on Cape York, which ended his north Queensland expedition. Aspirations for a second expedition to Cape York and Mornington Island never eventuated.

Previous research (Ferrier 1999, 2002, 2006) on Mjöberg's rainforest expedition focused on reconstructing his travels in the rainforest region and the ethnographic rainforest material he took back to Sweden. His diaries had not been located at the time of the original research (1999), and as a result, it was mostly based on Mjöberg's published works (1918, 1925). In addition, a small number of letters and journal articles were found in Swedish archives, which were analysed and used to piece together his rainforest expedition. The research established two general collecting areas in the rainforest region: the Tablelands and the coastal lowlands around Cairns (Ferrier 1999, 2006). The investigations within each area focused on trying to find out where he travelled and the types of Aboriginal material culture he collected at each location. Items of material culture were relatively clearly provenanced, and the research showed that a relatively high proportion were collected at a location referred to as Cedar Creek (Ferrier 1999, 2002, 2006).

Analyses of Mjöberg's diaries support previous research results (Ferrier 1999, 2002, 2006). Diary entries show that he arrived in Cairns on 3 January 1913, and embarked on what was to become the main component of his expedition, the exploration of the rainforests. Mjöberg's first diary entry from far north Queensland describes the rainforest scenery as he travelled from Cairns to Atherton by train:

> 3/1 Friday We arrived in Cairns, which is nothing more than a small village, at 5 am. I took the 7 am train up to Atherton. The scenery on the way up is stunning, steep hills are covered with dense dark scrub, palms and vines and steep ravines, small mountain creeks play and jump down its steep bases. Clearings are now and again visible. Also visible on occasion inside the dark scrub are green crowns of eucalypt trees, visible high above the dominant scrub vegetation. I arrived at 2.30 pm in Atherton and checked in at the Barron Valley Hotel with great trepidation (Mjöberg 1913a, Diary 1).

Staying at the Barron Valley Hotel brought him unexpected good fortune:

> This turned out to be lucky because here I met with Mr Arena, a prospector, who promised to take me on a trip to unknown scrub areas for a week. In addition, Mr Drew, a surveyor and Mr Maguise, who promised to lodge me for a week or so, giving me an opportunity to collect *Dendrolagus* [the tree kangaroo] which according to my sources are relatively common in the area. Drew's address is <u>Malanda</u>. This is a fantastic opportunity to photograph and collect specimens. I will have my own camp and tent and black fellows. Good, good, thus I will be amongst *Dendrolagus* and possums in tropical scrub, it will be excellent (Mjöberg 1913a, Diary 1).

The diary shows that surveyors and prospectors helped Mjöberg plan and execute his many rainforest expeditions. For example, they assisted him in finding Aboriginal guides and took him to areas of undisturbed rainforest where he collected animals and insects. Excited about how his first day on the Atherton Tableland had turned out, he started to organise his expedition:

5/1 Next week I will be going out into the scrub and follow the track of the timber cutters and camp with them. According to information I have received, there are areas of newly felled scrub also at Drew's place. The location, where I will go to with Arena, is on the Great Dividing Range from where you get a beautiful view over the lowlands in the west towards the sea of Carpentaria. This area of scrub has so far not been surveyed and the country is classified as 'new country' (Mjöberg 1913a, Diary 1).

He soon realised the difficulties of working in rainforest:

Sunday 12/1 1913 The leeches are terribly mean. They attack without any consideration and suck one's blood with a never-ending appetite. Working in the scrub [rainforest] is almost like visiting hell: ticks and leeches, sharp and thorny vines as well as stinging bushes make life very difficult. The rain has not stopped for days, making life in the scrub miserable to say the least, and my scrub itch is getting worse (Mjöberg 1913a, Diary 1).

The rainforest region was also struck by a tropical cyclone in the early phase of his expedition and Mjöberg became confined to a small hotel in Herberton for several days, cut off from the outside world. It became clear to him that conditions in the rainforest during the wet season were going to seriously affect his progress. In addition to the difficult terrain and weather, at times his health deteriorated with fevers and tropical ulcers, which slowed his work down (Mjöberg 1913a, Diary 1).

Despite the generous help he received from local settlers and prospectors, Mjöberg was generally very critical of the Europeans he encountered in the rainforest region and of Australian society in general. He commented on the general lack of good character and bad behaviour of Australians:

The country is exaggerated with its democracy, here you see the priest riding a bike, going to the pub getting drunk together with hooligans and playing tennis etc. The doctor in the village is an ordinary little man who visits the bars and who is an equal to everybody else (Mjöberg 1913a, Diary 1).

The diaries provide insight into Mjöberg's thoughts on how civilised (i.e. white) people should behave according to class and occupation. He, like many others at the time, believed that the extinction of Aboriginal people was inevitable with the arrival of European civilisation (Mjöberg 1913a, Diary 1). As a result, he wrote sympathetic accounts about Aboriginal rainforest people in his travel account. His preconceived ideas about 'Stone Age people' and 'natives' living in exotic locations such as the rainforest region, strongly influenced his ethnographic work. While it is beyond the scope of this research to present any detail on the differences between Mjöberg's diaries and his published travel account (1918, 2015), when the two sources are compared there are some clear differences. One is his lack of recognition of the assistance given to him. In the travel account he sometimes mentions 'a white gentleman' accompanying him but fails to acknowledge the extent to which Europeans and Aboriginal people guided him to places in the rainforest where he was able to collect and document flora and fauna and Aboriginal material culture items. Another difference lies in the way he describes European settlement on the Tablelands. For example, in the chapter on Cedar Creek in his travel account, it is suggested that very little European settlement had taken place. In fact, a pub already existed, which he occasionally visited, two stores were in operation, and there were more than 300 selectors in the area (North Cedar Creek Settlers Group 1908; Ravenshoe Writers' Group 1999). Selections of land had been available since 1907 and European family homes had been built on the banks of Cedar Creek (Smith 2001; E. Dingwall, pers. comm., 2005).

Encounters with Aboriginal people

Mjöberg spent the first weeks of January in rainforests outside of the town Atherton, where he stayed with his newly acquainted prospecting friend Arena at his place 'somewhere in the scrub' (Mjöberg 1913a, Diary 1). Moving away from the settled areas around Atherton, Mjöberg set out to find rainforests untouched by the timber cutters. He regularly accompanied surveyors in his rainforest sojourns and for the rest of the time, he hired Aboriginal guides:

Friday 17/1 Set out once again to the rainforests together with the surveyor. However, heavy rain stopped our journey and we returned by 2 o'clock. On Monday I will start a journey to Mt Lavery [sic] with two pack horses and a few black fellows. Cedar Creek is rumoured to be very good. (Mjöberg 1913a, Diary 1).

Diary entries show that within weeks of arrival he had heard about Cedar Creek, where according to his European sources, Aboriginal people were living in traditional campsites at the edge of undisturbed rainforests. He later noted in this diary:

In Cedar Creek I encountered a traditional wet-season native rainforest village used by a large group of native people that inhabit rainforests around Cedar Creek and Tully River (Mjöberg 1913a, Diary 2).

Some of Mjöberg's Aboriginal guides appear to have spoken relatively good English and his failure to question them about Aboriginal rainforest culture and society past and present probably reflects his lack of training in ethnographic and anthropological research. He spent most of his time with young Aboriginal boys and men, who would have had more limited cultural knowledge compared to the more senior Aboriginal men and women. It is also quite possible that the older people avoided him. Similar to his predecessor Meston, Mjöberg sometimes noted the Aboriginal name for an object or animal. A list of Aboriginal words and their meanings is provided in the third diary but it is generally unclear who provided information on the Aboriginal names for various things. The type of limited information he documented is demonstrated in the following diary extract:

9/1 I will tomorrow hire some Negroes and start collecting. –mabi=Dendrolagus sp. (Mjöberg 1913a, Diary 1).

For the most part, no information on the names of Aboriginal groups he encountered or observed in the rainforest can be found in the diaries. This means that the only way of interpreting whose traditional land he was travelling in is by finding out the names of the locations he visited.

Change and continuity in cultural trajectories

Historical information shows that, by the time of Mjöberg's visit in 1913, traditional Aboriginal society had already changed a great deal because of European settlement in the region. Mjöberg's previously unanalysed diaries, therefore, have the potential to contribute information on change and continuity in traditional Aboriginal rainforest culture and society during the transitional contact period. As a result, the following analysis reflects on change and continuity in the trajectories identified in Chapter 1: material culture and technology, subsistence strategies and rainforest settlement patterns, between circa 1880–1913.

Material culture and technology

When Michael O'Leary arrived in the upper Tully River area in the early 1880s, he observed many of the typical organic material culture rainforest items described in the ethnographic literature in use:

Before the white man's time those people had no utensils for boiling water. They had a bag made from the nupa bark that they used for carrying honey, etc. It was sometimes used for water purposes. The native bee supplied them with honey and also wax, so that the fastenings where string was used could be made more secure. This vessel was called the nupa, and the honey and wax was known as myee. Water would be mixed with the honey and then it would be lapped up with the aid of pieces of vine that they had purposely chewed into shreds. This nupa tree came in for a good many purposes. The shoots or saplings supplied them with very strong rope. From the bark they made their blankets. The tree when dead decomposed very quickly and it was a favourite timber for the beetles to deposit their larvae in. When hatched they formed into grubs, and, of course, provided those people with food. This grub is known to them as the chambonne. Before using, the bark is carefully smoked. Those trees [nupa] are often ringbarked so as to cause their decay. The young vine tree [Calamus spp.] is somewhat similar to the nupa. From it they get material for ropes, blankets, vessels, and the tree is often stripped for making humpies (Coyyan 1918, part X:2).

He observed that men manufactured most of the equipment used to hunt and fish as well as more domestic items mostly used by the women:

> The weapons that those scrub blacks have in use are a fair load to carry, the shield and sword being rather cumbersome. The task of making fishing nets, turkey nets, dilly bags, vessels for holding water, and the catching of large game, such as the possom [sic], tree climbing kangaroo and cassowary, is monopolised by the males. All their weapons, swords and spears of all descriptions, woomeras, waddies and boomerangs, are made from varieties of hard timber that is also very durable. The shield is made from a very light and soft timber. It has also to be tough enough to turn or stop a flying spear. During the heavy wet months of the year the wood supply entailed a fair amount of labor [sic], as their stone axes were a very primitive implement (Coyyan 1918, part X:2).

References to stone implements in the ethnographic literature are rare and the naming and use of some stone implements on the upper Tully River suggests little contact with Europeans:

> The stone axe is called Moan, but the name mostly used is Puddy. All quartz is called Coyyan, but each kind has its own name. Stones are called Tebun, but here too they apply the word to stones in general; having different words to designate different material, as basalt, granite etc. Flewen means the sapphire or any transparent stone. Before glass and metal was available to those abos. [sic] a sharp piece of quartz was used in slicing and cutting, much like a knife (Coyyan 1918, part VI:2 & part VIII:3).

This extract shows that artefacts made from quartz were used at the time of European arrival. Later on, glass and metal replaced quartz as the raw material used in the activities described above.

Mjöberg collected a small number of Aboriginal stone implements (Ferrier 2002). His diary shows that Europeans presented him with most of these and informed him that they were no longer in use by the Aboriginal people at Cedar Creek or elsewhere in the rainforest. Based on his own observations, Mjöberg wrote that European axes were common amongst the Aboriginal men, as many of them worked for European timber cutters and surveyors as trackers and tree climbers. The diary demonstrates that on many occasions, information on Aboriginal rainforest culture was based on hearsay and not on first-hand observation. In addition, the diary shows that during Mjöberg's visit to Yarrabah mission he came across previously published works about the rainforest Aborigines:

> Have with great interest read Matthews work, as well as Spencer and Gillen, Roth and others. They are available here at the station in addition to Lumholtz. –For comparative purposes, I can borrow a lot of information provided by Mathews and Spencers. According to sources, the children were carried in a piece of bark and a lawyer cane vine around the forehead (Mjöberg 1913a, Diary 2).

Thus, it appears that Mjöberg used a variety of sources to try to piece together a picture of 'traditional' Aboriginal rainforest culture for his travel account.

Acquisition of material culture items

A sword and two spears labelled 'Atherton' in the Swedish Museum of Ethnography collection were paid for by Mjöberg with money. There is no mention of who they were purchased from when he wrote '1/1 Bought a beautiful sword and two spears' (Mjöberg 1913a, Diary 1).

One possibility is that the items purchased in Atherton were made by Aboriginal people who were selling them as a source of income. It is equally possible that he purchased them from European collectors. A number of the material culture items from Cedar Creek were bought directly from Aboriginal people:

> 25/3 <u>Tuesday</u> A day extremely rich in results. My workers arrived and work is in full swing. –My steps went towards the black fellows' camp, where I quickly acquired a few items. In every camp I observed a primitive grinding stone implement, a simple flat piece of rock and a cobble stone. I bought three samples of these, as well as headache stones. In the camps at Cedar Creek I saw a large number of shields, swords and some spears as well as a beautiful club, a few grinding stones and some music sticks as well as several dilly bags, some beautifully painted with red ochre. I hope to acquire a bark blanket,

these were made and used in the old days but some people still know the method of how to make them. Similarly, I will acquire an eel net, a turkey net, an eel spear and eel trap made of lawyer cane (Mjöberg 1913a, Diary 1).

Mjöberg's reference to bark blankets and stone axes made and used in the 'old days' are the only two examples in the diaries where he mentions a change in Aboriginal material culture resulting from European arrival.

Some material culture items were 'collected', i.e. stolen, from campsites and on the rare occasion, he traded, or promised to supply, European goods in return for Aboriginal artefacts:

27/3 In the afternoon, I continued on to the Negroes camp where I previously found and collected a large nice dilly bag and seven nulla nullas. The Negroes were all at the camp, they had hidden the eel spear and sword, but after a lot of negotiation I managed to exchange the large shield with the promise of a few pipes in return. It is a ceremonial fighting shield and has spear marks from the corroboree. They were very hesitant to separate themselves with it because it requires a lot of work to make a new one. It has been cut out by using a stone axe and is very old, and is the pride and joy of its owners. I also discovered oval stones, somewhat bigger than a hens' egg, hidden along the walls in the huts and carried around by the women in their lawyer cane baskets. They are painted with a layer of wax or resin of some sort. They are apparently used to cure headaches with. The women are quite unwilling to separate themselves from the stones which are believed to have magical powers. I managed to acquire a sample of them from their baskets when they were out collecting food (Mjöberg 1913a, Diary 2).

One contact item in the Mjöberg collection is a fishhook made of iron, which was collected at Cedar Creek. Its presence demonstrates the inclusion of European items into the traditional material culture of the Aboriginal people living at Cedar Creek. Some of the material culture items were commissioned by Mjöberg. Mjöberg received (from an unknown source) a gigantic slate axe head which was later fitted with a new flimsy lawyer cane handle by Tommy, one of the Aboriginal boys working with him during his stay at Cedar Creek (Fig. 3.8).

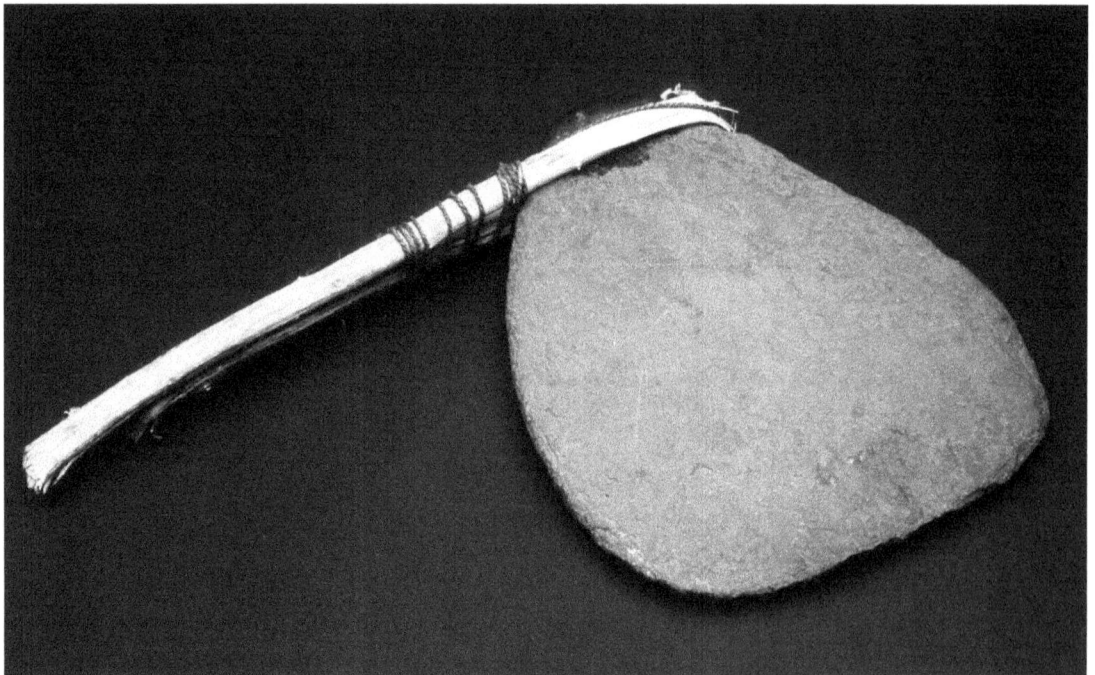

Figure 3.8 Large slate axe with a new lawyer cane handle, Cedar Creek.
Source: Courtesy Museum of Ethnography, Stockholm.

Mjöberg did not document what this type of axe would have been used for in the past, possibly because his source was not able to inform him on the uses of pre-European Aboriginal artefacts. The surface is covered with ochre, which suggests that one of its uses was to process ochre, or perhaps it was once painted with ochre for some unknown reason. Diary entries indicate that stone artefacts were generally no longer in use at Cedar Creek with the exception of flat basalt rocks used as grinding stones accompanied by a small cobble. Combined, they served as an important tool in the preparation of nuts, fruits, and roots, as well as for grinding ochre. Mjöberg also acquired two previously undocumented types of baskets. One was made from eucalypt bark and another from grass, which indicate the inclusion of raw materials from an open forest environment. With the location of Cedar Creek at the western margin of the rainforest region, Mjöberg suggested that the Aboriginal people in this area utilised raw materials from two different environments (i.e. semi-dry open woodlands and rainforests) in manufacturing of their material culture (Mjöberg 1918:447).

Subsistence strategies

The historically documented use of toxic walnuts and other rainforest food plants are discussed in more detail in the context of the Urumbal Pocket archaeological plant assemblage (Chapter 6). The following extracts from Coyyan's column (1918) titled 'Their Food' provides information on additional food sources and subsistence strategies in use in the upper Tully River area in the early contact period:

> When the abos. [sic] are preparing for a journey they always prepare a bountiful supply of food. Yams, ground nuts, the succulent part of the lawyer vine, the grass tree and every other sort of vegetable food that these people use have to go under some preparations before they can be used. The yams have a fair amount of energy expended on them. The *toe-kerroe* is a plum tree. The fruit is a large white nut, forms on the trunk of the tree, and when ripe, can be eaten without preparing. The Davidsonian plum grows on a small bush, and is strictly confined to our high land scrubs. On account of its bitter, acid taste it is not eagerly sought for (Coyyan 1918, part IX:1).

The use of the grass tree again demonstrates that food plants outside the rainforest were used. O'Leary's descriptions on the types of animals hunted provide additional insights into rainforest subsistence:

> When the turkey season is on it becomes a busy time for the abos. [sic]. Nets have to be made for trapping the birds, they lay their eggs at the same time. Those nets are made from the fibre of a small sapling, carefully scraped with some sharp stone. When finished the net is taken to the desired spot and set. Some koah nuts are then broken and distributed both inside and outside the net. The turkey and scrub hen provide the most food. The cassowary is often caught when young and it will get that tame that it will follow the tribe into different camps. When a large bird has been killed it gives the tribe a good feast. The tree-climbing kangaroo (mappey) is about the best flesh that those people get. They require dogs to hunt these animals. In those scrubs there is a species of black and brown dingo. It is a puzzle how they came into those scrubs. The abos. [sic] claim to have tamed and used them for hunting before they secured dogs from the white man. When they have an abundance of this food they will erect a stage about three or four feet high and on it they will spit the mappey. Next on the flesh list is the wallaby. There are two or three species of scrub wallaby and the abos. [sic] generally trap them by making pits on their regular pads. Then comes the bandicoot, but it is not a favorable [sic] dish of the abos. [sic]. Next on the list are the rodents. The two large species are game for the males; they are the turkim and the yarrey; all the smaller species (the muccah and mookin) are left to the females. There are two or three sorts of possums and the scrub one is a very large species; its color [sic] is black. They all provide food for the abo [sic] but at times it requires a considerable amount of climbing before they secure their prize. Both the carpet snake and a large black snake are eaten by those people. There are also several large lizards and iguanas in those scrubs that supply food for the abo. [sic]. They made cooking a profession, disembowelling all game before committing it to the fire. The scrub black will carefully dress his food and cook it properly, providing they are in a camp and have the time at their disposal (Coyyan 1918, parts IX:2–X:1).

Thus the traditional diet of the *Jirrbal* Aboriginal people was varied and, as with their material culture, incorporated plants and animals from two different environments: the rainforest and nearby open sclerophyll forest. Fish also played a significant role in the Aboriginal rainforest diet and O'Leary described different methods of catching fish:

Fish plays an important part with those people. From the rivers great quantities are caught. Their method is to form small eddies with stones on the river rapids. His device for throwing them out of the water is made from the lawyer vine, and is in appearance like two big fans joined together. Members at the camp will have fires prepared. The fish are placed in leaves and then baked in the hot ashes. When cooked the whole fish remains intact. Those people can turn their food out of the ashes entirely free from dirt. Another plant of the abos. [sic] is to form a wall of stones across rapids. At prepared openings they will place dilly-bags for the fish to enter. Then there is their pastime of fishing with hook and line. The line is made from the Boombal and is fairly strong, and hooks are made from a very hard timber that has been seasoned in the fire. Fish bones are also converted into hooks and another variety is obtained from a certain kind of shell. Nature supplies hooks in abundance from a species of lawyer vine. This species is known as the jaggan. Then comes that method which is the king of sport, spearing with a fish spear and woomera. In the shallow creeks is the home of the eels, and the abo [sic] has a tube made from lawyer vines for catching them. One end is closed the other is bell-shaped. In the night they will traverse those watercourses by the aid of torches known as the chillo, the tree is known as the bin-dan-new. The eels are apparently attracted by the flare of the torches, and are easily decoyed into the lawyer tube (wongar). In those waters are also the tortoise and the crayfish or lobster. In those scrubs there is a very large frog that is known as the tang-go. They are cooked on the fire (Coyyan 1918, parts IX:2–X:1).

Mjöberg's diary entries show that some toxic rainforest foods were still being processed and consumed at Cedar Creek in 1913. He, like O'Leary, specifically documented the importance of *Calamus* sp. (the lawyer vine) as a raw material in the manufacture of many material culture items but also for other purposes:

> Thursday 25/3 Took photographs of their mimi. Each family usually have their own hut (during the wet season) during the dry season they protect themselves with branches and leaves. At times, families join together and build a family mimi (majmaj) which has two openings. – The smoke escapes through an opening in the ceiling (Mjöberg 1913a, Diary 2).

> Saturday 28/6 Another new use of the lawyer cane may be added to all the previous ones, they eat many of the new shoots. Thus, also a source of food! (Mjöberg 1913a, Diary 2).

Mjöberg concluded that the lawyer vine must have played an important role in Aboriginal rainforest adaptation, and continued to play an important role in Aboriginal rainforest occupation in 1913. Both O'Leary and Mjöberg observed that many animals and plants had to be collected from the treetops, which was achieved with a climbing rope:

> Those blacks would climb the tallest tree with ease. They used a pliable lawyer vine for climbing and it was known to them as the 'Cambey'. Where the scrub was very dense, and the limbs overlapped each other, those blacks would take advantage and climb from tree to tree (Coyyan 1918, part II:3).

One annual rainforest activity during the drier months was to hunt large grubs, which involved burning dead and decaying tree logs on the rainforest floor:

> There was one yearly custom that they would indulge in. During the cold months, when the chambonne (tree grubs) were plentiful and fit for eating, a number of the tribe would gather and go on a chambonne hunt. When they came to the desired spot, fires would be set going and the fallen trees or decayed timber would be burst into fragments. Some would be cooking the grubs, and at a signal all hand would partake of the food in a hurried manner, and then amid much laughter they would rush through the scrub, until another patch of decayed timber was found. This would happen during the dry and cold months (Coyyan 1918, part VIII:2).

This suggests that fire was an important tool in traditional rainforest subsistence strategies. Mjöberg's diary shows that in addition to the Aboriginal camps at Cedar Creek, he also visited camps on European Tableland properties, where Aboriginal people worked for the landowners:

> 5/4 I walked over to the Negros [sic] camp where Tommy lives [on private land near Malanda] and talked to him. On the fire was a complete roasted Dendrolagus [tree kangaroo] with the skin left on. The intestines had been removed. I received a water bag and bark of the stinging tree which they use to sieve honey. They spread out one piece in the bottom of the container, place one in the middle and finally two pieces that act like mesh on the top (Mjöberg 1913a, Diary 2).

He sometimes referred to the Aboriginal people living at Cedar Creek as the 'Tully River mob' and documented that the people occupying the wet season camp at Cedar Creek would at certain times of the year travel to the Tully River to catch eel, a seasonally important food source.

The diary documents some of the food consumed by the rainforest people he met:

> Thursday 24/4 Jack has also showed me food, yam, a type of plant with wide leaves. The tube stock is very long and tastes like sweet potato according to Jack. They call it chokoll. They dig them out of the ground at a depth of 2 feet. Received five nuts from a type of tree which they eat and that they call Agkon, these they grind like walnuts and prepare a type of porridge (similar to dough). They cook a type of cake from the walnut porridge (Mjöberg 1913a, Diary 2).

This brief account on rainforest food sources lends support to the suggestion that Mjöberg fleshed out his published travel account with other historical sources, in which Aboriginal food sources and subsistence strategies were discussed in more detail. It is also possible that the lack of references to traditional food sources in Mjöberg's diary reflects the use of European food items at the Cedar Creek camp in 1913.

Rainforest settlement patterns

As the prospectors headed for the upper Tully River area and the Culpa goldfield in the early 1880s, they tried to follow Aboriginal tracks. Prospecting in dense rainforest without any local knowledge proved difficult:

> You would often strike one of their pads running in the direction you wanted to go. You would naturally follow it but you would not go for long before you would come to a standstill. Your beautiful track had run you into the tangled-up mass of a windfall or a dense cluster of vines After the abos. [sic] joined us and we began to understand them we soon learnt where to find the proper track. You would notice where a young tree had been cut down at some time and a bunch of green shoots had grown. Just brush yourself through them and you would find yourself once more on the clear pad. It was a clever device, and I suppose often assisted them to escape from an enemy (Coyyan 1918, part VII:2).

In time, the prospectors learnt many of the skills of the rainforest Aboriginal people. They also instigated contact with the Europeans sometime after their arrival in the area, perhaps as a result of events taking place on the coast. O'Leary's descriptions of Aboriginal rainforest settlement and use include the construction of camps and tracks:

> It was only during heavy spells of wet weather that they made a decent camp and even then it would require some everyday improvement to keep it rain proof. The males seldom assist in camp-making: this work belongs solely to the females. This allows the males to be able to hunt for game. In the early days, while the Abos. [sic] were in their wild state, I have come across camps, or huts of theirs that would easily hold 40 or 50 persons. These camps were built in semi-circle fashion, and were held or strengthened by what we would term props. Those camps were well built, and would stand the roughest of weather. In those dense scrubs their pad will always be on the leading spurs. There are two reasons for them adopting this method. First, the scrub is not so dense on high lands, and second, because it avoids the broken country, and is therefore easier for travelling. The scrub tracks must naturally be crooked, as it never was the abos. [sic] game to hew down trees to gain a straight track: their plan was to go round them (Coyyan 1918, part II:2).

In March 1913, Eric Mjöberg witnessed and described Aboriginal people building wet-season huts in a large clearing at Evelyn, north of Ravenshoe:

> They have the best huts on the continent regarding quality as well as form. Considerable time and effort is involved until the hut becomes pleasant to use as a dwelling. The location of a camp is always near a small creek, often at the edge of the rainforest to avoid the constant dripping from trees and dead branches falling down. Some camps used during their travels are found inside the rainforest and here they clear a large semi-circular area. The first step in making a hut is to build an oval or circular dome-shaped frame out of tough rainforest vines. The frame is held together with split lawyer cane vines and gets covered in layer after layer of large palm leaves, tied down with more split lawyer cane

vines. Stones are placed here and there on the ground to fill any gaps. Sometimes several of them are connected together and you can walk from one to the next through a covered path. The openings are always oriented facing the calm side and away from wind and rain and are kept closed during cold nights with a large piece of bark. They are completely waterproof, even against the heaviest rainstorms imaginable. A large family hut houses around 30 people. Their mostly used kitchen tools are on the ground, the others are attached to the wall and a fire is constantly burning in the middle of the hut. A ditch is dug around it to steer water away during heavy rain. How long these huts are occupied for is unknown but I assume that they are used at least for a few years since there is considerable time and effort involved to build them (Mjöberg 1918:429–432).

Weatherproof huts built out of rainforest plants thus remained in use for some time into the post-contact period. Most likely they were preferred because of their superior quality compared to huts made from European materials. Construction of weatherproof huts appears to have been a significant component in pre-European Aboriginal rainforest occupation, allowing local Aboriginal people to remain on the Tablelands throughout the wet season. This in turn would have allowed access to an abundance of important rainforest plant foods available at this time of year.

Ceremonial gatherings

The words corroboree and bora ground are commonly used in the ethnohistorical literature in reference to large ceremonial gatherings that were observed at contact. Some details of the significance of these ceremonial gatherings were described by O'Leary:

> The corroboree is called Bullbah. In speaking of their meeting places or Bora grounds, they say Bullbah. The word booyah-booyah means a fight and, of course, tribal differences are settled at these places. Those old time bullbahs meant a lot to those blacks. It was there that marriages would be arranged, and things in general would be fixed up to the satisfaction of all parties interested. Want of food would generally be the means of breaking up those meetings, and often the visitors would be last to leave the bullbah ground. The blacks who acted as messengers would carry a passport to ensure their safety. After the messages were delivered, business would become very brisk with the owners of the bullbah ground. Camps would be erected at one end of the ground in the adjacent scrub, so as to be clear of the numerous missiles that would be hurled during the fray. The cleaning of their bora grounds was generally the work of old males and females. The site chosen would be on the cap of a ridge or fairly level ground, and it was there that the rival parties would meet and adjust their differences. Mummies, spare weapons, and hiding places for edible nuts would be stored at the bullbah grounds. The ground is properly cleaned and prepared for action. Then there was the preparing of food, a task that would keep all the female members pretty busy. Huge piles of the various eatable nuts would be ground and made into food. Tree-climbing kangaroos would be caught and preserved either by half-roasting or perhaps they would be lucky enough to keep it alive until the eventful day. Sometimes when food would be very plentiful, they would congregate in large number. The visiting tribe would always travel by the main tracks that led through this dense jungle, and would arrive at the opposite side to where the camps were erected (Coyyan 1915:1).

In addition, some of the weapons used during a ceremony were described and named:

> Their war implements consisted of a heavy wooden sword (bacckur), shield (pekin) and spears (tuli). Boomerangs were not much in use among those scrub blacks, as their weapon was almost useless in the dense jungle, and I think that it must have come into use among those blacks in recent years, as none of the scrub blacks were adepts either in the making or using of this weapon. As the sword and shield were very heavy and cumbrous, it was no light task for those people when they were called on to carry them about (Coyyan 1915:35).

Thus, the aim of the *bullbah* was, amongst other things, to settle disputes between participating tribes through ceremonial dance, and to trade goods and arrange marriages.

Having heard rumours of ceremonies recently taking place at Cedar Creek in the summer of 1913, Mjöberg travelled to the area to seek out the local Aboriginal population and to witness a ceremony first-hand:

Monday 24/3 1913 To Tumoulin and from there to Cedar Creek, the location for the last remnants of natives in the area. Here they fight bloody battles during corroborees, a couple of months ago the heads on two boys were speared with the result that their brains seeped out. Saw a few water carrying devices made of bark and shield and spears (Mjöberg 1913a, Diary 2).

As it turned out, Mjöberg never observed a ceremony first-hand and comments in his published travel account of the activities are based entirely on hearsay:

Thursday 24/4 He brought with him a native, Jack, with an unusual capacity to talk and understand conversation. He told me the circumstances around the corroboree. When a native dies he leaves behind him a spirit. The killer will at the following corroboree be challenged to a fight. The defender of the dead person takes his leg bone, and attaches the sharp end of the bone to the tip of a spear. He thereby spears the offender who receives the spear with his shield, which the bone penetrates. The spirit of the dead is transmitted to the speared person who has a fit and runs around like crazy rolling his eyes in a wide circle only to return and fall into a type of coma. Everybody comes running over to him and throws cold water in his face in order for him to come back to sanity. At the next corroboree event they spear him with a normal spear and that settles the dispute (Mjöberg 1913a, Diary 2).

This information suggests that ceremonies were still being held at Cedar Creek during the wet season, a suggestion that is supported by *Jirrbal* oral traditions and historical documents (Police Department, 1914: A/38015; M. Barlow, pers. comm., 2004; L. Wood, pers. comm., 2004).

Mjöberg returned to Cedar Creek in early August after a journey to Chillagoe, west of the rainforest region (Fig. 2.1). He noted in his diary that the 'black fellows' he had camped next to at Cedar Creek in March and April had left:

Thursday 7/8 1913 I went over to visit the [sic] camp but no sign of its inhabitants.
Saturday 9/8 still no sign of the black fellows (Mjöberg 1913a, Diary 2).

It appears that Mjöberg made no attempt to find out why they had left or where they had gone. However, oral traditions show that during the winter months, *Jirrbal* people visited neighbouring groups to trade and participate in ceremonies (M. Barlow, pers. comm., 2004). Thus, in 1913, it appears that the *Jirrbal* people from Cedar Creek were allowed some degree of mobility. A newspaper article (cited in Berry 1999), two years after Mjöberg's visit, demonstrates how Aboriginal people 'gathered from all parts' at Cedar Creek:

January 23 1915 'Northern Herald'

Numerous blacks gathered from all parts, danced, gesticulated, threatened, threw a few spears and boomerangs on Sunday and afforded an interesting and expectant afternoon to the white onlookers, but nothing striking happened (cited in Berry 1999:27).

This shows that the *Jirrbal* people of Cedar Creek, and their neighbours, adapted their lifestyle and traditions according to changes brought about by European settlement, and continued to transform their culture and society into the post-contact period. By the early 1920s, the *Jirrbal* people of Cedar Creek were living in 'town camps' on farm properties around Ravenshoe, their ceremonial ground becoming part of a golf course that was constructed around this time.

Mjöberg left the rainforest region on 12 August when he travelled to Cairns and prepared for an expedition to Laura and the Coleman River on Cape York. In a statement sent to Sweden and published in the Swedish Society for Anthropology and Geography journal *Ymer* (1913b), Mjöberg outlined some of the results of his rainforest expedition:

I have studied the native people of the country with an open eye. The Tribes I have encountered in the rainforest have as a rule been in contact with white civilisation but have with a high degree of toughness remained unchanged in all of the essential aspects of their traditional society. I will bring home a select collection of their weapons and tools, which in regards to manufacture and practicality are advantageously different from tribes in Central and Western Australia (Mjöberg 1913b:336).

The analysis of Mjöberg's diaries shows that his statement 'unchanged in all of the essential aspects of their traditional society' mostly refers to Aboriginal people and rainforest occupation he observed at Cedar Creek. Here many of the characteristic organic rainforest items were still in use, and people were still occupying their traditional campsites. Documenting the rapid changes taking place in Aboriginal rainforest culture and society at the time of his visit was of little interest to Mjöberg.

Summary

From the available ethnohistorical evidence, it appears that, at the time of European arrival to the rainforests of far north Queensland, Aboriginal people had developed a culture and way of life well adapted to the rainforest environment. O'Leary's first-hand observations of Aboriginal subsistence strategies demonstrate that many types of rainforest plants were gathered and consumed but that other food sources such as fish, eel, mammals, birds and reptiles significantly contributed to the diet, including food items collected outside of the rainforest. The analysis has shown that during the wet summer months, Aboriginal people in the study area became more sedentary and hosted large ceremonies when large quantities of rainforest nuts were collected and consumed. Aboriginal campsites and rainforest tracks were kept clear of vegetation and the maintenance of large open pockets, connected by an elaborate network of tracks through the rainforest, allowed for large ceremonial gatherings to take place. Open forest pockets also allowed some larger mammal species to live in the rainforest region.

The analysis of Eric Mjöberg's diary from 1913 has shown that he received information from Europeans on aspects of Aboriginal culture that he could not have observed himself. Evidence also suggests that when he wrote his published travel account (1918, 2015), he had to use ethnohistorical information recorded earlier in the contact period, because of the many changes that had taken place since first contact. His diary demonstrates that he focused on collecting traditional Aboriginal rainforest material culture, some items given to him by European settlers, and others commissioned or acquired through trade with Aboriginal people. The Cedar Creek diary, however, supports previous research in that Aboriginal people at Cedar Creek were still occupying their traditional campsites, collecting rainforest plants, processing toxic rainforest tree nuts, and using their pre-European ceremonial ground in a large open pocket at Cedar Creek to host ceremonies during the wet season. From the historical evidence, it appears that the existence of open forest pockets in the rainforest were an important aspect of Aboriginal rainforest settlement at the time of European arrival. One hypothesis that presents itself from the analysis is that significant archaeological evidence may be present in open forest pockets within rainforest, allowing for investigation into long-term Aboriginal rainforest occupation.

4

Urumbal Pocket

Gumbulumba means a sacred place,
Far above the plains,
high in the forest ranges,
To which women came,
To make their special business,
And share their wise old tales,
Of ancient history of the tribe,
Away from ears of males,
They shared their hopes for happiness
And shared their troubles too,
And talked of sacred women's things,
I can't reveal to you.
They learnt about bush medicine,
Passed down from times of old,
And sat around their fires,
And of the Spirits told.
And sang the praise for all the days,
For their children and their birth.
As they sat beneath the shady trees,
Eating of their fruit.
Where the sparkling waters tumble,
Flowing on down to the sea,
You can feel their spirits present,
And know that they still be,
Sharing Gumbulumba,
For all eternity.

Jean Phillips, Ravenshoe Writers' Club

Introduction

The principal site used to investigate the pre-European archaeological record of the Evelyn Tableland is the open site of Urumbal Pocket located on Koombooloomba Dam (Fig. 1.1). The aim of constructing a long-term history of Aboriginal occupation at the Urumbal Pocket open site is to create a small window of images into a pre-European Aboriginal rainforest society. Urumbal Pocket's long-term occupation history is used here as a backdrop to the construction of occupation histories at two archaeological sites used in the more recent past by Aboriginal people, discussed in Chapters 7 and 8. This chapter commences with a background to the archaeological investigations at the Urumbal Pocket open site, describing the methods employed in the excavations. This is followed by a discussion of the site's stratigraphy and chronology. The assemblage analyses are presented in Chapters 5 and 6.

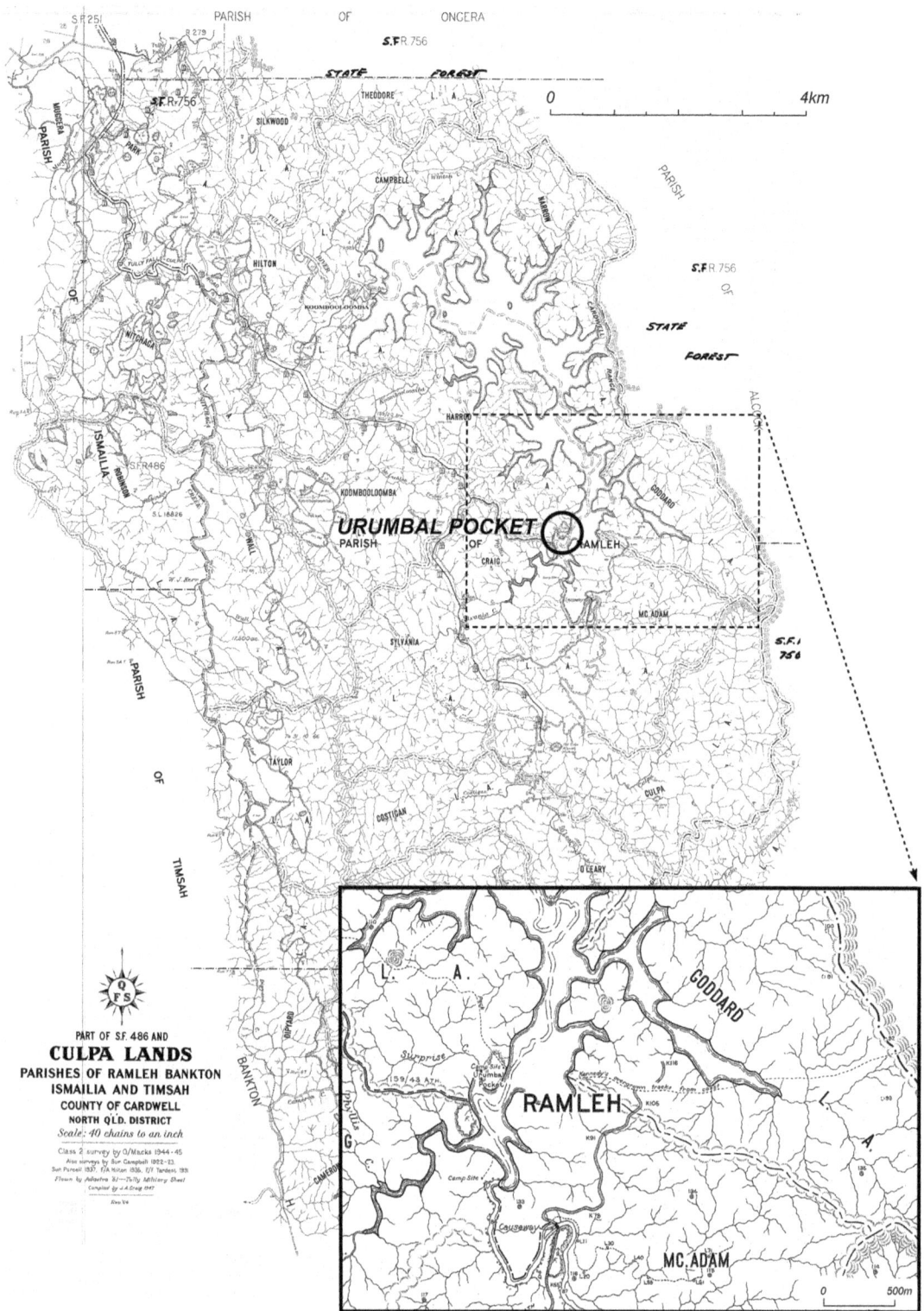

Figure 4.1 Map of Culpa Lands (historical gold field) in the upper Tully River region and the location of the Urumbal Pocket open archaeological site (circled) on Koombooloomba Dam.

Source: Courtesy of L. May.

Background to the excavations

The name 'Koombooloomba' was originally given to the area around the Culpa goldfields on the upper Tully River by gold prospector Michael O'Leary (Fig. 4.1), whose bush diary was discussed in Chapter 3. According to O'Leary, the name Koombooloomba came from the *Jirrbal* word *Gumbulumba*, meaning 'sacred women's place', which is supported by *Jirrbal* oral traditions (Coyyan 1915; M. Barlow, pers. comm., 2004). The first European believed to have stopped and camped in the area of Urumbal Pocket was Edmund Kennedy, whose fatal journey was referred to in Chapter 3. Many of the streams in the Koombooloomba area bear the names of members of the Kennedy party, for example Carron Creek (after a botanist) and Goddard Creek (after a convict) (Fig. 4.1).

Historical reconstructions of Kennedy's journey in the rainforest region described by Beale (1977) indicate that the party crossed the upper Tully River in the vicinity of Urumbal Pocket:

> The next day they crossed the Upper Tully at a spot where they could ford it more easily. Some of the men waded over first, stumbling amongst the round submerged rocks; the horses were then driven across, and caught and hobbled as they emerged on the other side; the sheep placidly followed. A camp was made on the west bank, and there they stayed a day resting the animals and their own bodies, weary and itching from leech-bites. Then on 12 August they set out again in order to get away from those eastern watercourses: it was a more than welcome experience for them, because they were able to go due west without serious obstruction (Beale 1977:181).

The Cardwell Range, with elevations greater than 1,000 m, separates the coastal plains from the Evelyn Tableland. Reconstructions of Kennedy's rainforest journey suggest that his party partly followed Aboriginal tracks to manoeuvre through dense rainforests in their journey into the upper Tully River area (Beale 1977:181–182). A track used by *Jirrbal* people to travel to the lower Tully River area, for ceremonies as late as the 1930s, was identified by elders as the probable route used by Kennedy's team to cross the difficult topography and dense vegetation of the Cardwell Range (Duke and Collins 1999). Campbell's 1922–23 survey maps of the upper Tully River district identify the same track as part of 'the main Aboriginal track to the coast' and other early maps show it as a 'pack track' (Craig 1947). In addition, during the clearing of the Misty Mountain Trail in the 1990s— a walking track that crosses the Tully River and the Cardwell Range to connect the Evelyn Tableland with the coast—many slate seed grinding dishes and slate and basalt ground-edge axes were observed on the ground along a track still visible through dense rainforest (A. Graham, pers. comm., 2007).

Whether or not Urumbal Pocket was where Kennedy crossed the Tully River is yet to be established, but what is clear is that Aboriginal people used this place in the past. An extensive stone artefact scatter on the surface and rich subsurface cultural deposits gave rise to a hypothesis that Aboriginal people used Urumbal Pocket, before and/or after crossing the river, to proceed along a track over the Cardwell Range and down to the coastal lowlands.

Urumbal Pocket has attracted some interest among local historians in recent times as an example of an open forest pocket within dense rainforest:

> Pockets' [sic], like Urumbal Pocket, were areas of land cleared in rainforest scrub by Aborigines using fire-stick farming methods. This allowed grass to grow and attracted fauna such as wallaby's [sic], used for food. They became resting places for early settlers to spell horses. Aboriginal tracks up from the coast linked one pocket to another and many small towns grew up on these sites. As examples, Yungaburra is sited on Allumbah Pocket and Priors Forest Pocket became Atherton (Ravenshoe Writers' Group 1999:29).

As discussed in Chapter 2, early European settlers took advantage of open forest pockets and tracks through the rainforest kept clear by Aboriginal rainforest people, thereby accelerating European settlement of the rainforest.

Cultural heritage investigations in the Koombooloomba area

Previous anthropological and archaeological surveys in the Koombooloomba area were carried out in the context of a cultural heritage assessment by Duke and Collins (1999). Their study was undertaken to assess the cultural heritage of selected areas, as part of background research undertaken for a proposed ecotourism project at Koombooloomba Dam. The report includes the results of an archaeological survey and an assessment of the archaeological evidence in a number of areas in the vicinity of the dam and around its shoreline. Urumbal Pocket is referred to as one of a series of pockets along this stretch of the Tully River, originally sketched by surveyor Campbell in 1922–23 (Fig. 4.2).

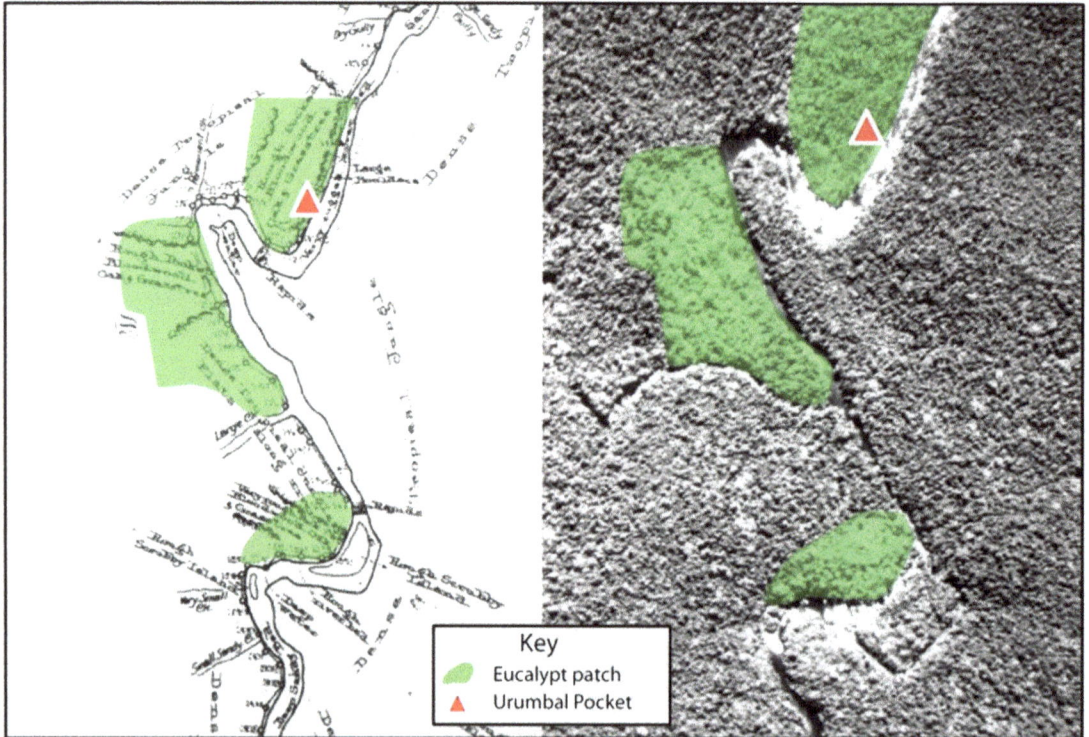

Key
🟢 Eucalypt patch
🔺 Urumbal Pocket

Figure 4.2 Campbell's survey map from 1922–23 (left) and aerial photograph from 1951. Red triangle indicates the location of the archaeological open site at Urumbal Pocket.

Source: Produced by J. de Lange.

Urumbal Pocket is not within the areas investigated in the ecotourism project and, as a result, was not visited by Duke and Collins. However, eucalypt forest pockets in the area (see Fig. 4.2 above) were generally considered to probably contain significant archaeological sites. This assumption was based in part on surveyor Campbell's note of a 'nigger camp' [sic] in another forest pocket along the river. It was also based on the discovery of a substantial archaeological open site opposite a series of pockets of which included Urumbal Pocket (Pentecost in Duke and Collins 1999).

Archaeological surveys

Koombooloomba Dam is located approximately 40 km south of Ravenshoe and was built in the late 1950s for the purposes of generating hydroelectricity. The dam wall is 35 m above the Tully River channel. As a result of dam construction, sections of the old course of the Tully River became submerged. In 2002, Richard Cosgrove and Judith Field undertook surveys along the exposed edge of Koombooloomba Dam, with a team of university students and traditional owners. A lack of rainfall in 2002 had resulted in dam water levels falling below 25% capacity, thereby exposing a band of bare soil (Cosgrove et al. 2007:155). The aim of the survey was to find archaeological open sites suitable for excavation. A second aim was to document Aboriginal surface finds, using a Global Positioning

System (GPS), to gain an understanding of past Aboriginal occupation in the upper Tully River area (R. Cosgrove, pers. comm., 2004). As a result of the survey, many Aboriginal stone artefacts were found on the band of bare soil exposed around Koombooloomba Dam (Fig. 4.3). In total, 31 artefact scatters, 66 axes, and 34 broken axes were recorded in approximately two thirds of the dam margin (Stevens 2004). The artefact scatters are composed of cores, flakes and broken flakes, mainly of quartz, crystal quartz, rhyolite, and small amounts of fine-grained raw materials such as chert, jasper, and silcrete. Ground-edge tools, particularly basalt and slate axes, are also common on the exposed soil surface (Fig. 4.4).

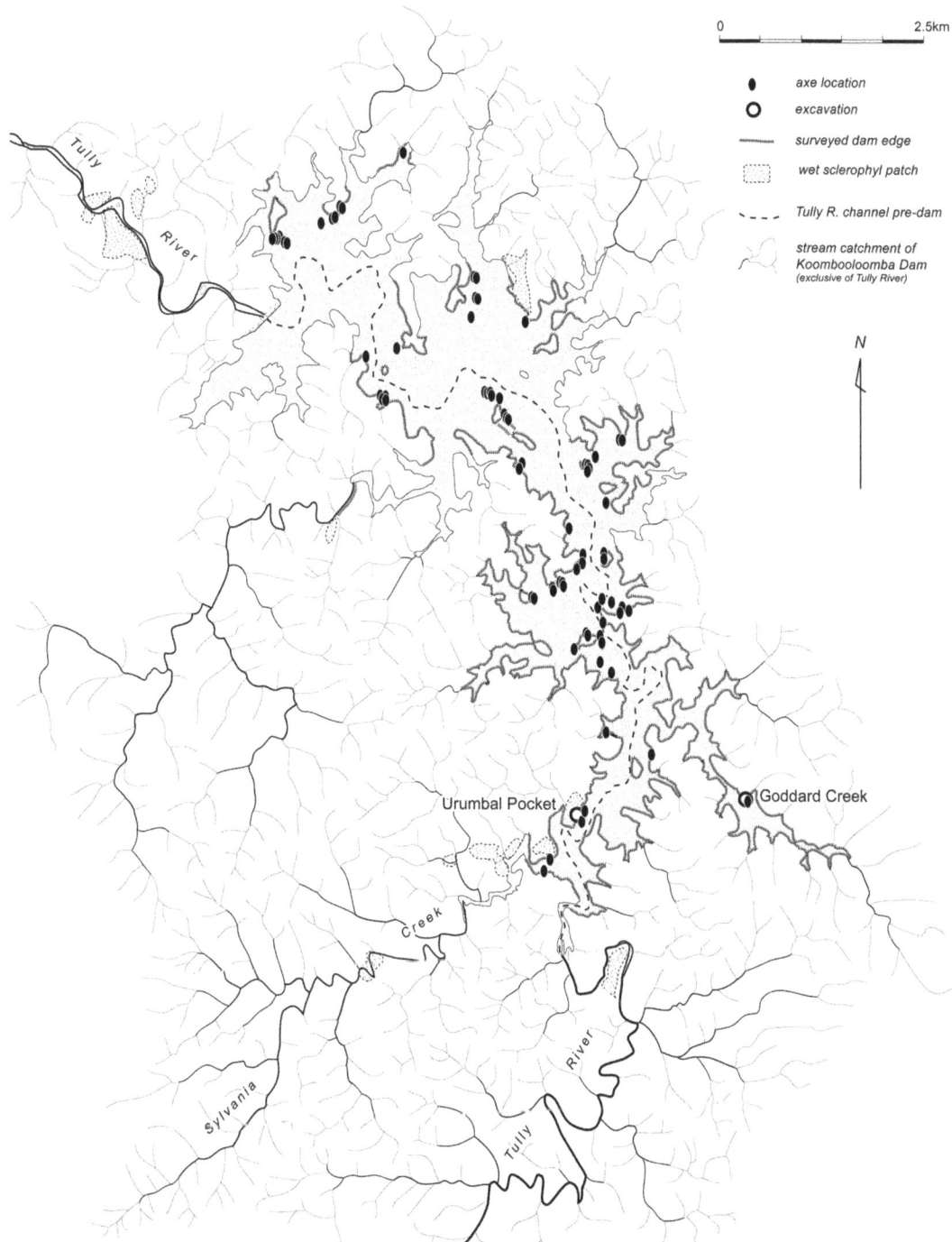

Figure 4.3 Surface finds and archaeological stratified sites located in surveys around Koombooloomba Dam during 2002–03.

Source: Courtesy of R. Cosgrove.

Other implements include complete and broken *morahs* or incised slate grinding plates (Fig. 4.5) and *moogis* or top stones—tools associated with toxic nut processing previously described in the literature (e.g. Colliver and Woolston 1966, 1980).

Figure 4.4 Example of a ground-edge basalt axe found on exposed soil at Koombooloomba Dam.
Source: Photograph by R. Cosgrove.

Figure 4.5 Example of incised slate grinding stone (*morah*) found on exposed soil at Koombooloomba Dam.
Source: Photograph by R. Cosgrove.

In addition to stone artefacts, pieces of flaked and unmodified glass were also located on the surface of the bare soil exposed around the dam's edge (Fig. 4.6). Their presence may be an indication of Aboriginal people using this remote area after the arrival of Europeans to the coast. This suggestion is supported by documentary sources and *Jirrbal* oral tradition (Duke and Collins 1994, 1999; M. Barlow, pers. comm., 2005). According to these sources, the area around the upper Tully River became a refuge area for Aboriginal people in the late 1800s (Duke and Collins 1994, 1999; M. Barlow, pers. comm., 2004). The archaeological surface record from Koombooloomba Dam thus demonstrates that this part of the rainforest was probably frequently used by Aboriginal people in prehistory and into the early contact period.

Figure 4.6 Flaked glass artefacts found on exposed band of soil at Koombooloomba Dam (scale=1 cm) (GK/7607, 7601, 7602, 7600).
Source: Photograph by P. Saad.

As a result of the surveys and analyses of documentary sources, two archaeological open sites, Urumbal Pocket and Goddard Creek, were identified at Koombooloomba Dam. One rock-shelter, *Murubun*, was relocated in the transition zone between sclerophyll and rainforest. All are within the traditional lands of the *Jirrbal* people. The Urumbal Pocket site has been the subject of the most extensive archaeological investigations. All excavation work at Urumbal Pocket was directed by Richard Cosgrove and Judith Field. The stone artefacts and the carbonised plant remains recovered from the excavations were subsequently made available for analysis as a component of the research presented herein.

Site description and setting

The eucalypt pockets that include Urumbal Pocket were first described by Campbell in 1922 as a patchwork of open sclerophyll forest and rainforest (Campbell 1923). The archaeological open site (Fig. 4.7) abuts a large pocket of *Eucalyptus* spp., *Casuarina* spp., *Xanthorrhoea* spp., and sedges, which in turn borders rainforest approximately 170 m from the archaeological site and the dam's current water edge. This vegetation structure marks the transition zone between a wet sclerophyll forest patch and dense rainforest (Cosgrove et al. 2007).

Figure 4.7 Location of the archaeological open site (arrowed) at Urumbal Pocket on Koombooloomba Dam, July 2003.

Source: Photograph by R. Cosgrove.

The spur located in front of the eucalypt pocket, which includes the archaeological site, is intermittently flooded and exposed depending on the fluctuating water levels in Koombooloomba Dam. Raw materials in the surface collection include quartz, crystal quartz, rhyolite, chert, slate, basalt, and glass. During the archaeological excavations, a series of 10 test pits were dug along a 150 m transect perpendicular to the site in order to establish the extent of archaeological deposits and stratigraphy away from the spur. The test pits were placed at the interior edge of the border between sclerophyll and rainforest, the wet sclerophyll pocket centre and the outer edge, respectively. The soil was sieved and charcoal samples were obtained from all pits and at various depths (R. Cosgrove, pers. comm., 2004). Radiocarbon dated charcoal samples recovered from the test pits suggest that fire has influenced the vegetation at Urumbal Pocket for about the last 8,000 years (Ferrier and Cosgrove 2012:113). No carbonised nutshell fragments or stone artefacts or other cultural materials were identified in the pits (Cosgrove et al. 2007:161).

Archaeological excavations

In total, six 1 x 1 m pits and one 50 x 50 cm pit were excavated in order to confirm the depth, age, and stratigraphy of the site, to establish the spatial distribution of cultural materials, and to facilitate identification of possible activity areas at the site (Fig. 4.8). All of the excavated sediments were weighed and then wet-sieved through 7 mm, 3 mm and 1 mm mesh. Stone artefacts, carbonised plant remains, ochre and charcoal were recovered *in situ* where possible. They were also collected from the sieves, and bagged and labelled on site. Soil colour, based on the Munsell soil colour charts, and soil pH level were recorded at the start of each new spit. Cultural material recovery processes, sorting, cataloguing, and the cultural material analyses are discussed in Chapters 5 and 6.

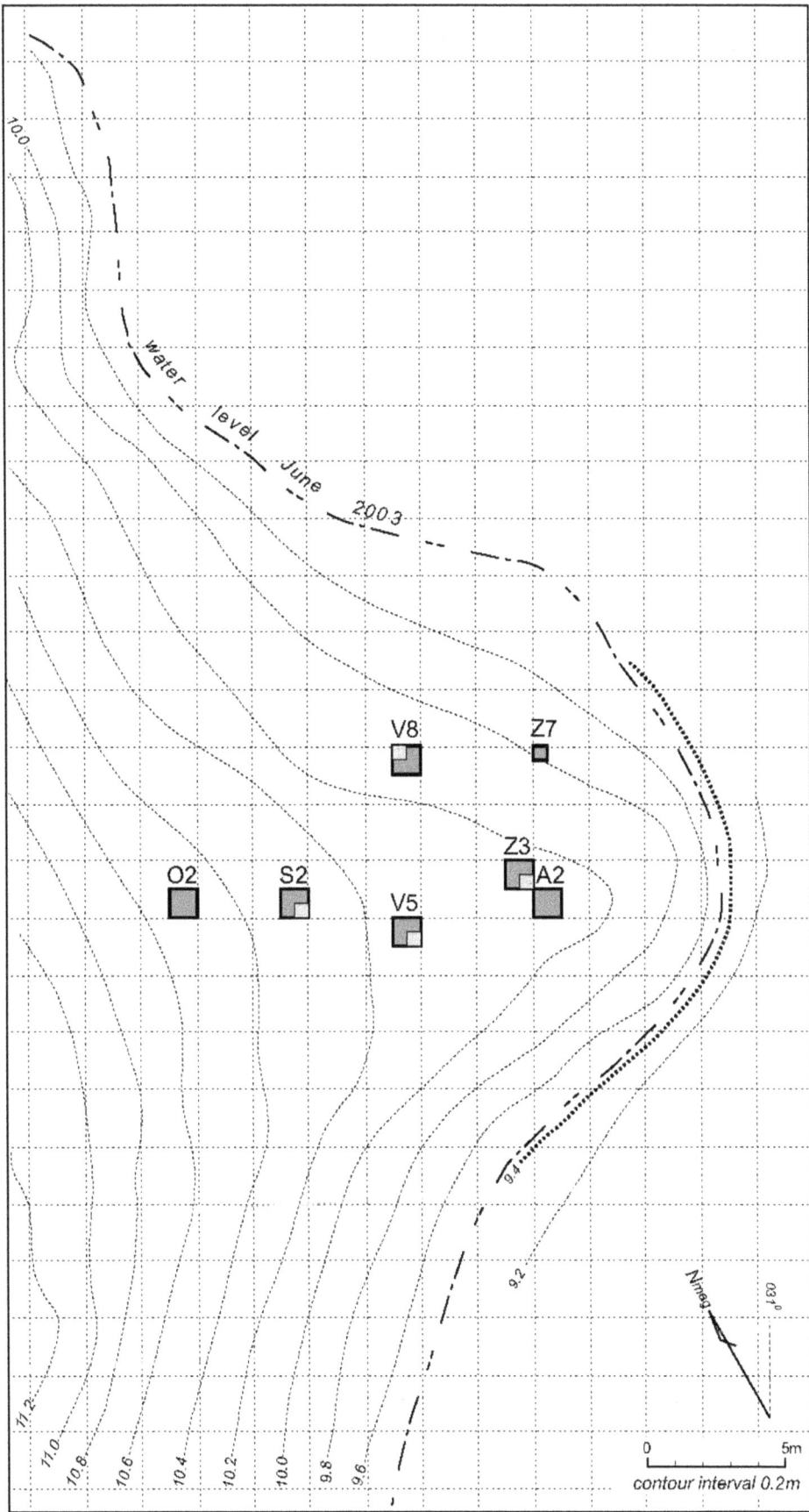

Figure 4.8 Location of excavation squares at Urumbal Pocket.

Source: Produced by R. Frank.

Square A2

The first phase of excavations at Urumbal Pocket took place in July 2002. One 1 x 1 m pit, square A2 (Fig. 4.8), located in the flat central area on the spur, was selected for excavation because of a concentration of surface artefacts in this area. Excavations in square A2 confirmed a presence of substantial accumulated cultural deposits in this area. A total of 139 artefacts with a maximum dimension of 10 mm or greater were recovered from spit 1. Square A2 was excavated in 5 cm spits, following the stratigraphy where possible. Excavation ceased at a mean depth of 60 cm, where an archaeologically sterile layer of weathered, decomposing granite bedrock was encountered (Fig. 4.9). The pH levels ranged from 5.5 in the top layers to 6.5 in the bottom layers. The total sediment weight for square A2 was 677.3 kg.

Figure 4.9 Square A2 showing the surface of spit 10 at a depth of 60 cm.
Source: Photograph by R. Cosgrove.

Two main stratigraphic units containing cultural materials were distinguished on the basis of colour and structure: an upper dark humic layer and an underlying lighter layer overlying granite bedrock. The soil is defined as Yellow Kandosol (McKenzie et al. 2004:246–247), and is common in the area. The deposit consists of an artefact-rich stratigraphic unit 1, which may be described as a homogeneous dark brown (5YR 1.7/1) unconsolidated sandy loam layer approximately 40 cm deep.

URUMBAL POCKET: SQUARE A2

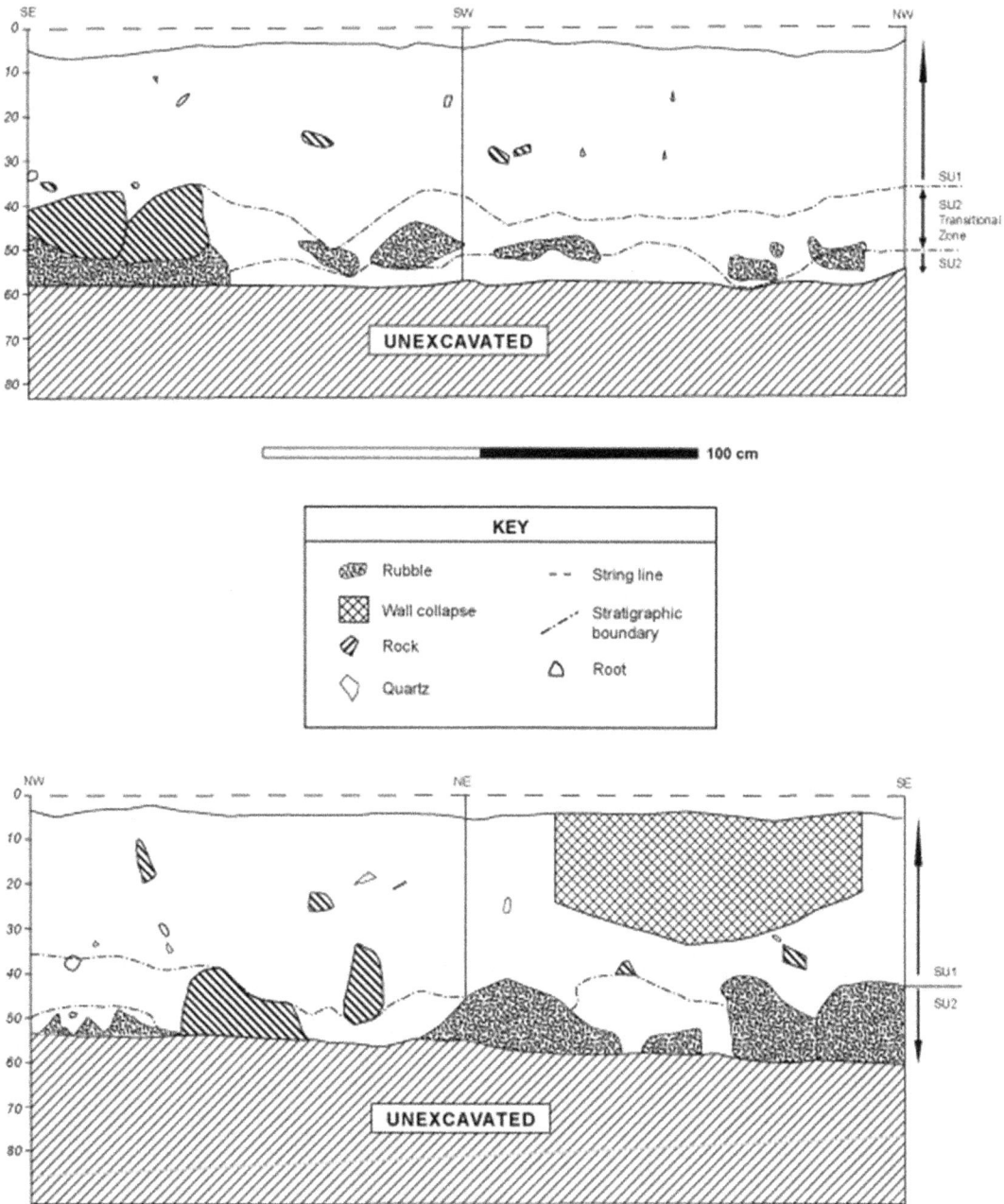

Figure 4.10 Stratigraphic sections in square A2.
Source: Drawing by Å. Ferrier.

A transition zone is located at an approximate depth of 40 cm, and consists of a dark brown (7.5YR 2/3) deposit with a slight tendency towards orange mottling and the occurrence of gravel. Cultural materials are present in lower quantities and charcoal becomes more fragmented throughout the transition layer. The deposit in stratigraphic unit 2 is increasingly gritty, with particles from the decomposing granite bedrock incorporated into the soil. Cultural materials cease at a depth of around 50 cm. It appears that the deposit in square A2 was relatively intact and no evidence of major post-depositional disturbance was noted during excavation. Figure 4.10 shows the stratigraphic sections in square A2 and all radiocarbon dates from Urumbal Pocket are listed in Table 4.1.

Square V5

Excavations at Urumbal Pocket continued in September 2002. It was decided to excavate a 1 x 1 m pit five metres west of square A2, within the perimeter of the flat central area on the spur (Fig. 4.8). This square, called V5, is located closer to the edge of the flat section, where the ground gradually begins to incline. This slope continues past the present-day edge of the eucalypt forest pocket. Square V5 was chosen in order to determine whether or not the richness of cultural deposits recovered from square A2 extended beyond the apparent central activity zone and to further investigate the stratigraphy, depth and age of the deposit. Another aim was to investigate site formation processes that may have affected the site's integrity, particularly water running over the surface during heavy downpours.

Excavation in square V5 proceeded in 5 cm spits, but ceased, due to time constraints, at a depth of 23 cm at the top of spit 5. Stone artefacts, carbonised plant remains, ochre and charcoal were recovered during the excavation. The pit was lined with plastic and backfilled. The investigators returned with a field crew in June 2003 and square V5 was reopened and excavated in 5 cm spits. When investigators encountered deposits with weathered granite rocks and rubble, similar in appearance to unit 2 in square A2, ongoing excavation was reduced to a 50 x 50 cm cell in the southeastern quadrant, to establish the depth of the basal layer of unit 2 (Fig. 4.11).

Figure 4.11 Square V5, surface of spit 12 at a depth of 65 cm (in southeastern quadrant).
Source: Photograph by R. Cosgrove.

The stratigraphic sequence (Fig. 4.12) to square V5 is similar to that in square A2 in that it consists of an artefact-rich stratigraphic unit 1, which may be described as a dark brown/black (7YR 2/2) unconsolidated and homogenous sandy loam layer approximately 40 cm deep. Below this was a thin transition zone with some orange mottling visible (2.5YR 2/3). Sediments then became increasingly gritty with particles from the decomposing granite bedrock incorporated into the soil. The total sediment weight for V5 was 625.7 kg. The transition zone indicates a change in the stratigraphy to stratigraphic unit 2, a dark reddish-brown (5YR 5/8) clay-dominated deposit. Orange mottling, decomposing granite and quartz grit gradually increased with depth. Stratigraphic unit 2 is more consolidated than stratigraphic unit 1.

URUMBAL POCKET: SQUARE V5

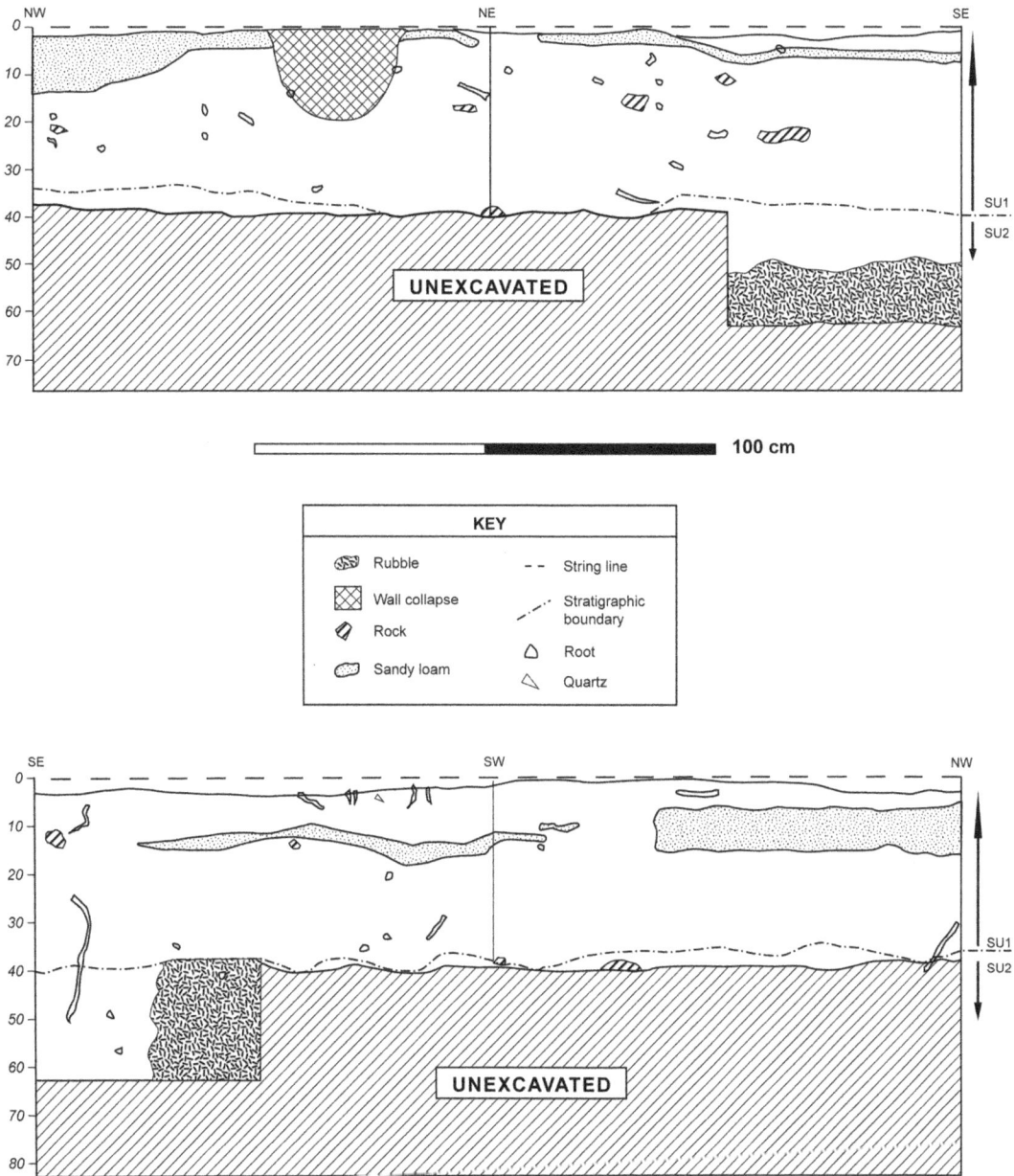

Figure 4.12 Stratigraphic sections in square V5.
Source: Drawing by Å. Ferrier.

Cultural materials are less dense and almost absent toward the base of unit 2, and charcoal becomes more fragmented throughout, when compared to unit 1. Cultural materials cease at a depth of around 50 cm. Below this level, deposits excavated from a 50 x 50 cm cell in the southeast corner of V5 change to a sterile clay structure, with a large quantity of rubble consisting, predominantly, of decomposed granite bedrock. Excavation was stopped at a depth of 65 cm, where the deposit turned into consolidated clay. The pH levels range from 6 in the top layers to 4–5 in the bottom layers.

At the completion of square V5, a decision was made to excavate in 2.5 cm spits. The approach was adapted in order to test whether a finer resolution, i.e. a change to smaller spits, would increase the ability to carry out temporal and spatial analyses on material culture remains in squares with strong chronological control. It was also to understand the effects of depositional and post-depositional processes on the deposit. In June – July 2003, the final excavation season at Urumbal Pocket, a further four 1 x 1 m pits (S2, O2, V8, Z3) and one 50 x 50 cm cell (Z7) were excavated (refer to Fig. 4.8). The location of excavation squares S2, O2, V8 and Z7 was chosen primarily to understand the extent of subsurface deposits away from the culturally rich area identified in the flat central area on the spur. It was also to assess the impact of cultural and natural depositional disturbances and processes on the deposits across a larger area. Square Z3, adjacent to square A2, was chosen in order to increase the sample size from an area previously established as artefact-rich, and to investigate variability in Aboriginal activities across the site.

Square S2

The surface of square S2 was patchy in appearance, probably as a result of soil and sand washing down the slope. Quartz and slate artefacts (n=91) were collected from the surface and from spit 1. At a depth of 2 cm, the deposit turned into a homogenous dark brown/black (7.5YR 1.7/1) sandy loam, similar in colour and consistency to unit 1 in other squares. Some small root intrusions were encountered. The pH levels ranged from 4–5.5 in the top layers to 4 in the bottom layers. The bottom layers of unit 1 were a reddish-brown colour (7.5YR 5/8) (Fig. 4.13). The stratigraphic sequence of S2 was also similar to other squares in that it consisted of an artefact-rich stratigraphic unit 1, a dark brown/black unconsolidated and homogenous sandy loam layer, approximately 35–45 cm deep. Below this lay a transition zone that marks a change to stratigraphic unit 2. This layer had a distinguishable orange mottling originating from underlying decomposing granite bedrock. The transition layer in square S2 was considerably thicker (by approximately 10 cm) than in the squares located in the flat central area approximately 10 m away.

Figure 4.13 Square S2, surface of spit 18 (top of unit 2) at a depth of 45 cm.
Source: Photograph by R. Cosgrove.

Stratigraphic unit 2 was a consolidated, dark reddish-brown (2.5YR 7/6) silty clay. The lower deposit became increasingly gritty with particles from the decomposing granite bedrock incorporated into the soil. Cultural materials were almost absent and charcoal became more fragmented throughout unit 2 compared to unit 1. Cultural material ceased at a depth of around 50 cm. The deposits excavated below this level, from a 50 x 50 cm cell in the southeast corner, changed to a sterile clay with a large quantity of rubble of decomposed granite bedrock and what appeared to be decomposing roots. The excavation in square S2 reached bedrock at an approximate depth of 70 cm, with 731.6 kg the total weight of removed sediment. The stratigraphic sections in square S2 are illustrated in Figure 4.14.

URUMBAL POCKET: SQUARE S2

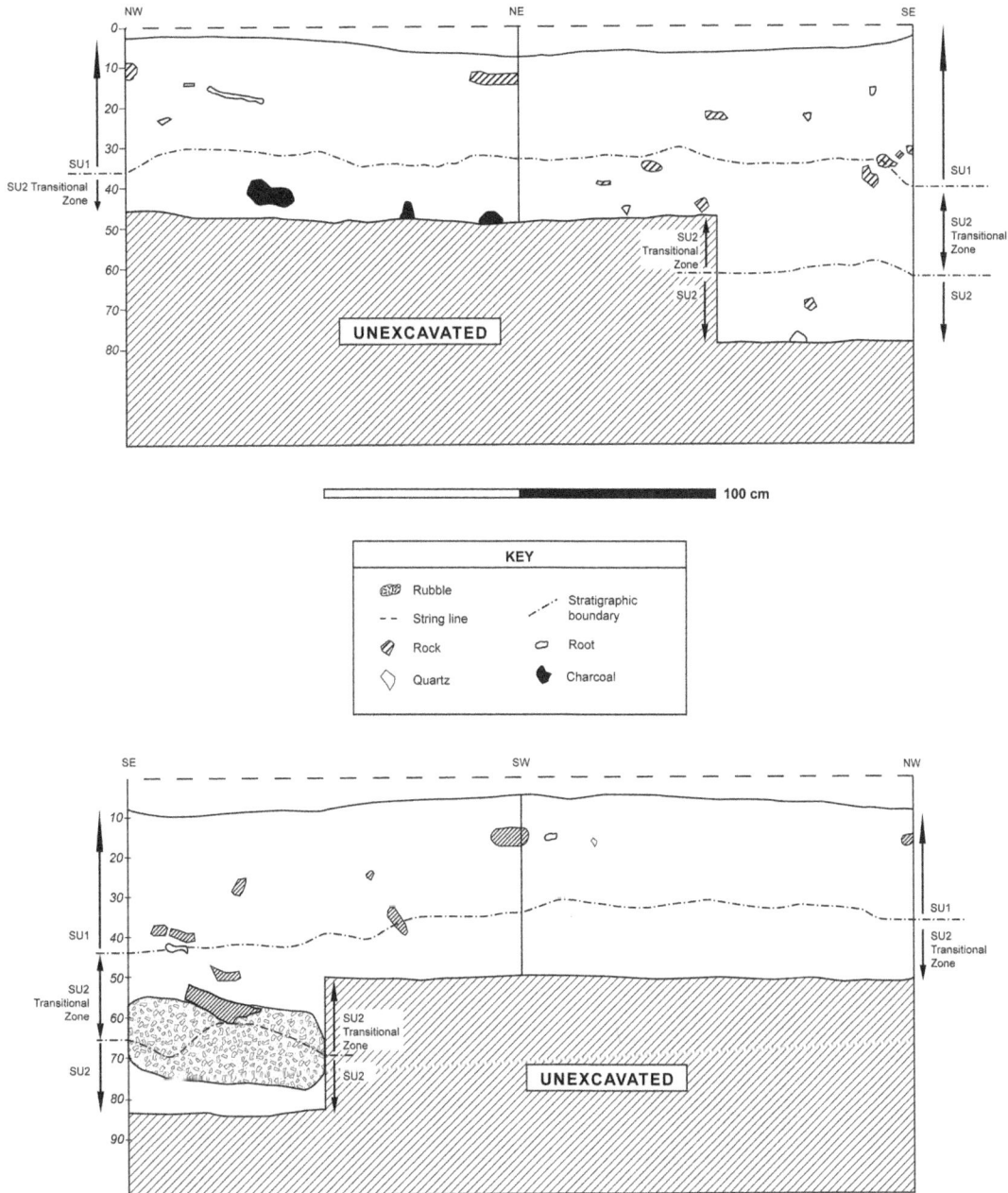

Figure 4.14 Stratigraphic sections in square S2.

Source: Drawing by Å. Ferrier.

Square O2

The surface colour of square O2 was patchy in appearance, with a mixture of light-coloured sand (2.5YR 8/1) and a darker red loam (7.5YR 1.7/1) washed in from the slope above. The pH levels ranged from 4 to 6 in the top layers. The mixed sand/loam deposit continued to a further 2.5 cm below, with small roots throughout.

Figure 4.15 Square O2, surface of spit 12 (top of unit 2) at a depth of 30 cm.
Source: Photograph by R. Cosgrove.

A concentration of charcoal was encountered in the upper layers in the southern section of the square but no cultural material was observed during the excavation. However, stone artefacts (n=93) were collected from the sieves. Stratigraphic unit 1 was a 30 cm thick, unconsolidated dark reddish-brown (5YR 3/3) layer with a pH of 4. Cultural materials were restricted to this unit. Below this was a 5 cm thick transition zone, identified by an increase in orange mottling, similar to that found in the other squares, with decomposing granite bedrock and a clay-like texture (Fig. 4.16). Overall, stratigraphic unit 2 was an archaeologically sterile, consolidated bright reddish-brown clay deposit (5YR 5/8) with decomposing granite gravel that increased in density and size with depth. The excavation in square O2 reached sterile layers at an approximate depth of 35 cm, with a total 225.9 kg of excavated sediment. The stratigraphic sections in square O2 are illustrated in Figure 4.16.

Square O2 was placed on the western boundary of the open site at Urumbal Pocket (Fig. 4.8). The topography of the landscape sets a natural boundary to its western and eastern limit, with slopes that form part of the Tully River bank as it existed before this section of the river was dammed. Similarly, the southern side has a natural boundary as it gradually slopes down towards the river. This topography led to a decision to focus the remaining excavation squares in the area with high surface artefact densities and to determine the site's northern limits.

URUMBAL POCKET: SQUARE 02

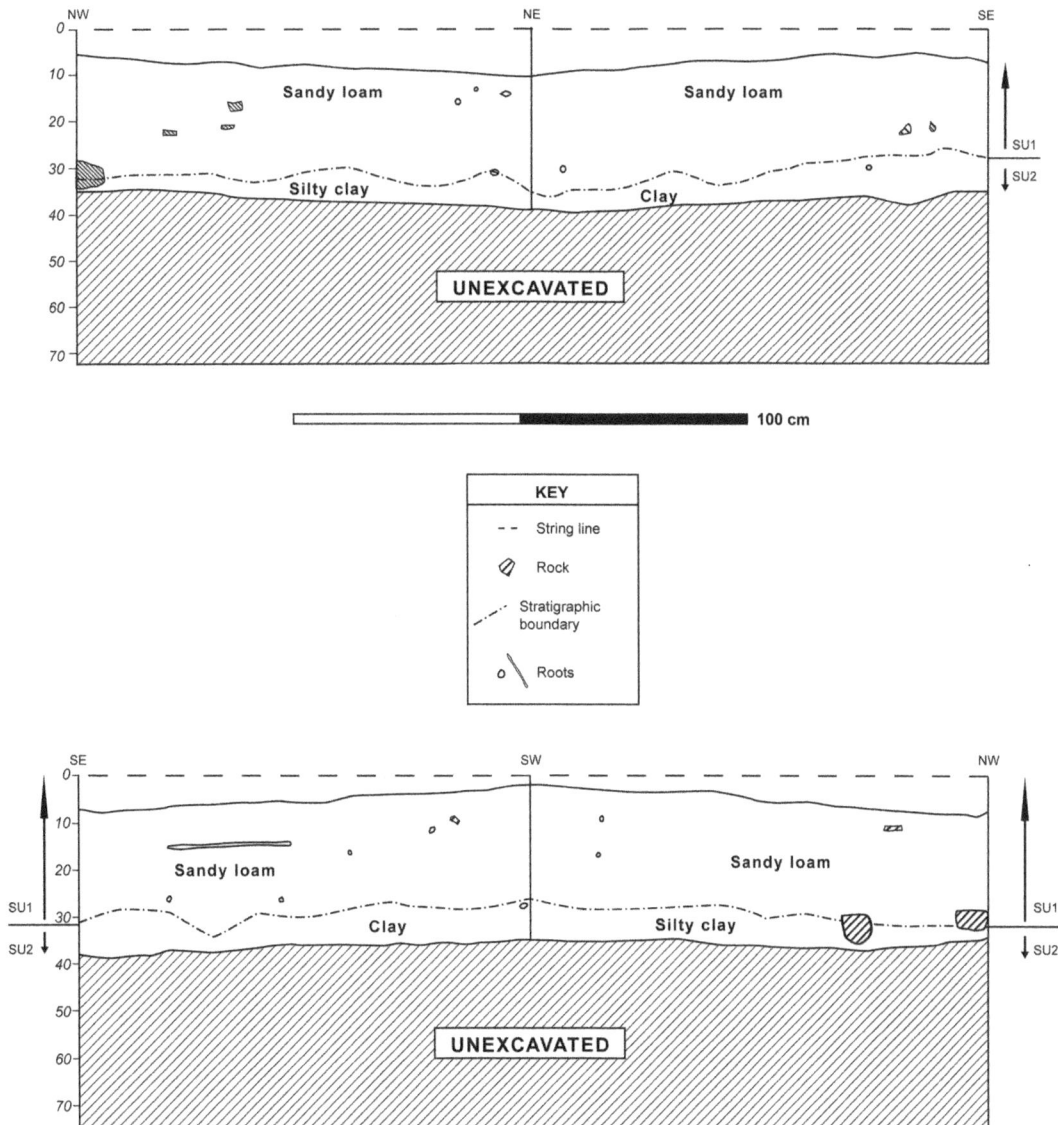

Figure 4.16 Stratigraphic sections in square 02.
Source: Drawing by Å. Ferrier.

Square V8

The deposit in square V8 was similar to previously discussed squares. It consisted of two stratigraphic units with a thin transition zone in between. Unit 1 may be described as a black (7.5YR 1.7/1) unconsolidated and homogeneous sandy loam layer approximately 30 cm deep. The pH levels ranged from 5.5 to 6. Some roots and large granite rocks were noted in the upper layers. Below unit 1 lay a thin transition zone that indicated a change in the deposits and the start of stratigraphic unit 2 at a depth of around 35 cm. The upper layers in unit 2 have some orange mottling and the sediments become increasingly gritty with particles from the decomposing granite bedrock being incorporated into the soil. Stratigraphic unit 2 consisted of a wet, brown deposit (5YR 5/8) with a pH of 6. Orange mottling and weathered granite and quartz grit gradually increased in density and size with depth (Fig. 4.17).

Figure 4.17 Square V8, surface of spit 12 at a depth of 30 cm.
Source: Photograph by R. Cosgrove.

Cultural materials were recovered in much lower numbers than elsewhere on the site and ceased at a depth of around 30 cm. The total weight of removed sediment for V8 was 364.4 kg. The stratigraphic sections in square V8 are illustrated in Figure. 4.18.

URUMBAL POCKET: SQUARE V8

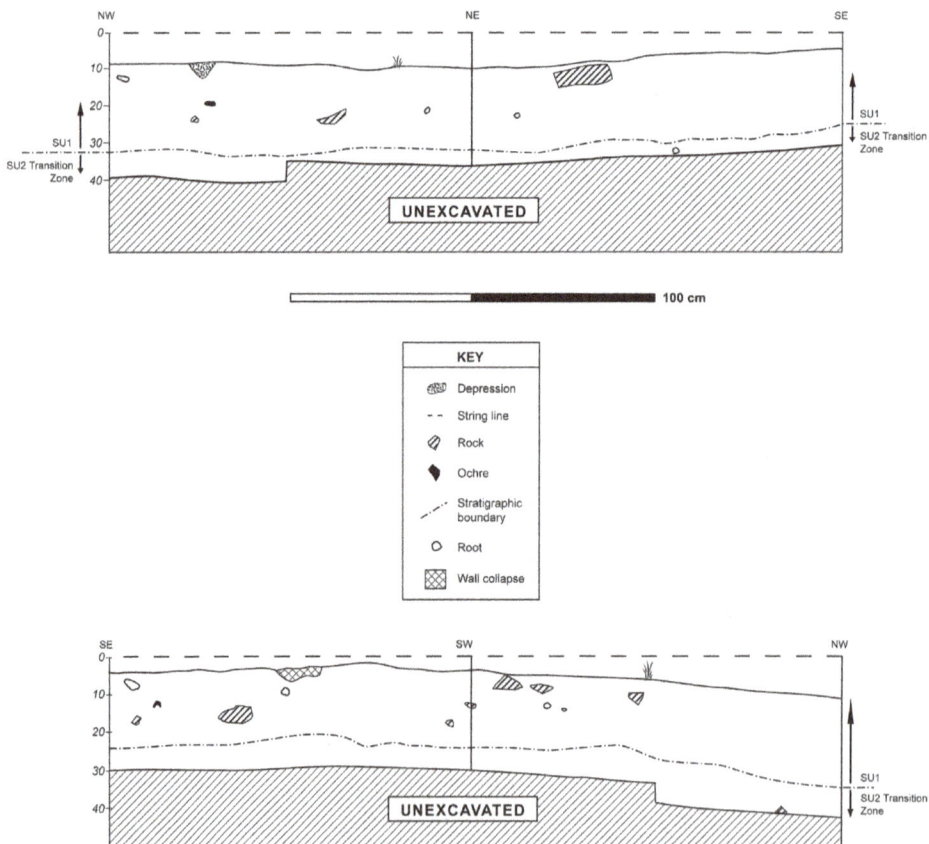

Figure 4.18 Stratigraphic sections in square V8.
Source: Drawing by Å. Ferrier.

Square Z3

Square Z3 was located in the flat central area on the spur (Fig. 4.8). It was selected for excavation in order to expand the sample of materials from a suspected central activity zone at the site. The stratigraphy in square Z3 was, in general, similar to that in squares A2 and V5. Two main stratigraphic units may be distinguished based on soil colour, texture and type; a distinct transition layer separated them. Unit 1 consisted of an artefact-rich dark brown/black loam, with the Munsell colour ranging from 10YR 1/7 in the top layers to 7.5YR 4/6 in the bottom layers. The sediments in unit 1 may be described as a homogeneous and unconsolidated sandy loam deposit with fine grit throughout.

The sediment was derived from the surrounding organic soil and lower layers were mixed with an increasing amount of grit derived from decomposing granite bedrock. The transition layer separated the two units and was distinguished by some orange mottling. Its top was situated at a depth of 35–40 cm and it was approximately 10 cm thick. Sediments in unit 2 became increasingly gritty and less homogeneous with depth, with particles from the decomposing granite bedrock becoming incorporated into the soil (Fig. 4.19).

Figure 4.19 Square Z3, surface of spit 18 (in south-eastern quadrant) at a depth of 55 cm.
Source: Photograph by R. Cosgrove.

In unit 2, granite rubble and rocks appeared in greater numbers and cultural material was less common than in unit 1. Cultural materials ceased to occur at a depth of around 45 cm. Excavations of a 50 x 50 cm cell established an archaeologically sterile granitic soil layer (7.5YR 4/4) below stratigraphic unit 2. Excavations were stopped at a depth of 55 cm, where bedrock was encountered. The total weight of removed sediment for Z3 was 3,667.1 kg. Figure 4.20 illustrates the stratigraphic sections in square Z3.

URUMBAL POCKET: SQUARE Z3

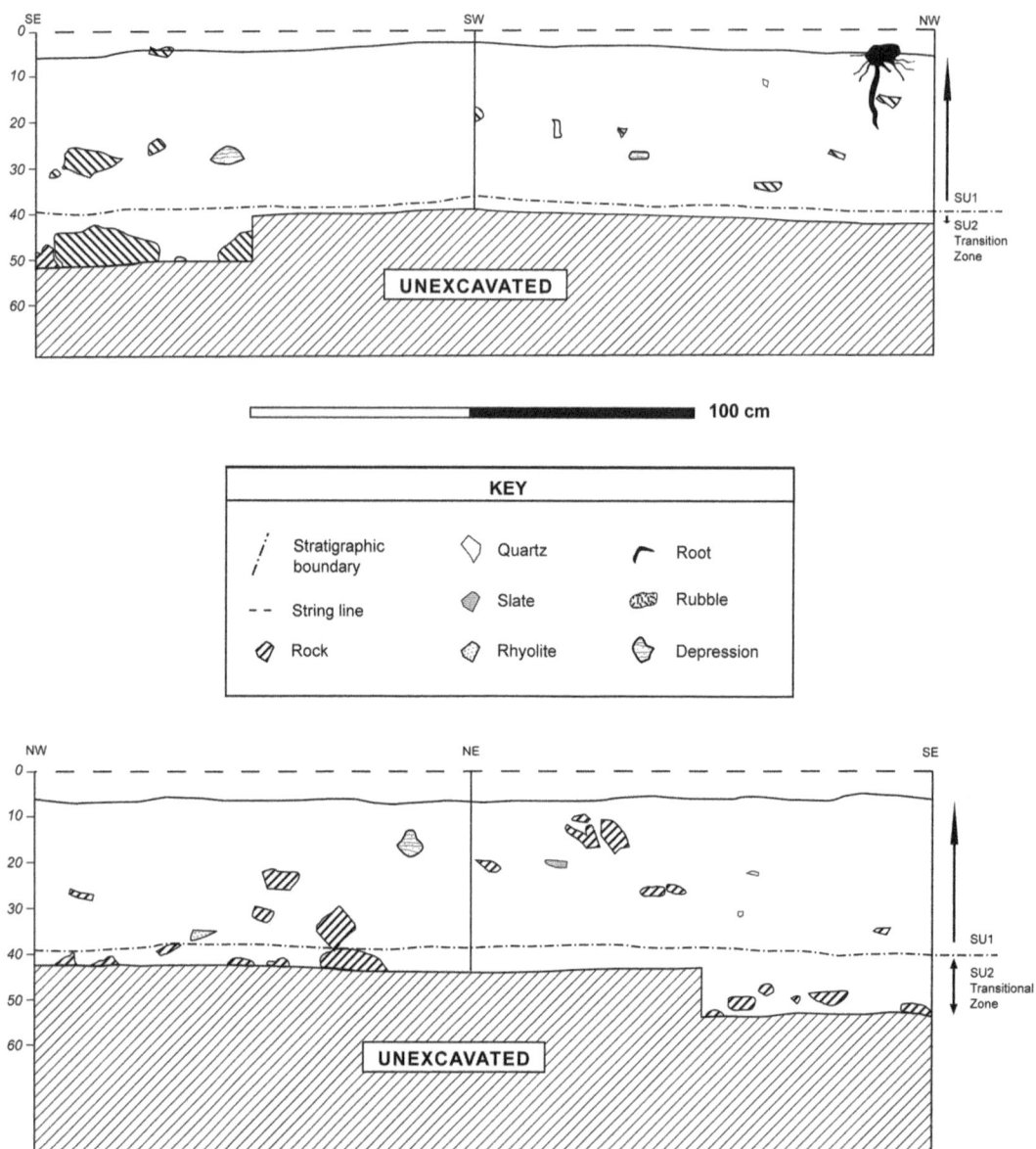

Figure 4.20 Stratigraphic sections in square Z3.

Source: Drawing by Å. Ferrier.

Stratigraphic summary

The excavations at Urumbal Pocket reached sterile layers with exposed bedrock in all squares except square Z7. As a result of its proximity to the edge of the dam, square Z7 became waterlogged when the transition layer between unit 1 and unit 2 had most likely been encountered. The excavation of square Z7, therefore, was stopped before bedrock or an identified sterile layer had been reached. For this reason, cultural materials recovered from square Z7 have not been included in the material culture analyses presented here. The average depth of cultural deposits is 45–50 cm in squares A2 and Z3, and somewhat less in the other squares. Large quantities of charcoal, stone artefacts, carbonised endocarp fragments, complete and partially complete seeds and small amounts of ochre were recovered from squares A2, Z3, V5 and S2. No bones were recovered. This may be a result of the acidic nature of the deposits, but it is possible that the site was mostly used for plant processing. Apart from some small hollows caused by insects and roots, no obvious evidence for post-depositional disturbance was observed during excavation. The size distribution of stone artefacts and plant remains in the deposits is discussed in the assemblage analyses (Chapters 5 and 6) in order to address the integrity of the deposits and assemblage formation processes. The spatial distribution of cultural materials recovered was also analysed as a component of the cultural material analyses and is discussed in Chapters 5 and 6. The excavation squares at the completion of the third season is shown in Figure 4.21.

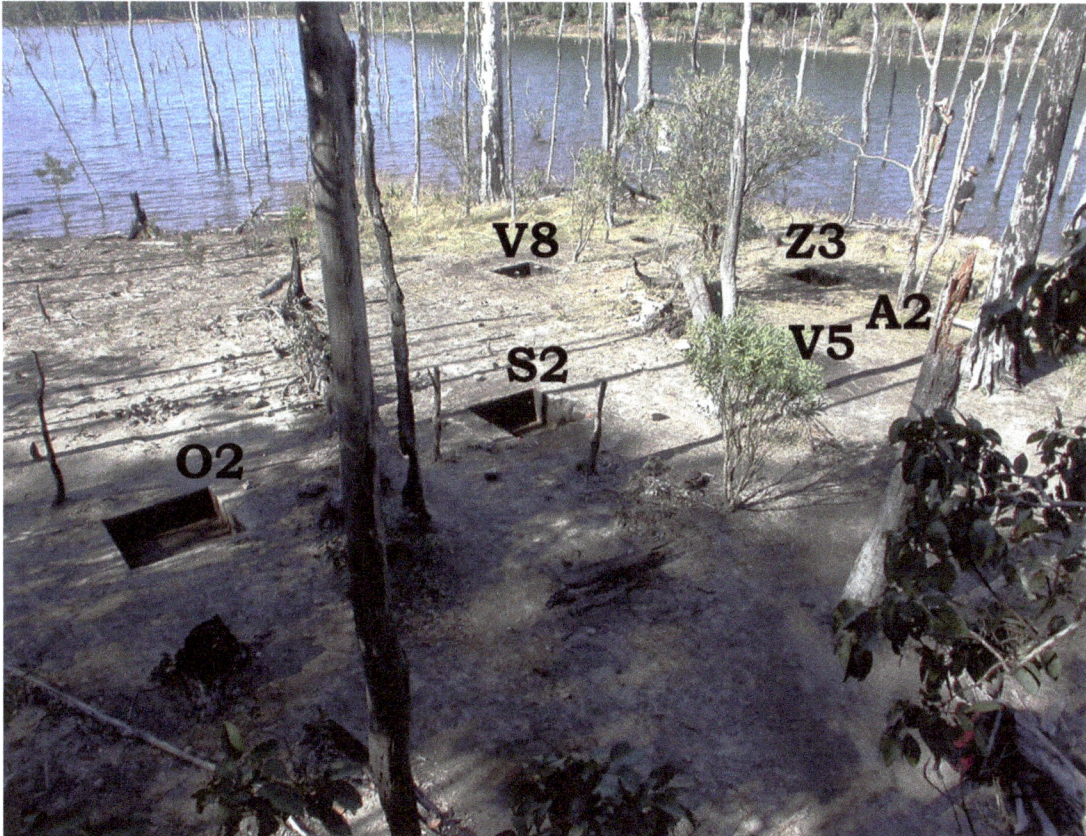

Figure 4.21 Excavation squares at Urumbal Pocket at the end of the third season. Squares A2 and V5 were excavated in season 1 and 2 respectively.

Source: Photograph by R. Cosgrove.

Chronology

Charcoal was recovered from all squares. A total of 23 radiocarbon dates were obtained (Table 4.1.). Of these, 17 were from samples of *in situ* charcoal pieces recovered during the Urumbal Pocket excavations. They show a correspondence between stratigraphic and chronological order and support the suggestion that the site is relatively undisturbed. About 70% of the dates are younger than 1500 BP. Six AMS dates were obtained from carbonised endocarp fragments that are believed to be the remains of past Aboriginal tree nut processing (discussed in Chapter 6). Five of these were from square Z3 and one was from V8. The sample from square V8 was a carbonised Lauraceae endocarp fragment, and could be from either the yellow walnut (*Beilschmedia bancroftii*) or the black walnut

(*Endiandra palmerstonii*). It was submitted for analysis to date early use of toxic plants at Urumbal Pocket, and dates to 1585±40 BP (OZJ718). This date is consistent with evidence for toxic plant use from other archaeological sites in the region, which all date to the late Holocene period.

At *Jiyer* Cave, evidence of toxic rainforest species within cultural deposits date to less than 1000 BP. At the Mulgrave River open site (Fig. 1.1), toxic nuts found in association with quartz artefacts have been dated to around 2000 BP (Horsfall 1987:268). Radiocarbon dates from these two sites were obtained on charcoal samples in layers associated with nutshell fragments. The dated endocarp fragments from Urumbal Pocket provide a more certain age for the appearance of toxic nut processing in the rainforest region. The five nutshell samples from the cultural deposits in square Z3 were selected, subsequent to the dating of charcoal pieces, to assist with interpreting the apparently intensive late Holocene occupation phase at Urumbal Pocket. The dates on the nutshell fragments broadly correlate with the dates on the charcoal samples, except in square V8 where there is a discrepancy between spits 8 and 9. These two spits have very low stone artefact numbers (n=8) and nutshell fragments. Some mixing of cultural materials may also have occurred in deposits dated to around 650 BP to 850 BP in square Z3, where approximately 10 cm of deposit separates the two dates. Such mixing of deposits is not surprising and may be related to the amount of human activity that appears to have taken place at Urumbal Pocket in the last 1,500 to 1,000 years.

Table 4.1 Conventional and calibrated radiocarbon dates for Urumbal Pocket. Codes followed by an asterisk are AMS dates.

Square	Spit	Material dated	Conventional age	Calendric age calBP	68% range calBP	Code
A2	3	Charcoal	514±51BP	569±48	520-617	Wk-11341
A2	5	Charcoal	1045±51BP	980±51	929-1031	Wk-11342
A2	8	Charcoal	3339±66BP	3579±82	3497-3661	Wk-11343
A2	10	Charcoal	4887±93BP	5627±111	5516-5738	Wk-11344
O2	7	Charcoal	422±40BP	449±62	387-511	Wk-13566
O2	10	Charcoal	2201±46BP	2229±69	2160-2298	Wk-13567
S2	13	Charcoal	1497±34BP	1381±30	1351-1411	Wk-13568
S2	15	Charcoal	1660±44BP	1573±54	1581-1627	Wk-13569
V5	7	Charcoal	1581±41BP	1472±47	1424-1519	Wk-13570
V5	9	Charcoal	7212±46BP	8052±65	7987-8117	Wk-13571
V8	6	Charcoal	1374±39BP	1304±21	1283-1325	Wk-13572
V8	8	Charcoal	2628±51BP	2762±34	2728-2796	Wk-13573
V8	9	Endocarp	1585±40BP	1474±47	1427-1521	OZJ718*
Z3	2	Charcoal	190±37BP	156±122	33-278	Wk-13574
Z3	4	Endocarp	470±60BP	502±44	457-546	OZJ719*
Z3	5	Endocarp	850±40BP	778±51	727-829	OZJ720*
Z3	7	Endocarp	720±40BP	676±21	655-697	OZJ721*
Z3	8	Charcoal	672±39BP	622±45	577-667	Wk-13575
Z3	11	Charcoal	1244±40BP	1181±64	1117-1245	Wk-13576
Z3	11	Endocarp	1605±40BP	1486±51	1434-1537	OZJ722*
Z3	13	Endocarp	1595±40BP	1480±48	1431-1528	OZJ723*
Z3	14	Charcoal	2143±48BP	2169±104	2065-2273	Wk-13577
Z3	16	Charcoal	7445±68BP	8273±67	8205-8340	Wk-13578

Source: Fink et al. 2004; Jenkinson 2007.

Occupation periods

The set of radiocarbon determinations (Table 4.1) indicates three periods of site use, with the last two phases corresponding with evidence for human occupation periods in archaeological sites excavated across the region (Cosgrove et al. 2007; Horsfall 1996). The earliest dates at Urumbal Pocket, 7445±68 BP (calBP 8273±67) (Wk-13578) and 7212±46 BP (calBP 8052±65) (Wk-13571) are from square Z3 and V5 respectively. The charcoal samples, found in the lower spits of unit 2 together with a small number of quartz artefacts, suggest that this part of the rainforest region was used by Aboriginal people in a very early phase of rapid but variable rainforest expansion that took place after the end of the last ice age (Haberle 2005). The archaeological remains associated with this early phase of rainforest use by Aboriginal people is modest, but nevertheless indicates that people were occasionally visiting the area, perhaps as early as 8,000 years ago.

Table 4.2 Calibrated radiocarbon dates from Urumbal Pocket, in descending chronological order, are broadly grouped into three phases of site use. Bold dates represent the transition zone within stratigraphic unit 2. About 70% date to Phase 3, after 1500 BP.

Stratigraphic unit 2		Stratigraphic unit 1
Phase 1: occasional visits ca. 8000–7000 BP	Phase 2: occasional visits ca. 5000–2000 BP (includes the transition zone)	Phase 3: intensive use after 1500 BP
8273±67BP		
8052±65BP		
	5267±111BP	
	3579±82BP	
	2762±34BP	
	2229±69P	
	2169±104BP	
		1486±51BP
		1480±48BP
		1474±47BP
		1472±47BP
		1381±30BP
		1304±21BP
		1181±64BP
		980±51BP
		778±51BP
		676±21BP
		622±45DP
		569±48BP
		502±44BP
		449±62BP
		156±122BP

Source: Produced by Å. Ferrier.

Table 4.2 shows how the grouping of radiocarbon dates from Urumbal Pocket suggests three phases of Aboriginal rainforest occupation and that about 70% date to after 1500 BP. The three phases are correlated with increasingly high numbers of cultural materials through time.

Summary

The Aboriginal cultural heritage in the Koombooloomba area and the association between people and open forest pockets are clearly significant in terms of understanding long-term Aboriginal rainforest occupation. Walking routes to and from the Evelyn Tableland across the Cardwell Range down to the coast, passed through this area (Duke and Collins 1999). Documentary sources and previously recorded oral-historical tradition indicate that the Koombooloomba area and remote locations in the upper reaches of the Tully River were places of great significance to the *Jirrbal* people and their neighbours at contact and subsequently became a refuge for Aboriginal people.

Excavations at the Urumbal Pocket open site consistently demonstrate that two main stratigraphic units exist at the site. They are represented by an artefact-rich stratigraphic unit 1, a 40–50 cm deep deposit, which is separated by a thin transition zone from stratigraphic unit 2. This unit has low levels of cultural material that drops off before sterile bedrock is encountered. For the purposes of the material culture analyses presented in Chapters 5 and 6, the transitional zone is included in stratigraphic unit 2, thus resulting in the construction of two analytical units.

5

The Lithics Analysis

Introduction

The significance of the archaeological record from Urumbal Pocket lies in the preservation of large amounts of cultural materials associated with a relatively high-precision temporal record. The archaeological evidence from Urumbal Pocket consists of two principal categories: a large stone artefact assemblage and a collection of carbonised plant materials (presented in Chapter 6). The analyses of the Urumbal Pocket archaeological material mainly relate to Aboriginal rainforest occupation before European arrival in and around the traditional lands of the *Jirrbal* people. The aims of the analyses are firstly to explore change and continuity in stone artefact typology and technology, raw material use and availability through time. Secondly, to investigate pre-European Aboriginal rainforest plant use by identifying and quantifying the archaeological plant remains. The analyses include investigations into assemblage formation and the relationships between contexts and the preservation of remains. Approaches and techniques used to understand the links between people occupying the rainforest in the past and the material culture are also discussed.

Aims and methods

The reductive nature of stone artefact manufacture is used to reconstruct the processes by which artefacts were made, thus the archaeological record has the potential to preserve the products from different stages of stone tool manufacture (Holdaway and Stern 2004:4). Applying a reduction analysis may also allow inferences to be made about technological responses to changing circumstances. Stone artefact analyses have the capacity to generate information relevant to research questions addressing small-scale issues. For instance, raw material representation, artefact types and artefact morphologies provide information about aspects of site use, including stone technologies, artefact manufacture, discard and function. At a larger scale, measures of reduction may provide information on past land use and settlement in a region, on mobility and on processes of trade and exchange (Clarkson and Lamb 2005:2).

The Urumbal Pocket stone artefact analysis consisted of the identification of artefact attributes which reflect the manufacturing technology, particularly the ways flakes were detached from a core, how they were further modified, and their reduction sequence. The analysis also investigated typology, choice of raw material and usewear. The artefact features were classified following Holdaway and Stern (2004) and the stone artefact database was created using the *EntrerTrois* program (McPherron and Holdaway 1997). The analysis was designed to make an inventory of the stone assemblage and establish the nature of stone artefact technology through time, as well as to explore human behaviours gleaned from the stone artefact assemblage to assist in the construction of a long-term Aboriginal occupation history of Urumbal Pocket. It was framed to answer a number of questions:

1. What is the size and character of the assemblage?
2. What spatial information can be derived from the sample?
3. What raw materials are represented and where are the sources for these raw materials located?

4. What technological information on reduction sequences can be inferred from the data?

5. Is there any evidence for usewear on the artefacts such as edge damage, retouch, or residue?

The surface artefact assemblage

Before excavations began, a number of artefacts on the surface of the site were recorded, collected and bagged separately. Square AB consisted of a 2 x 2 metre surface area. It incorporated square A2, which was subsequently excavated, and squares A1, B1 and B2, which were not excavated. These connected with square A2 and formed part of the inferred main zone of activity in the flat central area on the spur (Fig. 4.8). The surface assemblage consisted of 64 artefacts. Raw materials were chiefly quartz (n=41) and rhyolite (n=16). Another seven raw material categories are represented by a single artefact each, including one piece of worked glass. Refitting of artefacts from surface square AB was attempted, but was unsuccessful. Because Koombooloomba Dam is used as a recreational fishing and camping area, it is quite possible that stone artefacts on the surface may have been picked up and removed from the site as souvenirs. As a result, the stone artefact analysis presented here focuses on the excavated assemblage.

Excavated stone artefacts

During excavation, all artefacts greater than or equal to 10 mm in maximum dimension were bagged individually and labelled according to excavation square and spit. All excavated sediments were weighed and then wet-sieved using 7 mm, 3 mm and 1 mm mesh to allow for small flakes and angular fragments to be collected. Most artefacts less than 10 mm in maximum dimension were collected from the sieves, recorded and bagged together according to excavation square and spit. The assemblage was sorted into two size categories according to the maximum dimension of artefacts: those less than 10 mm, referred to in the text as 'small artefacts', and artefacts greater than or equal to 10 mm, referred to as 'large artefacts'. The small artefacts were sorted into raw material types, counted and weighed together according to square and spit. This data is presented following the results of the technological analysis of the large stone artefact assemblage. There was no further analysis of the small artefact assemblage. However, during the sorting process it was noted that the small artefacts were comprised of angular fragments, flake fragments and complete flakes. The spatial and temporal frequencies of the small artefacts are examined with the aim of complementing the large artefact distributions.

Sample size

A total of 33,624 stone artefacts were recovered in the excavation of the six 1 x 1 metre trenches and the one 50 x 50 cm pit. Of all the stone artefacts in the assemblage, two thirds (n=22,628) were less than 10 mm in size. The remaining one third (n=10,997) were made up of flaked artefacts greater than or equal to 10 mm in size, pieces of ochre, and a small number of stone implements of other types. Stone artefacts recovered from square Z7 (n=187 ≥ 10 mm and n=551 < 10 mm) were also analysed, however the results are omitted from the following discussion because the trench filled with water before excavation was completed. In addition, eight non-artefacts have been omitted as well as 57 pieces of ochre which are discussed separately. This left a sample size of 10,745 stone artefacts greater than or equal to 10 mm in size.

Analytical Units

In order to explore variability in stone technology through time, the spits from each of the six squares were assigned to two analytical units defined for Urumbal Pocket. Analytical Unit 1 and Analytical Unit 2 are considered to have temporal significance, with the lower Analytical Unit representing the period from circa 8000 BP to 2000 BP and the upper Analytical Unit representing the last 2,000 years. The spit correlations for the two Analytical Units from each square are shown in Table 5.1.

Table 5.1 Spits in each square attributed to Analytical Units 1 and 2.

Square	Spits	
	Analytical Unit 1	Analytical Unit 2
A2	1–6	7–11
Z3	1–12	13–17
V5	1–7	8–12
V8	1–9	10–13
S2	1–13	14–20
O2	1–12	13–15

Source: Author's data.

Numbers of large artefacts per Analytical Unit

Table 5.2 shows the frequency of large stone artefacts in Analytical Unit 1 and Analytical Unit 2 for each square, and their percentages from all squares.

Table 5.2 Large stone artefacts per Analytical Unit, in absolute numbers and in percentages of the entire assemblage for all squares.

Square	Analytical Unit				Total	%
	1		2			
	n	%	n	%	n	%
A2	3,339	31.1	269	2.5	3,608	33.6
O2	93	0.9	-	-	93	0.9
S2	1,282	11.9	45	0.4	1,327	12.3
V5	1,682	15.6	68	0.6	1,750	16.2
V8	522	4.9	2	0.0	524	4.9
Z3	3,296	30.7	147	1.4	3,443	32.1
Total	10,216	95.1	529	4.9	10,745	100.0

Source: Author's data.

As seen in Table 5.2, Analytical Unit 1 contains the bulk of stone artefacts recovered from Urumbal Pocket, accounting for 95.1% of the assemblage (n=10,216).

Numbers of small artefacts per Analytical Unit

Table 5.3 shows the numbers and percentages of small artefacts per square and per Analytical Unit. It demonstrates that more than 90% of the small artefacts occur in Analytical Unit 1. The highest numbers were recovered from squares Z3 and A2, followed by squares S2 and V5. This distribution in numbers of artefacts correlates well with the distribution of the large artefacts discussed above.

Table 5.3 Numbers and percentages of small artefacts <10 mm in maximum dimension, per square, per Analytical Unit.

Square	Analytical Unit 1		Analytical Unit 2		Total	
	n	%	n	%	n	%
A2	4,721	87.4	680	12.6	5,401	24.5
Z3	6,520	90.4	692	9.6	7,212	32.7
V5	2,893	89.3	346	10.7	3,239	14.7
V8	1,484	98.7	20	1.3	1,504	6.8
S2	3,992	94.0	253	6.0	4,245	19.2
O2	456	95.8	20	4.2	476	2.2
Total	20,066	90.9	2,011	9.1	22,077	100.0

Source: Author's data.

Distribution in numbers of large and small artefacts

Varying spit depths used in the excavations (2.5 cm and 5 cm) was discussed in Chapter 4. They do not allow for a grouping and comparison of materials from a particular spit across all six squares that would allow for an analysis of spatial stone artefact distributions at the site. To overcome the problem of varying spit depths, it was decided to group artefacts from two 2.5 cm spits in squares Z3, V8, and S2 into one single spit of 5 cm. These three squares have large numbers of artefacts and a similar stratigraphy, and are on relatively level ground. Whilst depth below surface is not considered a reliable guide to contemporaneity, by grouping this spit data, the distributions of material culture for these squares can broadly be compared and contrasted with those for squares A2 and V5. The stratigraphy in square O2 is different from the other squares. However, a general lack of artefacts throughout square O2 when compared to the other five squares has been interpreted as a boundary of the site and numbers of artefacts per composite spit in square O2 are therefore included in the analysis for comparison.

Distribution of large artefacts

In Table 5.4, the numbers of large artefacts per composite 5 cm spit for each of the six squares are shown. The numbers of artefacts per (composite) 5 cm spit per square (Table 5.4) form the basis for the analysis of the Urumbal Pocket stone artefact distribution pattern from each square. Figure 5.1 shows the distribution in number of stone artefacts in each composite 5 cm spit (1–12) across the site with a concentration evident in the numbers of artefacts in the central flat area on the spur.

Table 5.4 Numbers of stone artefacts ×10 mm per 5 cm (composite) spit, per square.

| Composite spit | Square | | | | | |
	A2	V5	Z3	V8	S2	O2
1	132	110	234	109	116	1
2	425	230	517	211	274	-
3	779	212	513	182	265	-
4	515	285	524	18	464	-
5	808	297	978	3	108	2
6	680	314	530	1	45	7
7	220	234	133	-	18	13
8	41	56	14	-	10	36
9	3	10	-	-	18	26
10	5	-	-	-	9	8
11	-	1	-	-	-	-
12	-	1	-	-	-	-
Total	3,608	1,750	3,443	524	1,327	93

Source: Author's data.

The number of artefacts in subsurface deposits in squares A2, Z3 and V5 suggests that these squares form part of a 'central activity area' at Urumbal Pocket and correlates with the high number of surface artefacts in this location. A pronounced increase in the number of artefacts per spit begins in composite spit 7 in squares A2, Z3 and V5. This trend continues in squares A2 and Z3, but the artefact density in square V5 remains relatively uniform throughout the spit sequence. For squares A2 and Z3, spit 5 has the highest numbers of artefacts in the whole sequence and coincides with the beginning of an increase in square S2, located at least 10 metres away from the central surface artefact concentration present in squares A2 and Z3. Square S2 yielded a relatively large number of tools (i.e. artefacts with usewear and residue) as well as a bipolar stone anvil. Based on these observations, it is proposed that square S2 provides possible evidence of stone- and wood-working activities being carried out away from an inferred central activity area. This area, believed to be represented by squares A2, V5 and Z3, is located in the flat section on the spur closest to the water. The expansion of the site continues in spit 4, with stone artefacts recovered from square V8 in addition to the other squares.

Results show that the lower-density scatter in square S2 consists of a higher percentage of tools, suggesting differences in the way space was used and organised at Urumbal Pocket in the past. Radiocarbon dating suggests that the pronounced increase in the number of artefacts in spit 7 of squares A2, Z3 and V5, dates to after 1,500 years ago. Most of the artefacts are contained in the final 1,000 years of Aboriginal occupation deposit at Urumbal Pocket. Almost 74% of large artefacts in square A2 were recovered from spits 1–5, and in square Z3 over 80% of the large artefacts are from spits 1–5. A small number of flaked glass artefacts and radiocarbon dating further suggests that the site was used by Aboriginal people until sometime in the mid- to late nineteenth century, which links in with the timing of European arrival in the coastal areas and on the Tablelands. Therefore, a decrease in artefact numbers in spit 1 may reflect the restrictions put on the movement of Aboriginal people across the rainforest region by Europeans at this time. The presence of a river crossing at Urumbal Pocket, increasingly used by Europeans, also may have resulted in Aboriginal people avoiding the location.

Distribution of small artefacts

All of the small artefacts were initially sorted and counted per square and spit to facilitate an analysis of stone artefact density distribution using the total assemblage. Numbers of small artefacts per composite spit for the six squares are presented in Table 5.5.

Table 5.5 Numbers of small stone artefacts <10 mm per 5 cm (composite) spit, per square.

Composite spit	Square						
	A2	Z3	V5	V8	S2	O2	Total
1	411	472	147	334	246	11	1,621
2	389	1,120	341	491	603	15	2,959
3	1,274	897	516	440	980	30	4,136
4	971	1,320	357	160	1,393	81	4,283
5	1,023	1,792	450	67	472	165	3,969
6	653	919	587	12	232	154	2,557
7	468	541	495	-	97	20	1,621
8	132	142	244	-	68	-	586
9	29	9	69	-	93	-	200
10	51	-	33	-	61	-	145
Total	5,401	7,212	3,239	1,504	4,245	476	22,077

Source: Author's data.

As Figure 5.2 demonstrates, there are relatively low artefact numbers in the lower spits. The beginning of an increase is apparent in spit 8, but only for squares A2, Z3, and V5.

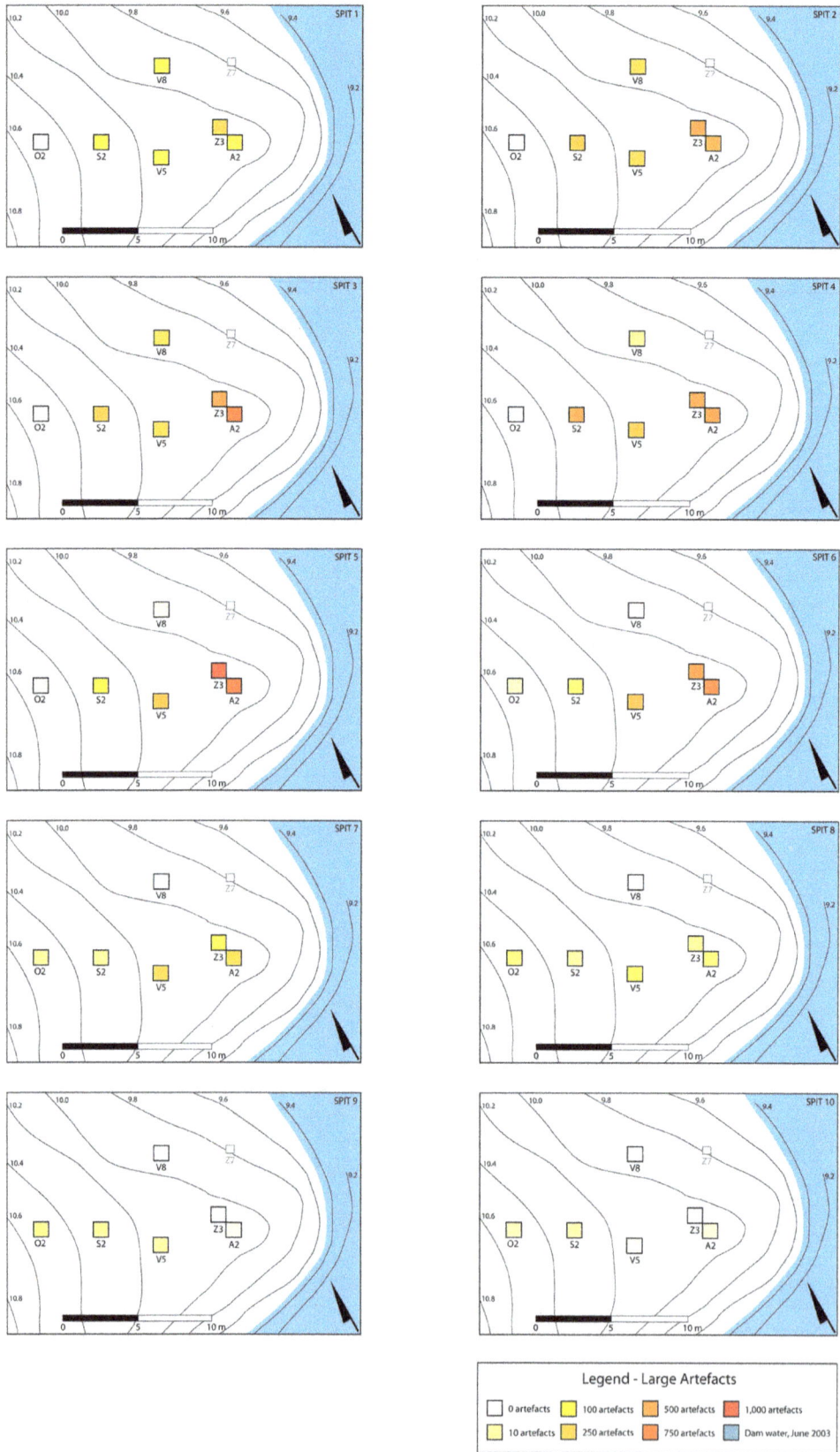

Figure 5.1 Numbers of large artefacts recovered from Urumbal Pocket, in composite spits 1–12, per excavated square.

Source: J. de Lange.

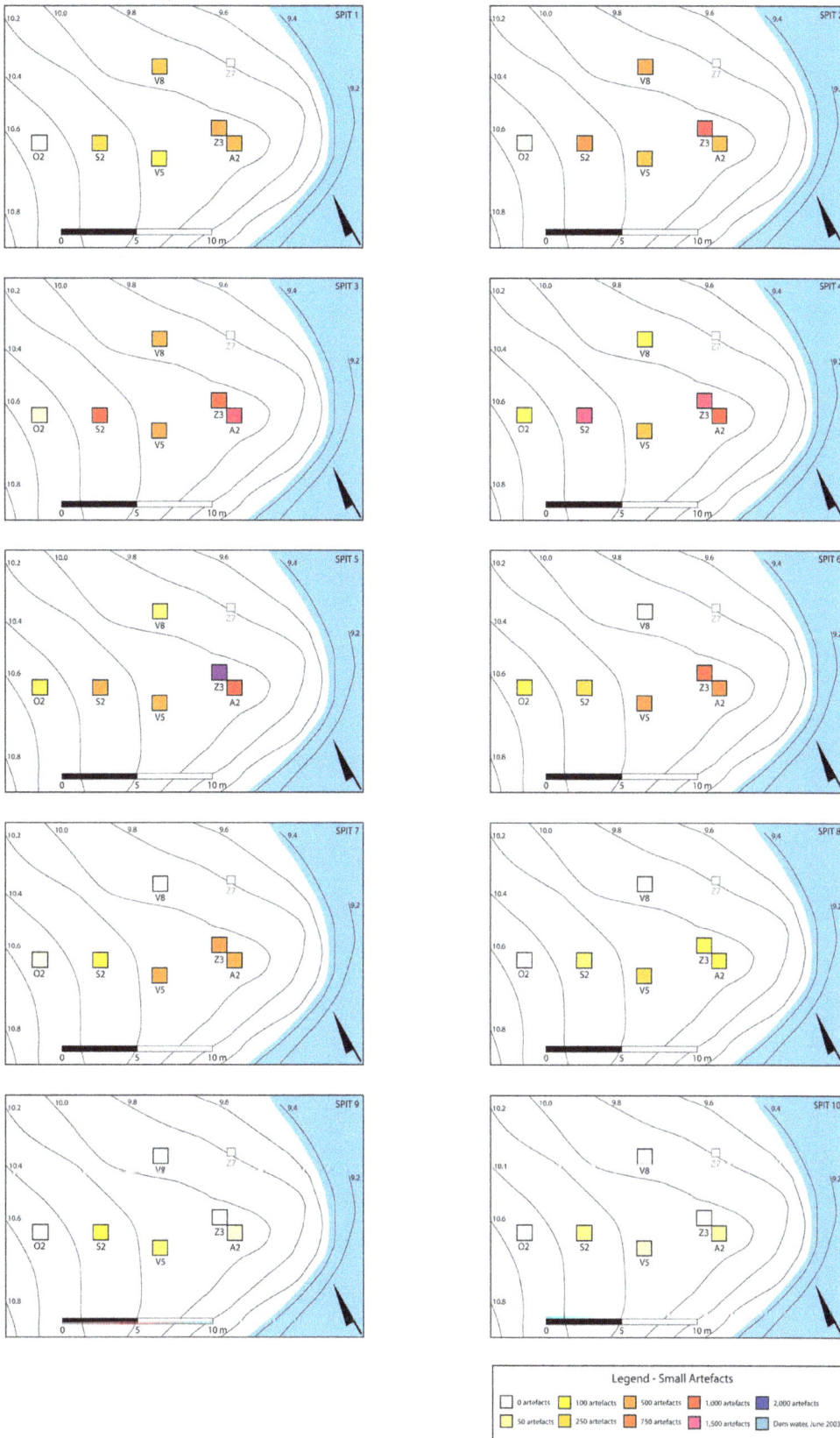

Figure 5.2 Numbers of small artefacts recovered from Urumbal Pocket, in composite spits 1–12, per excavated square.

Source: J. de Lange.

By the time the sediments contained in spit 8 were deposited, artefact discard was concentrated on the front flat area of the spur. Composite spits 2–6 have the highest numbers of artefacts in all of the squares. An increase in numbers of artefacts appears in spit 6 in square S2, and in spit 5 in square V8. Both squares are located about 5 m from the other three. The results show that the site expanded in area over time, as seen in the large artefact distributions.

Table 5.6 Large and small artefact distributions per composite spit in squares A2, Z3, and S2.

Composite spit	A2		Z3		S2	
	×10 mm artefacts	−10 mm artefacts	×10 mm artefacts	−10 mm artefacts	×10 mm artefacts	−10 mm artefacts
1	132	411	234	472	116	246
2	425	389	517	1,120	274	603
3	779	1,274	513	897	265	980
4	515	971	524	1,320	464	1,393
5	808	1,023	978	1,792	108	472
6	680	653	530	919	45	232
7	220	468	133	541	18	97
8	41	132	14	142	10	68
9	3	29	-	9	18	93
10	5	51	-	-	9	61
11	-	-	-	-	-	-
12	-	-	-	-	-	-
Total	3,608	5,401	3,443	7,212	1,327	4,245

Source: Author's data.

When the large and small artefact distributions per composite spit and per square are compared (Table 5.6), the results show that the numbers of large and small artefacts are consistent over time. The small artefacts represent 60% of the total assemblage in square Z3, almost 33% in square A2, and around 24% in square S2. This may suggest that there were no significant cleaning activities on site, which might have resulted in the preferential removal of larger artefacts.

Raw material representation

The large artefact assemblage

A summary of the raw material represented (including ochre) in each of the six squares is shown in Table 5.7. The principal raw materials in the assemblage are quartz (88.5%), crystal quartz (4.9%) and rhyolite (2.6%). Slate and phyllite are grouped as metamorphic stone materials while igneous raw materials include basalt, granite and other, unidentified igneous material. The fine-grained raw materials include chert, silcrete, chalcedony and jasper, as well as other unidentified fine-grained material. There is a distinction between materials that were opportunistically exploited from local sources, such as quartz, and materials such as rhyolite, that were brought into the site from further afield.

Table 5.7 Total raw material representation in numbers of artefacts, including ochre, 10 mm and above per square.

Raw material	Square						Total
	A2	Z3	V5	V8	S2	O2	
Quartz	3,244	3,089	1,532	466	1,187	81	9,599
Crystal quartz	135	166	87	33	100	9	530
Rhyolite	66	123	47	15	30	1	282
Metamorphic	88	48	16	8	6	2	168
Igneous	53	1	42	0	0	0	96
Fine-grained materials	5	6	20	2	3	0	36
Indeterminate/other	17	8	6	0	1	0	32
Glass	0	2	0	0	0	0	2
Ochre	27	4	23	0	3	0	57
Total	3,635	3,447	1,773	524	1,330	93	10,802

Source: Author's data.

When quartz and crystal quartz are grouped, they make up 93.7% of the total assemblage. This is not surprising since open sites and rock-shelters in the rainforest region generally show quartz to be the most commonly used material in artefact manufacture (Cosgrove et al. 2007:155; Cosgrove and Raymont 2002; Horsfall 1987; Wright 1971). The high percentage of quartz (including crystal quartz) is consistent with the fact that it was available in creek beds of the Cardwell Range, a relatively short distance from Urumbal Pocket, and could probably be easily procured and opportunistically exploited, as discussed further below. The second most common raw material represented in the assemblage is rhyolite, a fine-grained igneous rock. Other raw materials are present in the deposits (for example silcrete and chalcedony) and provide significant clues to the types of exotic raw material (i.e. stone materials sourced outside the rainforest region) that were available and used by the Urumbal Pocket occupants. Identification of the sources of the raw materials represented at Urumbal Pocket is important for understanding human exploitation of different stone materials and is discussed below.

Quartz

Depending on the origin of quartz, a range of internal structures may be found that form the basis of a more detailed classification system, including, for instance, crystal and vein quartz. Vein quartz can be successfully worked by exploiting internal flaws but its products are very difficult to distinguish from natural weathering (Witter 1992:43). Most of the quartz artefacts excavated from Urumbal Pocket are of a white quartz variety with a relatively fine crystalline structure. It has relatively predictable flaking characteristics and may be described as good quality white quartz. Quartz is not available in the immediate vicinity of the site, which removes the problem of trying to separate naturally occurring quartz debris from artefacts produced by the Urumbal Pocket occupants. To date, the exact location of the quartz source(s) has not been established. The closest known source is the Cardwell Range (B. Wyatt, pers. comm., 2006), the mountainous area located to the east of the site. Today, the range is covered in dense rainforest vegetation and there are currently no access roads into the area. Pebbles of similar shape and size to those that were recovered in the excavations have been reported across the range in the many small tributaries of the Tully River, where tin and gold prospecting took place in the late 1800s and later in the twentieth century (Coyyan 1915; B. Wyatt, pers. comm., 2006). Attempts to source white quartz of a similar quality were also carried out on the western side of the Tully River. Although numerous cobbles and pebbles were found in small creeks and on the banks of the Tully River and tested, no fine crystalline quartz or crystal quartz was identified on the west side of the river (personal observation, 2006).

The quartz pebbles collected by Aboriginal people in the past and brought to Urumbal Pocket typically have smooth waterworn cortex but are relatively angular in shape (Fig. 5.3). In contrast, quartz cobbles found on the banks of the Tully River and in nearby creeks are much larger in size and round or oval in shape. This suggests that the pebbles used in artefact manufacture at Urumbal Pocket had not been rolled in high velocity flowing water (i.e. the Tully River), but probably in small, relatively low-energy creeks. One crystal quartz core on a large river cobble was recorded on the exposed band of soil at Koombooloomba Dam during surveys, which suggests that crystal quartz could have been sourced locally (Fig. 5.4). However, the relatively small amount of crystal quartz at Urumbal Pocket may indicate that it was more difficult to procure than white quartz and the cobble may have been brought in from elsewhere.

Figure 5.3 Broken quartz pebble recovered in the excavations at Urumbal Pocket (scale=1 cm) (UP/Z3/10/4961).
Source: Photograph by P. Saad.

Figure 5.4 Crystal quartz core recorded on the banks of Koombooloomba Dam (scale=cm).
Source: Photograph by R. Cosgrove.

Rhyolite and fine-grained raw materials

The presence of rhyolite, chert, and other fine-grained raw materials at Urumbal Pocket indicates that stone was transported to the site from drier areas with different geology located to the west of the rainforest region, where these raw materials are available (Bultitude et al. 1997:236; Henderson and Stephenson 1980). No known outcrops or exposures of rhyolite are found near the site. The closest known source is in the drier sclerophyll area located to the west of the Evelyn Tableland (Cosgrove et al. 2007:155). At contact, this area was also within the traditional lands of the *Jirrbal* people. The presence of rhyolite may, therefore, point to the use of both open, drier areas and rainforests by Aboriginal people occupying the southwest corner of the rainforest region in the past. It has previously been noted, based on the ethnographic material culture record and from *Jirrbal* oral traditions, that people living at Cedar Creek had access to two very different environments at the time of Eric Mjöberg's visit in the area in 1913 (Ferrier 1999:96). The presence of raw materials from sources outside of the rainforest region at Urumbal Pocket may also be a result of trade with non-rainforest groups in the past. The evidence does not offer a preference between these two interpretations of the presence of non-local raw materials at Urumbal Pocket. However, the combined evidence strongly points to the Urumbal Pocket occupants' utilisation of two very different environments.

The low numbers (n=282) of rhyolite artefacts in the deposits that are small, and show an absence of cortex and extensive retouch, may suggest that this material was being curated by its owners (see for example Binford 1979; Gould 1980:234). That is, it was a stone material retained and reused, or was unpopular in artefact manufacture. Both options may be a result of the distance rhyolite had to be transported. It is possible that quartz was not only locally available but also the raw material favoured for use in stone working by Aboriginal rainforest people, as observed by Michael O'Leary in the early contact period (Coyyan 1915). It was beyond the scope of the research to source other raw materials, represented by very small numbers of artefacts, such as the chert and other fine-grained materials.

Metamorphics

The metamorphic raw material group, comprising phyllite and slate, is associated with grinding technology and occurs mainly in the form of ground and incised tools such as axe bevels and incised grinding stones. It has been suggested that their presence in the rainforest indicates interaction and some form of trade with coastal rainforest groups, where this raw material is available (Stevens 2004). At the time of European contact, it was recorded that interactions between tableland and coastal groups were an integral part of the seasonal cycle of ceremonial gatherings with host groups occupying different areas in the rainforest region, as discussed in Chapter 3. The metamorphic artefacts in the Urumbal Pocket deposits may provide evidence for the development of late Holocene interactions between groups occupying different areas of the wider rainforest region.

The small artefact assemblage

A summary of the raw material of the small artefacts represented in each of the six squares is shown in Table 5.8. The small artefact assemblage is represented, as might be expected, chiefly by quartz (n=20,365; 92.2%; weight=1,323.3 g), crystal quartz (6.3%) and rhyolite (1.0%). Slate and phyllite are grouped as metamorphic stone materials and represent 0.4% of the small artefact assemblage. Other raw materials in the small artefact assemblage include one artefact each of chert and chalcedony and two artefacts that are of an indeterminate raw material.

Table 5.8 Raw material representation in numbers of stone artefacts <10 mm, per square.

Raw material	Square						
	A2	Z3	V5	V8	S2	O2	Total
Quartz	5,071	6,517	3,015	1,405	3,923	434	20,365
Crystal quartz	255	565	160	90	293	34	1,397
Rhyolite	23	98	56	7	23	8	215
Metamorphic	52	31	7	2	4	0	96
Other	0	1	1	0	2	0	4
Total	5,401	7,212	3,239	1,504	4,245	476	22,077

Source: Author's data.

Crystal quartz artefacts were recovered from all squares and represent just over 6% (n=1397) of the overall assemblage, with the highest numbers in squares A2, Z3 and S2. Rhyolite accounts for 1% of the assemblage (n=215), with the highest numbers in squares Z3 (n=98) and V5 (n=56). A small number of slate (n=54) and phyllite (n=42) probably represent fragments that broke off during tool maintenance and/or use of incised grinders and edge-ground axes, and lend support to the suggestion that these tools were being used at the site.

Attributes of the large artefacts

All of the large artefacts were classified following Holdaway and Stern (2004). Each of the large artefacts was given an identification number and classified according to artefact type. Square and spit were recorded for each artefact. Other attributes recorded for each artefact include raw material type, amount of cortex (in percentage increments) on the dorsal surface of flakes and on cores, and the absence or presence of residue that could be seen with the naked eye. The number of edges with modification (retouch/usewear) was also documented. The primary dimensions (length, width and thickness) of oriented complete flakes, complete split flakes and tools were measured. The maximum dimension of all other types of artefacts were measured, and all artefacts were weighed. A number of other measurements and attributes were recorded and included in the database (Ferrier 2010) but are not discussed here because they are unrelated to the aims of the stone artefact analyses presented in this chapter. Artefact illustrations are labelled according to site/square/spit/identification number.

Represented artefact types

Artefact type describes a combination of the completeness of an artefact, its form and its technological attributes. Table 5.9 lists and defines the artefact types represented in the large artefact assemblage.

Table 5.9 Definitions of stone artefact types represented in the Urumbal Pocket assemblage.

Artefact type	Definition
Complete flake	An artefact exhibiting a ventral and dorsal surface, platform and termination.
Proximal flake	A broken flake with a platform but without a termination.
Medial flake	A broken flake without a platform or termination but with at least one medial section of a lateral edge.
Distal flake	A broken flake with a termination but without a platform.
Complete split flake	A flake with a platform and a termination that is split down the percussion axis.
Flake fragment	A split or otherwise broken flake with no platform or termination.
Core	An artefact that exhibits a series of negative flake scars, each of which represents the removal of a flake.
Bipolar core	A core exhibiting crushing on both proximal and distal margins, sometimes with crushed lateral edges indicating rotation on an anvil.
Core fragment	A broken core that exhibits at least one negative flake scar which represents the removal of a flake.
Complete tool	A complete flake with evidence for use in the form of residue, usewear and/or retouch.
Proximal tool	A proximal flake with evidence for use in the form of residue, usewear and/or retouch.
Medial tool	A medial flake with evidence for use in the form of residue, usewear and/or retouch.
Tool fragment	A flake fragment with evidence for use in the form of residue, usewear and/or retouch.
Angular fragment	Unidentified fragments that sometimes resemble flakes but lack the characteristic diagnostic features of conchoidal fracture.
Flaked cobble	A stone with water-rounding cortex and negative flake scars from flake removal.

Source: Author's data.

Cores were divided into a number of types:

Unidirectional core

Cores with scars originating from a single platform, and all the flakes have been struck from the core in the same direction (Holdaway and Stern 2004:180).

Bidirectional core

Cores with two platforms, one opposite the other. Flakes have been struck from each of the platforms and thus from opposite directions (Holdaway and Stern 2004:180).

Multidirectional core

Cores with two or more platforms and there is no clear pattern, either in the orientation of the platforms or in the orientation of the scars resulting from the striking of flakes from those platforms (Holdaway and Stern 2004:180).

Bipolar core

Cores that were flaked using an anvil (Holdaway and Stern 2004:196). The resulting artefact exhibits crushing on both its proximal and distal margin and often on its lateral margins, when it has been rotated on an anvil.

Tools

Tools were classified according to shape and the location and character of any edge with retouch or usewear. Based on the observations at other sites in the rainforest region, the high representation of quartz artefacts resulted in low expectations of finding many retouched implements in the assemblage (Cosgrove et al. 2007; Horsfall 1987; Wright 1971). In addition to the flaked artefact types described above, a number of other stone tools (n=9) were recovered. This category consists of one edge-ground axe, one utilised cobble, three cobbles (manuports), one bipolar anvil and three incised slate fragments or grinding stones. Table 5.10 lists the total numbers of artefacts of each type represented in the large stone artefact assemblage.

Table 5.10 The total numbers and the percentages of large artefacts per artefact type.

Artefact type	Number	Percentage
Complete flake	3,516	32.7
Proximal flake	890	8.3
Medial flake	173	1.6
Distal flake	443	4.1
Complete split flake	1,423	13.2
Flake fragment	556	5.2
Core	355	3.3
Bipolar core	527	4.9
Bipolar core fragment	68	0.6
Core fragment	135	1.3
Complete tool	57	0.5
Proximal tool	2	0
Medial tool	1	0
Tool fragment	39	0.4
Angular fragment	2,542	23.7
Flaked cobble	9	0.1
Other stone implement	9	0.1
Total	10,745	100

Source: Author's data.

Stone artefact categories

The numbers and percentages of large artefacts recovered from each of the six squares were grouped into four general categories: (i) flakes (including all forms of broken flakes); (ii) cores (including all forms of complete and broken cores); (iii) angular fragments; and (iv) tools and other stone implements (Table 5.11). Dividing the large stone artefact assemblage into these four categories provides an overall characterisation that satisfactorily addresses the research questions.

Table 5.11 Flakes, cores, angular fragments, tools and other stone implements 10 mm and greater in size, by number and proportion of the assemblage, per square.

Square	Flakes		Angular fragments		Cores		Tools and other stone implements		Total	
	n	%	n	%	n	%	n	%	n	%
A2	2,210	20.6	1,084	10.1	274	2.5	40	0.4	3,608	33.6
Z3	2,290	21.3	706	6.6	359	3.3	88	0.8	3,443	32.0
V5	1,143	10.6	397	3.7	176	1.6	34	0.3	1,750	16.3
V8	318	3.0	111	1.0	76	0.7	19	0.2	524	4.9
S2	833	7.7	218	2.0	161	1.5	115	1.1	1,327	12.3
O2	62	0.6	12	0.1	11	0.1	8	0.1	93	0.9
Total	6,856	63.8	2,528	23.5	1,057	9.8	304	2.9	10,745	100.0

Source: Author's data.

As seen in Table 5.11, the assemblage is dominated by flakes and angular fragments (including complete flakes and all types of broken flakes), which together make up 87.3% of the assemblage. Cores make up 9.8% of the assemblage, tools and other stone implements 2.9%. Squares A2 (n=3608) and Z3 (n=3443) are the richest, accounting for two thirds of the total assemblage. Squares V5 and S2 are also relatively rich in stone artefacts compared to squares V8 and O2.

Stone artefact types represented in Analytical Units 1 and 2

The lowest spits in squares A2, V5, and S2, in Analytical Unit 2, contain very small numbers of quartz artefacts and no other raw materials are represented. However, artefacts in the upper spits in squares A2, V5 and Z3 (Analytical Unit 2) show that other raw materials like chert, rhyolite, and slate were also used. The occurrence of different types of artefacts in Analytical Unit 1 and 2 is illustrated in Tables 5.12 and 5.13. These tables show that no distinct temporal differences in stone technology could be identified on the basis of a comparison between the small artefact sample in Analytical Unit 2 and the much larger sample in Analytical Unit 1.

Table 5.12 Artefact types, 10 mm and greater, per square in Analytical Unit 1, by number and percentage.

Square	Angular fragment		Core		Flake		Tool/other		Total	
	n	%	n	%	n	%	n	%	n	%
A2	988	29.6	258	7.7	2,058	61.6	35	1.0	3,339	32.7
O2	12	12.9	11	11.8	62	66.7	8	8.6	93	0.9
S2	209	16.3	156	12.2	805	62.8	112	8.7	1,282	12.5
V5	385	22.9	167	9.9	1,101	65.4	29	1.7	1,682	16.5
V8	111	21.3	76	14.6	316	60.1	19	3.6	522	5.1
Z3	678	20.6	341	10.3	2,197	66.7	80	2.4	3,296	32.3
Total	2,383	23.3	1,009	9.9	6,539	64.0	283	2.8	10,214	100.0

Source: Author's data.

Table 5.13 Artefact types, 10 mm and greater, per square in Analytical Unit 2, by number and percentage.

Square	Angular fragment		Core		Flake		Tool/other		Total	
	n	%	n	%	n	%	n	%	n	%
A2	84	31.2	16	5.9	152	56.5	17	6.3	269	50.6
O2	0	0	0	0	0	0	0	0	0	0
S2	9	20.0	5	11.1	30	66.7	1	2.2	45	8.5
V5	12	17.6	9	13.2	42	61.8	5	7.3	68	12.8
V8	0	0	0	0	2	100.0	0	0	2	0.4
Z3	28	19.0	19	12.9	93	63.3	7	4.8	147	27.7
Total	133	25.0	49	9.2	319	60.1	30	5.6	531	100.0

Source: Author's data.

Technological analysis

In the following data summary, artefacts made on chalcedony, jasper and basalt are excluded because there are no complete cores on these metamorphic raw materials. Therefore, comparisons are made between two raw material categories: (i) quartz and (ii) the non-local raw materials grouped together, including rhyolite, chert, and unidentified igneous raw materials.

Mean size and weight of non-utilised flakes and cores

The mean weight and size of complete flakes (including complete split flakes), and of complete cores, can provide information about the intensiveness of reduction of different stone raw materials. Previous studies on quartz show that flaking consistently generates large quantities of debris (Bird and Frankel 2005; Dickson 1977; K. Akerman, pers. comm., 2007). The large amount of small artefacts recorded in the excavations suggests intensive reduction applied to quartz, or alternatively is a result of the tendency of quartz to fracture into small pieces.

Table 5.14 Mean weight (g) and size (mm) of complete flakes, including complete split flakes, and cores 10 mm and greater, on quartz and non-local raw materials grouped together. In this case size refers to the length of flakes and the maximum dimension of cores.

Artefact type	Quartz	Non-local	Quartz	Non-local
	Mean weight (g)	Mean weight (g)	Mean size (mm)	Mean size (mm)
Flake	0.7	0.9	14.0	12.8
Core	4.6	9.2	20.9	30.0

Source: Author's data.

As demonstrated in Table 5.14 the complete flakes on quartz are, on average, slightly larger in size than those on non-local materials but, on average, weigh slightly less. Cores on quartz are smaller and weigh less than cores on non-local materials. The analysis of the average weight and size on complete flakes and cores of two raw material categories, local versus non-local, suggest that a variety of raw materials were brought to the site and intensively worked by the Urumbal Pocket occupants. It appears, however, that the intensity of reduction did not depend on the raw material used. One hypothesis that presents itself is an extensive use of bipolar reduction technology on a variety of raw materials, allowing for the production of small flakes. However, with some exception (n=4), there is no evidence of non-quartz cores having been reduced using bipolar technology. Jasper, silcrete, and chalcedony are only represented by flakes and/or angular fragments, the latter also only represented by one core fragment. It is possible that the low numbers of non-quartz artefacts is a reflection of curation and that non-quartz cores may have been transported away from the site.

The results show that quartz was intensively worked and that the pebbles were highly reduced from their original size of 60–70 mm range in maximum dimension, a size estimate based on flaked pebbles excavated from Urumbal Pocket (Fig. 5.3). Technological attributes show that hard-hammer percussion as well as the bipolar technique were applied to quartz and also to other fine-grained materials, such as chert. Overall, the results show that all stages of stone reduction are represented, on a variety of raw materials. The remainder of the technological analysis focuses on the quartz artefacts because they represent over 95% of the stone artefact assemblage.

Size/weight range on non-utilised flakes and cores

The size/weight range on complete flakes and cores (i.e. the minimum to maximum size and weight) are presented in Table 5.15.

Table 5.15 The size (mm) and weight range (g) (minimum and maximum) of complete non-utilised flakes and complete cores on quartz and non-local raw materials. Size in this case refers to the axial length of flakes and the maximum dimension of cores.

Artefact type	Quartz		Non-local		Quartz		Non-local	
	Min size (mm)	Max size (mm)	Min size (mm)	Max size (mm)	Min weight (g)	Max weight (g)	Min weight (g)	Max weight (g)
Flake	4.0	50.5	5.0	44.5	0.1	19.9	0.1	26.8
Core	11.0	65.0	18.0	60.0	0.4	117.1	0.9	43.0

Source: Author's data.

The results (Table 5.15) show that not all raw materials brought to the site were intensively worked because there are large cores and flakes in the assemblage. To explore this further, the range in weight distribution of cores on quartz is presented in Fig. 5.5.

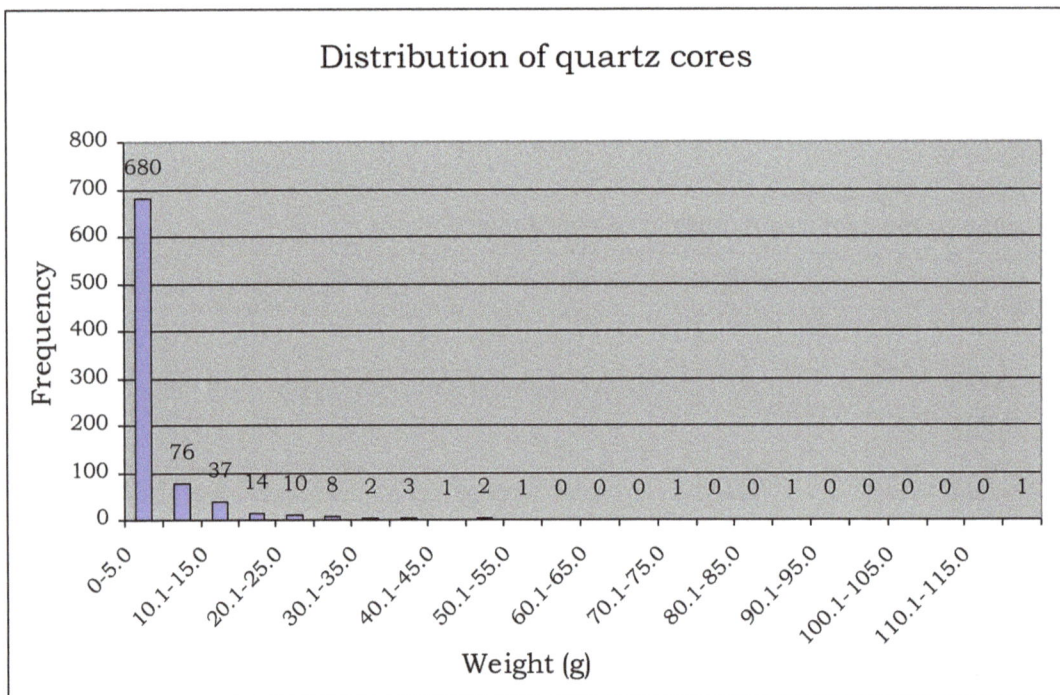

Figure 5.5 The distribution of complete cores, including bipolar cores, on quartz, in numbers of artefacts in 5 g intervals.
Source: Author's data.

Almost 80% of the complete quartz cores weigh less than five grams. The few heavy cores are 'pulling' the mean weight value upwards. Even with a relatively modest mean weight of 4.6 g for quartz cores, almost two thirds of cores fall below the mean weight with one third above it. Whether large cores, including the flaked pebbles, were discarded as a result of poor raw material quality or left at the site for future stone working episodes, is unknown. The cores provide significant information on the different reduction stages represented at Urumbal Pocket and demonstrate that not all of the quartz brought to the site was utilised in the same way. A similar pattern is present on complete rhyolite cores with a small number of large cores (n=3) pulling the mean weight value upwards, whilst complete cores on other non-local raw materials all fall below the mean size and weight.

Cortex

In order to examine different stages of stone reduction at the site, the amount of cortex remaining on the dorsal surface was recorded according to a series of percentage classes (Table 5.16) for each artefact (Holdaway and Stern 2004). Table 5.16 shows the percentage of cortex recorded in three raw material categories: quartz, rhyolite, and other non-local raw materials.

Table 5.16 Proportion of artefacts by raw material category, of the total number of artefacts, by different cortex percentage categories.

Raw material	Percentage of cortex present					
	0%	1–24%	25–49%	50–74%	75–99%	100%
Quartz	68.2	18.1	7.2	2.4	1.4	2.7
Rhyolite	76.9	13.8	5.7	1.1	1.1	1.4
Other non-local	90.2	7.5	1.5	0	0.7	0
Total	78.4	13.1	4.8	1.2	1.1	1.4

Source: Author's data.

Overall, 78.4% of artefacts in the assemblage have no cortex. Percentages per raw material category are: 68.2% of quartz artefacts; 76.9% of rhyolite artefacts; and 90.2% of other non-local raw materials. The high proportion of artefacts with no cortex indicates that early stage reduction is relatively rare in the assemblage. The lower overall proportion of non-local artefacts with cortex may suggest that non-local materials were more intensively reduced than quartz. However, the mean weight of quartz artefacts compared to other raw material types does not support this conclusion. The size/weight range on complete flakes and cores (Table 5.15) supports the notion that non-local raw materials were being reduced prior to discard on site, perhaps initially decorticated at their source to reduce the weight of cores in transportation. Given that quartz had been locally available, it was expected that a greater proportion of quartz artefacts would have some cortex, when compared to non-local materials. The quartz artefact assemblage does indeed show a lower percentage of artefacts without cortex when compared to artefacts made from non-local raw materials. This is probably a reflection of the local availability of quartz pebbles, which are portable items that could have been brought to the site complete. However, the amount of cortex is small, with most quartz artefacts (93.5%) having less than 50% cortex. This suggests that the Urumbal Pocket occupants were initially reducing the quartz pebbles and cobbles elsewhere, perhaps at the raw material source, before bringing them to the site.

Quartz flaking and the bipolar technology

With a large number of complete and broken bipolar cores in the assemblage (n=595), a review of previous studies on quartz and bipolar technology was undertaken to assess its potential significance in Aboriginal rainforest occupation. Results from experiments in quartz flaking previously undertaken by Dickson (1977:97) show that translucence and lustre are important indicator qualities in terms of flaking properties. Dickson found that the flaking properties of quartz improve with increasing translucence (Dickson 1977:102). Furthermore, he observed that workable quartz has a tough, cohesive nature that requires some specialisation of flaking technique. In direct hand-held percussion, a heavy hammer-stone was found to work best. When the core approached a size beyond which hand-held percussion was no longer possible, a limit that was reached between 60 and 90 g, the core had to be worked on an anvil to obtain flakes (Dickson 1977:103). This technique results in bipolar cores. Dickson (1977:103) found that similar artefacts may, however, be formed when using wedge-like pieces of quartz as stone-working chisels. Dickson's final observations (1977:103) were that bipolar core size is determined by the size of the stone knapper's fingers and that he could find no convincing evidence that they were deliberately made for use as tools. Bipolar cores have also been described by White (1968:665) as residual cores and the end product of the reduction of larger pieces. Although this is generally agreed upon, it has been suggested that they also may have been used as implements (Flenniken 1981; Lampert 1971:47). This resulted in further investigations on the bipolar cores excavated from Urumbal Pocket.

Bipolar cores—residual products or implements?

A total of 527 complete bipolar cores (Table 5.10) and 68 broken ones were recorded. A bipolar stone anvil of an unidentified igneous raw material was also recorded (Fig. 5.6). It has a roughly conical pit in the centre that is surrounded by a pecked area, identical to the features on a stone anvil that was used in a bipolar experimentation project (Dickson 1977:99). There are a total of 856 complete flakes in the assemblage that exhibit crushed platforms which may be a result of bipolar technology.

Figure 5.6 Stone anvil of an unknown volcanic raw material type excavated from Urumbal Pocket (scale=1 cm) (UP/S2/SP1/25).
Source: Photograph by P. Saad.

The average maximum dimension of complete bipolar cores is 15.3 mm with a mean weight of 1.8 g (Table 5.17). This is consistent with size data for bipolar cores at the point of discard in sites around Australia (Dickson 1977). In addition, unmodified flakes are in higher numbers than other forms of quartz debris, which is the expected outcome for bipolar technology (Dickson 1977:97).

Table 5.17 Average weight (g) and size (mm) (refers to maximum dimension in this case) and the minimum and maximum size of complete bipolar cores and non-bipolar cores in the assemblage.

Artefact type	Mean weight (g)	Min weight (g)	Max weight (g)	Mean size (mm)	Min size (mm)	Max size (mm)
Bipolar core	1.8	0.2	15.0	15.3	10.0	40.0
Non-bipolar core	8.0	0.3	117.1	23.6	10.0	65.0

Source: Author's data.

Most of the complete bipolar cores in the assemblage are quartz (n=464, 88%). Bipolar cores on crystal quartz are consistently slightly smaller than white quartz bipolar cores, which have a mean size of 12.0 mm and of 15.7 mm in maximum dimension, respectively. This indicates that crystal quartz bipolar cores were reduced or used beyond the point when quartz bipolar cores were discarded. This may be a result of the superior flaking quality of crystal quartz which allows for a better control over the flaking product, or the fact that crystal quartz is harder to come by, or a combination of both. A small number (n=5) of complete bipolar cores on non-local raw materials were recovered: two on rhyolite; one on chert; one on an indeterminate volcanic raw material; and one on glass (Fig. 5.7).

Figure 5.7 Complete and broken bipolar cores on (L–R) glass, crystal quartz, quartz, and rhyolite, excavated from Urumbal Pocket (scale=1 cm) (UP/Z3/1/5835, UP/A2/4/6560, UP/A2/2/5773, UP/V5/6/3397).
Source: Photograph by P. Saad.

Unmodified flakes and angular fragments on these rarely represented raw materials occur in very small numbers, and it may be that bipolar cores of non-local raw materials were used as implements.

Frequency of bipolar to non-bipolar cores in Analytical Units

It has been suggested that bipolar knapping is an advantageous technology to apply when mobility is low. This is because the main consideration for sedentary groups is to have adequate usable stone available at locations where it is needed. Whereas for mobile populations a portable tool kit is a primary concern (Parry and Kelly 1987:300). Therefore, the relative abundance of bipolar cores may be interpreted as a measure of residential mobility (Hiscock 1996:151). Parry and Kelly (1987) have suggested that, in North America, bipolar technology became more frequent in late prehistoric assemblages where it is associated with low residential mobility. One possible explanation for low residential mobility is that non-portable large, heavy anvil stones were being used in late prehistory. However, the relatively small size of one bipolar anvil stone excavated from Urumbal Pocket (Fig. 5.6) indicates that anvil stones in this region were as portable as cores. Therefore, low residential mobility may not necessarily explain an increased use of bipolar technology.

The frequency of complete bipolar cores to complete non-bipolar cores in Analytical Units 1 and 2 was explored in an attempt to evaluate the reductive technologies at Urumbal Pocket. Namely, to test if bipolar technology increases in Analytical Unit 1 might be expected if Aboriginal rainforest occupation became more permanent and, as a result, mobility decreased in the late Holocene period.

Table 5.18 Numbers and percentages of bipolar cores and non-bipolar cores represented in Analytical Units 1 and 2.

Core type	Analytical Unit 1		Analytical Unit 2	
	n	%	n	%
Bipolar core	500	48.3	27	55.1
Bipolar core fragment	65	6.3	3	6.1
Non-bipolar core	340	32.8	15	30.6
Non-bipolar core fragment	131	12.6	4	8.2
Total	1,036	100	49	100

Source: Author's data.

Based on the percentages of bipolar cores to non-bipolar cores the data from Urumbal Pocket do not support the notion of a more frequent use of bipolar technology in Analytical Unit 1. This suggests that during the last 1,500 to 2,000 years, a period when Australian Aboriginal rainforest occupation has been interpreted as becoming more permanent, residential mobility did not decrease, unlike the pattern proposed for North America (Parry and Kelly 1987:300). Alternatively, the results indicate that bipolar technology is not a good proxy for mobility studies. These results should, however, also be taken with some caution given the overall small number of stone artefacts in Analytical Unit 2. In addition, given the fact that bipolar cores possibly represent tools rather than cores, the potential link between bipolar cores and the degree of mobility becomes uncertain. One possibility for the increased frequency in numbers of stone artefacts in Analytical Unit 1 is that it reflects people returning to the site for short periods but more frequently after 2000 BP. This assumes that Aboriginal people were regularly using Urumbal Pocket as a short-term camp where stone-working and other activities such as toxic nut processing were carried out. Significantly, the presence of one bipolar core on glass unequivocally demonstrates that Aboriginal people were still visiting Urumbal Pocket at the time of European arrival and bipolar technology continued to be used on glass, at least in the early contact period.

Tool classification and tool types

In this research, a flaked artefact is a tool if it exhibits retouch or usewear along one or more edges, or it exhibits residue (Table 5.9). It should be noted that the term retouch is used here with caution. Since the majority of the artefacts are made of quartz, it was extremely difficult to establish whether edge modifications represent deliberate retouch or usewear damage, especially on the edges of inferred 'scraping implements'. Previous experimental studies on quartz (e.g. Dickson 1977; K. Akerman, pers. comm., 2008) have suggested that it is difficult to discriminate between retouch and usewear on flaked quartz artefacts (see also Bird and Frankel 2005). With a high proportion of quartz artefacts in the assemblage, the expectation of finding many retouched implements was also low because retouch on quartz is generally believed to be rare in archaeological sites in eastern Australia (V. Attenbrow, pers. comm., 2007).

The relatively good quality white quartz from Urumbal Pocket allowed a macroscopic assessment of edge modifications. Artefacts exhibiting continuous crushing to one or more edges were examined under magnification (7–40X) to further investigate whether the edge damage was deliberate retouch, usewear, or a result of bipolar technology (i.e. the crushing caused by the artefact that had been resting on a stone anvil). In the research presented here, usewear on a flaked artefact is defined as a continuous series of crushing in the shape of macroscopic edge damage. When magnified, this damage appears as micro-sized flake scars along one or more margins. Artefacts with crushed edges, resulting from bipolar technology, frequently have more than one crushed edge, i.e. complete flakes with crushed platforms and terminations. The crushing is often non-continuous and appears different to artefacts that exhibit edge damage as a result of use. Therefore, in the following discussion, flaked artefacts that exhibit one or more modified edges have been considered to be tools. Tools are classified into tool types according to morphological characteristics consistent with their function and use.

Scraper

Scrapers are generally flakes or parts of flakes with one or more margins that exhibit morphological characteristics consistent with a function and use as a scraper (Holdaway and Stern 2004:230). The Australian ethnographic record indicates that the majority of scraping tools used were not retouched into shape by their makers (Flenniken and White 1985:150).

Notched tool

Notched tools are flakes or parts of flakes that exhibit one or more small areas of retouch, each forming a concave edge on the lateral or distal margins (Holdaway and Stern 2004:236–238).

Notched scraper

A notched scraper is a type of tool that exhibits one or more notches. It has at least one edge that exhibits morphological characteristics consistent with use as a scraper. Notched tools are not generally separated from other types of scrapers (Holdaway and Stern 2004:238).

Burin

A type of engraving tool with a very strong, chisel-like edge that is usually created by snapping or retouching one end of a flake (Holdaway and Stern 2004:241). Sometimes artefacts with a burin-like appearance are also the casual product of bipolar flaking (Kamminga 1978:266–267).

Other stone tools

In addition to the flaked artefact types described above, nine other stone tools were recovered from the excavations. They consist of three incised slate fragments (of grinding stones), one edge-ground axe, one utilised cobble, three small, unmodified cobbles (manuports), and the bipolar anvil described previously. The incised slate fragments recovered from the Urumbal Pocket excavations demonstrate that toxic food processing was most likely carried out at the site in the past, and is discussed in more detail in Chapter 6. Incised slate grinding stones are unique to the rainforest region and can be distinguished from other grinding stones by a series of incised sharp grooves running perpendicular to the axis of the artefact. The incised slate grinding stone was traditionally used together with a small cobble. Maisie Barlow relates that a sharp piece of quartz was used to create the grooves by scraping the relatively soft slate surface (M. Barlow, pers. comm., 2004). It has also been suggested that the grooves were made using a bone point or an edge-ground axe (Horsfall 1987; Mjöberg 1913a). Woolston and Colliver (1973) have suggested, based on a statement by an Aboriginal woman, that the incised grinding stones were used in a rolling crushing motion rather than grinding motion (Field et al. 2009). The fragment shown in Figure 5.8 was recovered in spit 5 in square A2, in a layer associated with walnut fragments and stone artefacts that date to around 1000 BP.

Figure 5.8 Fragment of incised slate grinding stone recovered from the Urumbal Pocket excavations (UP/A2/SP5/1022).

Source: Photograph by R. Frank.

Figure 5.9 Edge-ground slate axe found *in situ* during the Urumbal Pocket excavations (scale=1 cm) (UP/Z3/SP12/5568).

Source: Photograph by R. Cosgrove.

One complete edge-ground axe made of slate was recovered (Fig. 5.9) with a maximum dimension of 139 mm and a weight of 402.5 g. The axe was recovered in spit 12 in square Z3, in a layer associated with walnut fragments and other stone artefacts. Radiocarbon dates on carbonised endocarp fragments excavated from spits 11 and 13 in square Z3 suggest that the layer in which the axe was found dates to somewhere between 1100 BP and 1500 BP. No complete edge-ground axe has previously been found *in situ* and the example therefore provides an approximate minimum age for the use of grinding technology in the rainforest region. A further 10 edge-ground slate fragments and one phyllite fragment were excavated. These cannot be assigned to a tool type because of their small size.

In a study of edge-ground axe assemblages on the exposed edge of the Tully River bank around Koombooloomba Dam (Stevens 2004), a recurring pattern of raw material selection was demonstrated and is broadly observed across the rainforest region. The axes recorded at Koombooloomba Dam are made of slate and basalt with suitable slate sources located along the coast (Stevens 2004:4). At least one basalt source is also available within the study area at Ravenshoe on the Millstream River. The average length of the metamorphic axes recorded from Koombooloomba Dam is around 160 mm (Stevens 2004:41) compared to 139 mm for the excavated axe recovered from Urumbal

Pocket. Stevens hypothesised that an artefact made on a non-local raw material should become smaller in size the further away it travels from its source. Stevens found that this correlation between size and distance was true, but not by very much. Stevens (2004:76) suggested that raw material selection was more likely a response to the requirements of task-specific activities rather than determined by the energy expended in raw material acquisition.

Table 5.19 Tool types represented at Urumbal Pocket, with number of modified edges (deliberate retouch or usewear) and the absence or presence of residue recorded for each tool. Bold numbers represent 'other implements' in the assemblage.

| Tool type | Number of edges with modification | | | | | | | | Total |
| | 0/Not recorded | | 1 | | 2 | | 3 | | |
	Residue absent	Residue present	Residue absent	Residue present	Residue absent	Residue present	Residue absent	Residue present	
Axe	0	0	1	0	0	0	0	0	1
Burin	0	0	2	0	0	0	0	0	2
Notch	0	0	36	1	1	0	0	0	38
Anvil	1	0	0	0	0	0	0	0	1
Utilised cobble	1	0	0	0	0	0	0	0	1
Manuport	3	0	0	0	0	0	0	0	3
Scraper	0	0	18	1	8	0	2	0	29
Notched scraper	0	0	3	0	2	0	1	0	6
Incised tool fragment	0	0	2	1	0	0	0	0	3
Ground tool fragment	8	1	0	1	0	0	0	0	10
Not classified	0	35	145	10	14	0	3	1	208
Total	13	36	207	14	25	0	6	1	302

Source: Author's data.

The total number of identified tools in the assemblage is summarised in Table 5.19. The table shows the number of tools for each type; the number of edges with all or part of the margin modified by secondary flaking; and the presence or absence of residue on each tool. Only 302 (2.8%) artefacts could be classified as tools. However, this result is most likely an underestimate of the number of tools in the assemblage. As discussed above, the extensive use of bipolar technology at Urumbal Pocket has resulted in many artefacts having crushed edges which may also be a result of use. Usewear analysis carried out on a small sample of artefacts from Urumbal Pocket by usewear analyst Richard Fullagar (2007) has shown, for example, that two of the bipolar cores in the assemblage were used as scraping implements in the past. To conclusively determine usewear on artefacts on the basis of edge damage requires an examination of each artefact by a usewear specialist, which was beyond the scope of the analysis presented here. Therefore, only a small number of flaked artefacts were classified as tools.

Table 5.20 Number and percentage of tools in each square.

Square	Numbers of tools	Percentage of tools
A2	40	13.2
Z3	86	28.5
V5	34	11.2
V8	19	6.3

Square	Numbers of tools	Percentage of tools
S2	115	38.1
O2	8	2.7
Total	302	100

Source: Author's data.

As shown in Table 5.20, square S2 has the highest number of tools (n=115), representing almost 40% of the tools recovered from the site. The stone anvil, indicative of bipolar technology, was also recovered from square S2. The results suggest that Aboriginal people were working stone and carrying out activities using stone tools in the area of highest artefact density, represented by squares A2, Z3, and V5. This suggestion is supported by evidence of little post-depositional disturbance and a relatively intact chronological record across the excavated squares (refer to Chapter 4). However, the highest number of tools is in square S2, which is some distance away from the area with the highest artefact density. Bearing in mind the long time scales involved, the results highlight the importance of sampling open sites outside areas of high artefact density, to allow for a more complete analyses of how space was organised and used by the occupants.

Ochre

Fifteen pieces of ground ochre (Fig. 5.10) were recovered from spits in Analytical Unit 1 in squares A2, Z3, V5, and S2. Ochre residue is also present on some of the stone artefacts recovered from this Unit (Fig. 5.11).

Figure 5.10 Piece of ground ochre recovered from the Urumbal Pocket excavations (scale=1 cm) (UP/Z3/11/5341).
Source: Photograph by P. Saad.

Figure 5.11 Quartz artefact with ochre residue (scale=1 cm) (UP/Z3/11/5339).
Source: Photograph by P. Saad.

Ethnographic material culture items like wooden spears, shields and other fighting tools collected from the study area during the contact period, were often smeared with ochre and elaborately painted using red ochre (Ferrier 1999). Other more domestic items, for example two types of baskets, were also traditionally painted with ochre. People also decorated their bodies using ochre. Thus, the ochre fragments recovered from the excavations may have been used for a variety of purposes.

Residue and usewear analysis

A number of artefacts with residue (n=51) were identified in the stone artefact analysis. For the purpose of this study, a usewear and residue analysis on a small sample of artefacts was conducted to explore stone artefact use and the types of activities carried out on site. Two distinct types of residue were noted: red ochre and a black, unidentified substance. Dr Richard Fullagar carried out a specialist residue and usewear analysis (2007) on four artefacts with a reddish-black, bubble-like residue on three quartz artefacts and one chert flake; the results of these analyses are presented below.

Chert flake (UP/V8/1/1606)

The residue on the chert flake in Figure 5.12 was found to lack any distinct fragments of plant tissue or clear cell structures. It appears that the residue has been 'melted' onto the rock, as might be expected in the case of a resin or other hafting substance. On one edge of the flake, there is a small prominence with massive rounding and broad striations perpendicular to the edge, indicating that the flake has been used for scraping (Fullagar 2007). This wear pattern extends along the edge, almost forming a slightly rounded bevel. The polish in this area is relatively bright and reticular, i.e. net-like. It is proposed that this wear pattern is very similar to wear patterns along edges of wood scraping and/or engraving implements examined previously (Fullagar 2007). The edge fractures are probably a result of the flake having been detached using an anvil, i.e. a consequence of the use of bipolar technology.

Bipolar core (UP/Z3/3/2567)

The bipolar core with a small proportion of waterworn cobble cortex shown in Figure 5.13 has scarring and slight rounding on two edges, possibly indicating use. The residue on this artefact has striations and is similar to the residue on the chert flake. The striations run parallel to a fracture that probably represents the removal of a main working edge. Given the morphology of the artefact, the location of the residue and the striations, it seems likely that the residue is a result of scraping or smoothing a wooden object that had this resin material in or on it.

Figure 5.12 Top: chert flake with residue (scale=mm) (UP/V8/1/1606). Bottom: magnified close-up of the residue showing its grainy, bubble-like texture.

Source: Photographs by R. Frank.

Figure 5.13 Top: bipolar quartz core with residue (scale=mm) (UP/Z3/3/2567). Bottom: magnified close-up of the residue showing its grainy, bubble-like texture.

Source: Photograph by R. Frank.

Quartz flake (UP/S2/6/523)

The small quartz flake, shown in Fig. 5.14 has a black with a reddish tinge resin-like residue very similar to the bipolar core discussed above, including similar striations but no cell structures. Given the morphology of the flake and the location of the residue, it appears likely that this flake was part of a hafted implement and that the striations were caused when it was detached from inside the haft.

Quartz flake (UP/A2/4/6543)

The small quartz flake in Figure 5.15 displays a distinct ridge with extensive crushing and undetached flakes indicate that hard-hammer percussion was employed (Fullagar 2007). The dorsal surface has the same black (slightly reddish tinge) residue described above. Assuming this residue is some sort of hafting material, the flake is probably a consequence of sharpening or reshaping a hafted implement or its edge (Fullagar 2007).

Figure 5.14 Top: bipolar quartz flake with residue (scale=mm) (UP/S2/6/523). Bottom: magnified close-up of the residue showing its grainy, bubble-like texture.

Source: Photograph by R. Frank.

Figure 5.15 Top: quartz flake with residue (scale=mm) (UP/A2/4/6543). Bottom: magnified close-up of the residue showing its grainy, bubble-like texture.

Source: Photograph by R. Frank.

The combined evidence of the residue characteristics, their distribution on the artefacts in question and the morphology of the artefacts suggest that the black residue is most likely the remnant of a hafting material, perhaps a gum or other type of plant resin (Fullagar 2007). Although the sample size is very small, the analyses suggest that implements made of quartz and tools of other raw materials were, occasionally, used in similar ways. In this case, they were used as scrapers (sometimes hafted) and on resin-coated wooden implements. Interestingly, the analysis also shows that bipolar cores were, at least on this occasion, used as scraping implements. The evidence suggests that these were probably not hafted, but rather used to scrape or otherwise smooth a wooden object. This indicates that bipolar cores may have functioned as tools in their own right, being discarded when they broke, or became too small to hold. It is not known whether quartz pebbles and other raw materials were deliberately reduced in order to produce small bipolar core 'scrapers', or whether cores produced in the context of flake production were used opportunistically as scraping tools.

Summary

The excavated stone artefact assemblage from Urumbal Pocket shows that quartz was the predominant raw material used in artefact manufacture at the site in the past, but other non-local raw materials were also utilised. Artefacts from all stages of freehand and bipolar stone reduction occur in both Analytical Units, suggesting that these technologies were employed throughout the entire period of occupation. In fact, no distinct difference in stone technology is evident between Analytical Units 1 and 2. This suggests that people visiting Urumbal Pocket ca. 8,000 years ago were already employing the flaked stone technologies represented at the site, and that they continued to do so until European contact. On the other hand, the development of unique rainforest stone tools, such as the incised grinder and nut-cracking stone, appear to have been later rainforest adaptations.

Although some separation in space at Urumbal Pocket has been inferred from square S2, there does not appear to be any clear spatial differentiation for different types of activities such as knapping or artefact use. However, as square S2 contained more tools than any of the other five squares, it is possible that it represents an area where tools were more often used, resharpened and discarded. These types of activities were also carried out in the central area of activity at the site, but with a much higher percentage of small artefacts in squares Z3 and A2, more stone knapping was perhaps taking place there. The densities in flaked artefacts across the six 1 x 1 m squares suggest that Aboriginal use of Urumbal Pocket began to increase around 1,500 years ago, and the site was intensively used thereafter. The density maps also show that the site expanded in size over time. These results are consistent with the higher proportion of radiocarbon samples dating to this time period.

6

The Archaeobotanical Analysis

Introduction

The analysis of carbonised plant remains recovered from Urumbal Pocket has two aims: (i) to identify the types of rainforest plants found in the archaeological record; and (ii) to investigate whether their presence in the archaeological record reflects human activity or site formation processes. The plant assemblage from Urumbal Pocket consists mainly of carbonised endocarp fragments, generically referred to as nutshells. Complete and incomplete seeds were also recovered and their identification was undertaken by using modern samples at the CSIRO herbarium in Atherton. The careful application of ethnographic analogy and comparison with a modern reference collection enabled the identification of many of the archaeological remains. The results are used to reconstruct Aboriginal plant use at Urumbal Pocket which provide longitudinal information on Aboriginal rainforest subsistence strategies.

Documented Aboriginal use of rainforest plant foods

Explorers, botanists, Aboriginal protectors, and naturalists (e.g. Lumholtz 1889; Meston 1889; Mjöberg 1918; Roth 1901–10) recorded the extensive use of plant foods by Aboriginal rainforest people. Historical documents and oral traditions (e.g. Mjöberg 1918:492–494; Pedley 1993; M. Barlow, pers. comm., 2004) have shown that plant foods comprised a significant proportion of the Aboriginal diet and included the collection, processing, and consumption of a large number of toxic and non-toxic rainforest nuts, an Aboriginal tradition that survived European contact. Much of the ethnohistorical literature on rainforest plant food has been summarised and discussed previously by Harris (1975, 1987), Horsfall (1987, 1990), and Pedley (1992, 1993). In addition, interviews with *Jirrbal* elders on the use of rainforest plants past and present confirms that a wide variety of species were being exploited at the time of European contact (Duke and Collins 1994; M. Barlow, pers. comm., 2004). However, the analyses presented here focus on those varieties which were retrieved archaeologically from Urumbal Pocket and are commonly referred to in the historical record. It is recognised that they represent only a small proportion of the rainforest plants utilised and consumed by rainforest Aboriginal people in the past. Historical records suggest that rainforest nuts were a staple food source in the Aboriginal rainforest economy at the time of European contact. They have high food value, high seasonal abundance and storage potential (both above and below ground) and, therefore, could be stored for later use in the seasonal calendar (Coyyan 1915; Harris 1975; Mjöberg 1918). Experimental work by Pedley (1993:179–180) and Tuechler (2010) has shown that the contribution of rainforest tree nuts to the diet of Aboriginal rainforest people was significant and that they were important sources of starch, carbohydrates, protein and fat in various quantities. It has been estimated that toxic rainforest tree nuts comprised around 10–14% of the diet to rainforest people in the study area (Pedley 1993).

Historical accounts on the processing of rainforest tree nuts

Historical accounts describing Aboriginal nut exploitation in the study area mainly refer to two types of walnut—*Beilschmedia bancroftii* (yellow walnut), *Endiandra palmerstonii* (black walnut)—a type of black pine nut *Sundacarpus amara,* and the black bean *Castanospermum australe* (Coyyan 1915; Mjöberg 1918). Michael O'Leary described some of the economically important plants used on Evelyn Tableland in the late nineteenth century:

> The principal food trees are the koah, burra, bean tree, tchupella and a number of smaller varieties; there are also a few vines or tree climbers that at times bear edible fruit. The bean tree is not often used by those people on account of its poisonous nature and the amount of work that is attached to preparing it. The nuts are pared into very thin slices, then there is a considerable time that it has to go under the water process and fire before it is fit for consumption. While other food is plentiful those people sacredly leave the bean tree alone. The tchupella is a smaller nut and grows on the trees we know as black pine. When the season is on the food is eagerly sought for by those people and they will travel over miles of country to partake of it. They also grind those nuts, into fire, but it does not require the water treatment, baking in the hot ashes being sufficient. The tchupella is an annual bearer, but is not too plentiful and is generally found on the high or tableland country. There are several other smaller nuts that supply food but they also have to be ground into flour and go through the fire and water process (Coyyan 1918 part IX:1).

The yellow (*burra* or *barra*) and black (*koah* or *goaj*) walnuts are available for around eight months of the year, mainly over the spring and summer months, and grow at altitudes ranging from 0–1,300 m. The black pine (*tchupella* or *tjubala*) has a considerably shorter fruiting period and is available only between October–December and has a more limited distribution, growing in altitudes ranging from 600–1,200 m (Cooper and Cooper 2004). The black bean tree (*wakki*) fruits between March and November and grows at altitudes between 0–840 m (Cooper and Cooper 2004:204). The yellow walnut and black pine are eaten by cassowaries and bush rats, whilst the black walnut is popular with white-tailed rats. Nuts that have fallen to the ground are preyed upon by these types of rainforest animals, leaving only a brief opportunity of time to collect them intact (personal observation). However, historical observations suggest that nuts were commonly collected by Aboriginal people who climbed into the tree canopy to collect them (Coyyan 1918; Mjöberg 1913a, 1918). Maisie Barlow recalls the types of plant foods her mother, grandmother and other *Jirrbal* women used to collect in the rainforest and process and consume during their travels to and from *Gumbulumba* around the turn of the nineteenth century:

> They would collect beans, brown [black] and white [yellow] walnuts and black pine nuts on the way out and on the way back to *Gumbulumba*. We had all of that and we had meat, the men hunted and the women collected and also processed the nuts. My grandmother knew where to get them. They give you lots of energy you know. It's like eating meat, fish and butter but all at once. You feel like you are full of beans! (M. Barlow, pers. comm., 2004).

Most of the plant varieties mentioned above are noxious and require complex detoxification processes before they can be consumed. Maisie describes the traditional way of processing two types of rainforest nuts in order to prepare them for human consumption, a process taught to her by her grandmother in the 1920s:

> When you cook the *barra* [yellow walnut] you have to boil it, grandmother used a kerosene tin, but in the old days they used to bake everything, they dig a pit in the ground, put a lot of leaves in it, a lot of wet ginger leaves, and they put the *barra* in that, put a lot of leaves on top and then make the fire on top. They had to be cooked twice that way. *Goaj* [black walnut] you can grate and mix in a bowl, they used to mix it on a sheet of bark, and then make like a damper out of it. But *goaj* you can throw straight on the coals and you can eat it straight away (M. Barlow, pers. comm., 2004).

The baking of *barra* using a ground oven, sometimes referred to as steaming, was also traditionally applied to *tjubala* (black pine nuts) and the *wakki* (black bean) (M. Barlow, pers. comm., 2004). Ethnohistorical accounts of Aboriginal subsistence strategies in the rainforest region (Coyyan 1918; Pedley 1992) similarly recount how people would dig earth ovens to bake tree nuts (and other foods, including meat and fish). At times, they would line the pit with pebbles as well as ginger leaves, placing the nuts in the pit and covering them up with more leaves and finally placing more hot coals on top. In April 1913 at the Cedar Creek campsite, Mjöberg recorded the use of two pieces of basalt (Fig. 6.1) to crack black pine nuts:

> I have observed nut-cracking implements at several locations around Cedar Creek and Malanda. When the blacks [sic] have nothing else to occupy their time with, they sit in their huts and crack large numbers of *tjubala*, which reportedly is from a tree called black pine but probably one of the *Cycas*-species. During rainy or cold days, this is what keeps them busy (Mjöberg 1918:437).

Figure 6.1 Nut-cracking stones (the largest is approximately 15 cm in maximum dimension) collected by Eric Mjöberg at Cedar Creek.
Source: Courtesy Mjöberg collection, Stockholm Museum of Ethnography.

Figure 6.2 shows a different type of nut-cracking stone implement unique to the rainforest region located in a survey on the Russell River. No such characteristic nut-cracking stones were recovered from Urumbal Pocket, but it appears that a couple of unmodified rocks might have sufficed in cracking the nuts open.

Figure 6.2 Stone artefact used in the cracking open of hard-shelled rainforest nuts found during surveys along the Russell River.

Source: Photograph by R. Cosgrove.

The next step in the detoxification process was grating (sometimes referred to as slicing or crushing) the seeds, which are enclosed within a hard nutshell layer (the endocarp). This was traditionally done by using a second stone implement unique to the rainforest region—an incised slate grinding stone (see Fig. 4.5). O'Leary refers to this stone implement as a *mo-an*:

> The *mo-an* is always carried with them when travelling as it is sometimes a difficult task to find the desired sort [of stone]. All those nuts are thrown into the fire. This toughens them and makes it easier for the miller (Coyyan 1918 part IX:3).

Eric Mjöberg was informed by a European settler at Cedar Creek that the incised slate grinding stones were exclusively used by the local Aboriginal people to process *barra*, the yellow walnut, at the time of European arrival (Mjöberg 1913a). In the final processing step, the grated pulp was put in lawyer cane dilly bags and leached for two to three days in a small running creek with a couple of rocks holding it in place (M. Barlow, pers. comm., 2004).

> The *barra* is ground into flour, sifted through the bottom of a dilly-bag until an evenness or suitable fineness is obtained, then it is cooked in the hot ashes (they make use of large leaves to protect their food from dirt), and when finished is restored again to the dilly-bag and placed in water. A very small quantity of water is allowed to filter through the bag, and after about twelve hours of this treatment it is fit to eat (Coyyan 1918 part IX:2).

Once leached of their toxins, the pulp was chewed and formed into a paste that was eaten raw or made into 'Johnny cakes' or flat cakes that were baked on hot coals (Coyyan 1918; Mjöberg 1918:492).

Materials, methods and results

The assemblage characteristics

The assemblage consists for the most part of nutshell remains in the form of robust endocarp fragments, which is the inner section of the fruit pericarp (Cooper and Cooper 2004:590). Archaeobotanical remains are generally rare in archaeological deposits, although they have been found in abundant quantities at Urumbal Pocket and other archaeological sites in the rainforest region (Cosgrove 2005; Cosgrove et al. 2007; Horsfall 1987). All of the botanical remains have been carbonised, transforming them into inert charcoal (Horsfall 1987, 1990). The nutshells may derive from a number of important food plants, referred to in the ethnohistorical literature as staple food sources for Aboriginal rainforest dwellers. What they have in common is that they consist of a hard shell (endocarp) that encapsulates a single seed.

Potential limitations of the data

It has been suggested that a good indication of the past cultural use of a plant species is its presence in high concentrations, a continuous presence through time in cultural deposits, and the state of the preservation of the remains (Minnis 1981)—criteria which are fulfilled at Urumbal Pocket. Generally, ethnobotanists also argue that it is safe to assume that charred plant remains are prehistoric (Minnis 1981:147), perhaps more so in tropical rainforests where natural fires are rare. Discriminating between cultural and natural plant accumulations in the archaeological record is important to the interpretation of the plant assemblage from Urumbal Pocket and of plant evidence found at archaeological sites in general (Beck et al. 1989). It has been suggested that criteria to consider include radiocarbon dating of plant remains, comparison of species represented in cultural soils compared to adjacent non-cultural soils, and a presence of high concentrations and good preservation of identifiable elements (Keepax 1977:226–228; Minnis 1981). To assist in the separation of cultural and natural plant accumulations in the archaeological record at Urumbal Pocket, shovel pits were dug in a 150 m transect perpendicular to the site to test for plant remains (discussed in Chapter 4). No nutshell or other cultural materials were identified in the pits. This is an important observation, demonstrating that adjacent non-cultural soils contain no charred nutshells and eliminating the possibility that the botanical remains were deposited at the site from natural bush fires and subsequent slope wash. In addition, none of the identified species are growing within the immediate vicinity of the site. The surrounding vegetation is currently dominated by eucalypts, suggesting that the archaeological plant remains are not the result of nuts and seeds falling into the site from overhanging vegetation. A further indicator that strongly supports the hypothesis that humans discarded the carbonised plant remains at the site is the lack of evidence for animal activity on the archaeological plant remains (see Asmussen 2008). Rodents and cockatoos often feed upon modern nuts and seeds of the species identified archaeologically, leaving distinct gnaw marks (Figs. 6.3 and 6.4). Scatters of chewed nuts are commonly found on the forest floor near nut trees (personal observation).

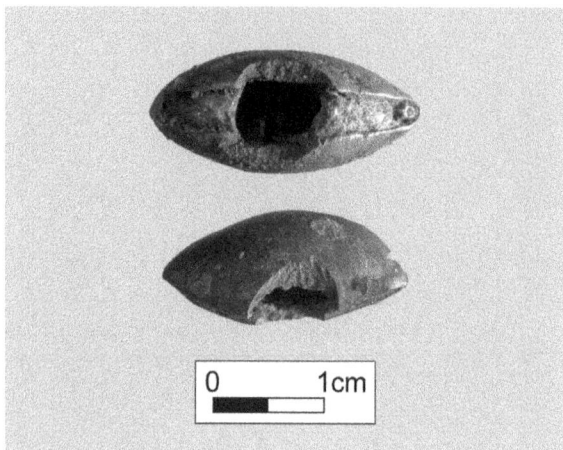

Figure 6.3 Rat gnaw marks on modern samples of *Pouteria* spp. (B. Grey, pers. comm., 2004) (scale=1 cm).

Source: Photograph by R. Cosgrove.

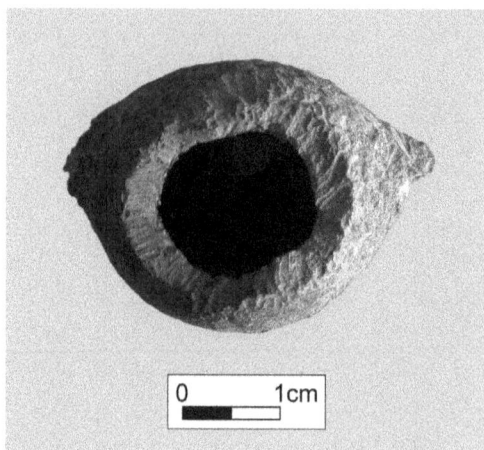

Figure 6.4 Rat gnaw marks on a modern yellow walnut, *Beilschmedia bancroftii* (scale=1 cm).

Source: Photograph by R. Cosgrove.

Experimental results

Experimental work on the taphonomic pathways of rainforest nuts and other plant foods may help explain how they became burnt and, as a result, survived in the archaeological record. Experimental work shows that nutshell fragments put on hot coals produced from a small log-fire burn fast and crumble almost immediately (personal observation). The carbonisation of the archaeological plant remains is therefore more likely a result of a low oxygen environment, whereby the nutshells were not subject to the high heat produced by a log-fire. Results from experimental work on traditional nut processing and cooking (Tuechler 2010; Tuechler et al. 2014) provide one explanation as to how the archaeological remains may have become charred. In the cooking experiments, a traditional ground oven was used to steam yellow walnuts and black pine nuts. The nutshells did not become carbonised during the cooking process, instead the cracked fragments became charred when incorporated as waste products into the coals of a dying fire during clean-up activities. These results compare very well with the archaeological remains.

The sample size

The excavations at Urumbal Pocket recovered carbonised macrofossil plant remains in relatively large numbers (n=9149) weighing a total of 422.7 g. Of these, 482 (5.3%) are diagnostic to family level, at least. The plant remains are highly fragmented. This is probably a result of nut-cracking during processing and other human activities at the open site, such as trampling and cleaning up, as described by Maisie Barlow (pers. comm., 2004):

> When we arrived at the campsite, the women would clean up the old leaves and sticks and burn it all. They liked it nice and tidy in camp. They repaired old *gunyahs* [huts] or burnt them and built new ones, collected lots of nuts and other food whilst the men went hunting. They started fires built on top of the old ones. Each hut had at least one fireplace and there was one big communal fire.

Maisie's childhood account highlights the activities carried out before the reoccupation of a campsite in the contact period, and the potential disturbance these activities may have had on any materials left from previous visits. This is particularly evident for plant remains which break easily, even when handled carefully (personal observation, 2004).

Recovery methods of the nutshell fragments and seeds

Large nutshell fragments with a maximum dimension greater than 10 mm were recorded *in situ* during excavation and smaller fragments and seeds were collected from the sieves. All soil excavated was wet-sieved on site. This allowed sorters to distinguish between small charcoal pieces, nutshell fragments, and complete and incomplete seeds, and prevented further breakage. The excavation teams were careful to protect fragments with diagnostic features that might facilitate identification. Any fragments or seeds considered potentially identifiable were wrapped in foil and placed in separate bags labelled according to square and spit and then stored in boxes. While this protected them from breakage, it also prevented contamination of radiocarbon dating samples. The material was then sorted into batches of fragments and seeds with and without diagnostic features, as discussed further below. At this stage, non-diagnostic nutshell pieces were counted (n=8667) and weighed (345.9 g) and bagged together according to square and spit. No further analysis was carried out on the unidentifiable fragments.

Creating a modern reference collection

To aid identification of excavated nutshell fragments, modern samples of yellow (Fig. 6.5) and black walnuts as well as black pine nuts were collected from underneath trees in the study area and in locations with a vegetation structure similar to that of pre-European times.

Figure 6.5 Modern yellow walnuts (*Beilschmedia bancroftii*) showing distinct morphological features that were used in the analysis of the archaeological plant remains (scale=1 cm).
Source: Photograph by R. Cosgrove.

Modern nut samples were collected from a number of locations on the Tablelands. This was to ensure that the modern reference collection was as comparable to the archaeological plant remains as possible and that, if a range in size exists in modern walnuts, this was taken into account in the analysis of the archaeological plant assemblage. In two instances, modern nut samples were collected from the same trees that Maisie Barlow's grandmother and other women collected nuts from in the 1920s and 1930s. A black walnut tree with an Aboriginal carving of unknown age (Fig. 6.6) grows in the vicinity of the *Jambilan* campsite (discussed in Chapter 7), which suggests that this area was used by Aboriginal people prior to European arrival as well as in the contact period.

Figure 6.6 *Jirrbal* elder Maisie Barlow next to the carved black walnut tree (*Endiandra palmerstonii*) discussed in the text.

Source: Photograph by J. Field, 2001.

Black pine nuts were also collected from the forest floor underneath a black pine (*Sundacarpus amara*) growing in an area now referred to as Mt Hypipamee National Park (Fig. 6.7). *Jirrbal* women collected nuts from this same tree in the 1920s and 1930s (M. Barlow, pers. comm., 2006).

Figure 6.7 The author next to the black pine tree (*Sundacarpus amara*) discussed in the text.
Source: Photograph by A. Simons, 2006.

The nutshells

To assist in the identification of the archaeologically derived endocarp fragments, the morphological features of 22 modern samples of yellow and black walnut and five modern samples of black pine nut were recorded. These attributes were then used as a guide to compare and contrast attributes recorded on the archaeological plant material. The key morphological features recorded for modern walnuts and black pine nuts are described in Table 6.1 and discussed below. The archaeological endocarp fragments selected for identification, i.e. fragments with distinctive features, were all greater than 10 mm in maximum dimension, and features were visible to the naked eye (Fig. 6.8). Surface structures were further compared using a standard binocular microscope (7–40 X).

Table 6.1 Morphological features recorded on modern walnuts and black pine nuts, compared with results from the archaeological nutshell fragment analysis.

Attribute	Modern yellow and black walnut	Excavated nutshell fragment	Modern black pine	Excavated nutshell fragment
Shape	Globose	Curved	Globose but slightly more oblong than walnuts	Slightly curved
Size (refer to section B below)	28-50 mm	25-50 mm	20-25 mm	<25 mm
Endocarp thickness	1-3 mm	1-3 mm	0.5-1 mm	0.5 mm
Surface ornamentation	Sharp protrusions on one or two ends, smooth surface with veins, ribbed or ruminate structures	Sharp protrusions on ends, smooth surface with veins, foveate, rough and ruminate structures	Lack protrusions on ends, overall smooth surface	Smooth surface

Source: Author's data.

A) Shape

In the modern samples, yellow and black walnuts have a globose form, i.e. they are spherically shaped. The main surface feature on the black walnut is a pointed and sharp apex with an opposite blunt base. On the yellow walnut the apex and base both have sharp protrusions. Black pine nuts are also globose in form, but are slightly more oblong, smaller and lack the pointed ends. In the first instance, large, curved endocarp fragments and fragments with distinctly pointed or swollen ends were selected for further analysis and identification.

B) Size measurements

Some size variability in the modern walnut samples was observed, similar to that recorded in the botanical literature of tropical rainforest plants (Cooper and Cooper 2004:242). In all cases, black pine nut samples were relatively small (20–25 mm) and fall outside the modern walnut size range (28–50 mm). A circle template was used to measure large, curved endocarp fragments in the archaeological assemblage so that the complete modern samples could be compared. This enabled the estimation of the size of the nut, including the complete seed surrounded by the endocarp layer. The modern sample sizes were used to assess the potential for endocarp shrinkage during the carbonising process, which might result in misidentification. Those samples that matched the modern walnut size were selected for further analysis. Fragments significantly smaller than the modern range of walnuts and without any other morphological indicators, such as endocarp thickness or surface ornamentations, were eliminated from the analysis and recorded as unidentified fragments. Black pine nuts are outside the walnut size range and, due to a lack of diagnostic morphological features other than size and shape, it was difficult to identify these fragments with any certainty.

C) Thickness of endocarp wall

The thickness of the endocarp was measured in millimetres using callipers. This was done to investigate whether or not fragments shrunk in the process of carbonisation, potentially making identification ambiguous.

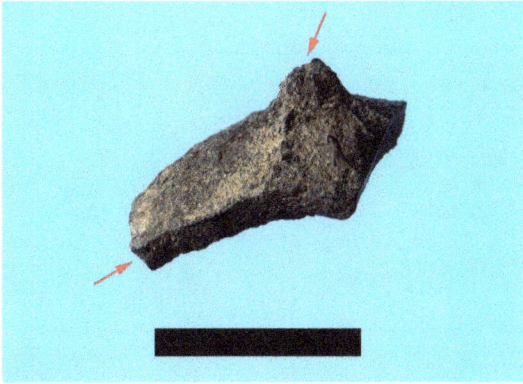

Figure 6.8 Walnut endocarp fragment showing characteristic morphological features discussed in the text (arrowed) (scale=1 cm).
Source: Photograph by R. Cosgrove.

Figure 6.9 Excavated nutshell fragments showing preserved parts of pointed apex and surface ornamentations (scale=1 cm).
Source: Photograph by R. Cosgrove.

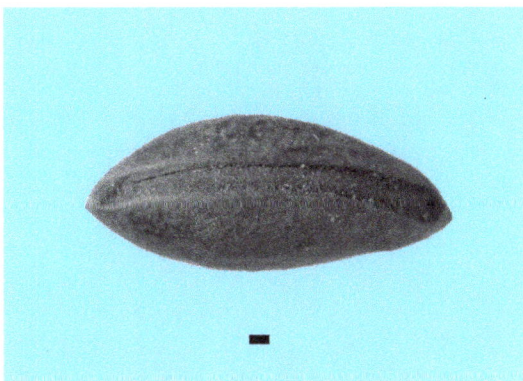

Figure 6.10 Excavated seed of *Pouteria* spp. showing characteristic groove running down the centre of its body (scale=1 cm).
Source: Photograph by R. Cosgrove.

The endocarp walls of the modern black pine nut are consistently thinner than those of the walnuts, making them susceptible to breakage and difficult to identify. Although some thin pieces of endocarp with a smaller circumference have tentatively been attributed to black pine, further microscopic analysis of cell structure is required for a conclusive identification. Therefore, nut endocarps resembling black pine have been excluded from the analysis.

D) Surface structures

Surface structures were carefully examined and recorded, following Anderberg (1994:9). Endocarp fragments preserving a complete or part of a pointed apex were easily identified to either black or yellow walnuts (refer to Fig. 6.8). Other surface structures recorded on modern samples were smooth surfaces with veins and surfaces with foveate, ruminate, rough and ribbed ornamentations (Fig. 6.9).

Complete and partially complete seeds

Also recovered in the archaeological deposits were a number of complete and incomplete seeds. The excavated seeds were identified by comparison with modern reference material held at CSIRO's tropical herbarium in Atherton and with samples collected in the field. A number of the seeds are identified as Sapotaceae, genus *Pouteria* (B. Grey, pers. comm., 2006). *Pouteria* spp. seeds have a number of key distinguishing features. They are ovate with one or two pointed ends and a smooth surface with a groove running down the centre of the body (Fig. 6.10).

The interpretation that *Pouteria* species were used and deposited in the sites by humans cannot be supported by reference to ethnographic analogy. A survey of the ethnohistorical literature and interviews with Aboriginal elders failed to find any historical evidence relating to the human use of *Pouteria* spp. in the rainforest region. Another variety, *Pouteria sericea*, is, however, commonly considered 'bush tucker' in field guides to vegetation of dry tropical areas in Queensland (Brock 2005:287). In this case, it is the fleshy pericarp that is consumed by humans. The presence of *Pouteria* spp. seeds in the deposits, and their association with nutshells, stone artefacts and other cultural material, strongly suggests that they were being discarded at the sites by people, rather than a result of animal activity. Modern *Pouteria* spp. seeds are often preyed upon by rodents and birds, which leave distinct gnaw marks on the seeds (refer to Fig. 6.3). The archaeological remains show no evidence of such animal activity, suggesting that their presence in the archaeological deposits is a result of human use, as people brought them into the site and probably discarded them into dying fires.

Another type of seed found in the archaeological deposits is a small, round to slightly oval seed, between 10 to 14 mm in diameter, with distinct surface ornamentations. The seed is enclosed within a thin, wrinkled, and woody endocarp (Fig. 6.11).

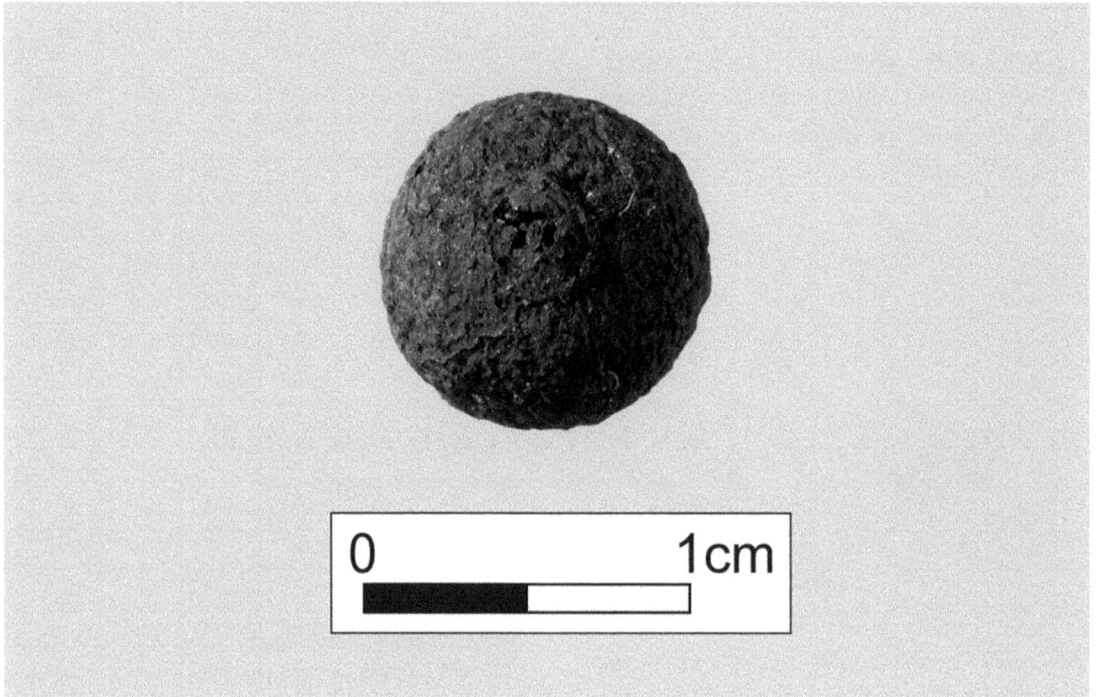

Figure 6.11 Excavated seed tentatively identified by B. Hyland as belonging to the Elaeocarpaceae family (scale=1 cm).
Source: Photograph by R. Cosgrove.

This type has tentatively been identified as belonging to the Elaeocarpaceae and is probably one of the *Elaeocarpus* (quandong) species (B. Hyland, pers. comm., 2006). The use of other *Elaeocarpus* species by rainforest dwellers was recorded in the contact period. For example, *Elaeocarpus bancroftii*, the Johnstone River almond (Harris 1975:39–43), although none of its remains were found at Urumbal Pocket.

Summary

The evidence presented above supports the notion that the charred plant remains found in the Urumbal Pocket excavations were brought to the site by Aboriginal people. To summarise, the evidence for this is:

1. The species represented were used by Aboriginal people in the contact period, according to oral traditions and ethnohistorical documents.
2. The plant remains are charred.
3. Pits dug outside the site contain no charred plant remains.
4. The remains have not been chewed by rats and other animals.

Thus, it appears that human agency is the most likely explanation for the presence of plant remains at Urumbal Pocket, with Aboriginal people bringing toxic nuts and other rainforest food to the site in the past.

Outcomes of the analysis

All of the 482 identified plant remains are from Analytical Unit 1 and account for 5.3% of the total plant assemblage excavated from six 1 x 1 m squares. An MNI (Minimum Number of Individuals) of 86 pieces of endocarp are derived from either *Beilschmedia bancrofti* (yellow walnut) or *Endiandra palmerstonii* (black walnut). Another 312 fragments are curved pieces of endocarp from a large type of fruit (greater than 25–30 mm in diameter). Given that the estimated size, endocarp wall thickness, and surface ornamentations of these partial remains are consistent with features recorded on modern walnuts, there is a strong possibility that these are also walnut fragments. Furthermore, modern and archaeological samples showed no significant difference in the size of the nuts or endocarp wall thickness and it is concluded that no major shrinkage occurred to the fragments at the time they were burnt, thus eliminating the possibility of misidentification. The remaining 98 identified specimens, which consist of complete and partly complete seeds, have been identified to Sapotaceae, and more specifically to species of *Pouteria*. A small round seed is also represented at Urumbal Pocket and has been tentatively identified to Elaeocarpaceae, probably one of the quandong species. Neither of these two taxa has previously been identified as economically important or historically documented as a food source by Aboriginal rainforest people.

Starch residue analysis

Linking food processing of particular plants directly to stone tools may be achieved through starch residue analysis (Cosgrove et al. 2007:163; Field et al. 2009). The grooves on incised grinding stones have great potential as 'residue traps' and preserve microfossils such as starch and phytoliths that can provide direct evidence for what types of plants were being processed on a particular stone artefact (Cosgrove et al. 2007:164). Past Aboriginal use of incised slate grinding stones in the rainforest region was discussed in Chapter 4. These stone tools, sometimes referred to as graters, are a type of stone tool found only in far north Queensland's rainforest region. Starch analyst Judith Field carried out starch grain analysis on an excavated fragment of an incised slate grinding stone from Urumbal Pocket. The starch recovered provided a clear indication of target species on the basis of maximum dimension measurements. It appears that the incised used surfaces of these grinding stones provide ideal locations for the preservation and recovery of starch granules (Cosgrove et al. 2007). The residue analysis of one incised slate grinding stone fragment excavated from Urumbal Pocket indicates the processing of toxic starchy seeds, consistent with the identification of carbonised yellow walnut (*Beilschmedia bancroftii*). This lead Field to suggest that yellow walnut was the plant likely to have been targeted for processing at Urumbal Pocket.

Summary of findings

The analysis of archaeological plant remains excavated from the Urumbal Pocket open site has demonstrated the following:

(A) Aboriginal people were bringing rainforest nuts to the site in prehistoric times. Distinct morphological features allow for a small proportion of these macrofossils to be identified and it has been established that they belong to the family Lauraceae, i.e. the yellow (*Beilschmedia bancroftii*) and black walnuts (*Endiandra palmerstonii*). Complementary starch analysis on an incised slate grinding stone fragment excavated from square A2 supports the Lauraceae identification and the suggestion that the carbonised nutshells reflect the use of nuts as a food source at Urumbal Pocket. It is likely that *Beilschmedia bancroftii*, the yellow walnut, was the primary economic species processed at Urumbal Pocket.

(B) Identification of the lowest excavated plant remains, in Analytical Unit 2, was not possible due to their fragmented state of preservation. However, the presence of nutshells in Analytical Unit 2 strongly suggests that Aboriginal people were also importing and processing nuts at the site before 2,000 years ago. The unambiguously lowest excavated Lauraceae fragment is from spit 9 in square V8 and dates to 1474±47 BP (OZJ718); it represents a minimum date for walnuts being brought to the site.

(C) Two other types of seeds were recovered in the excavations. One was identified to a species of *Pouteria* and the other a species of Elaeocarpaceae, probably one of the quandongs. Neither is referred to in the ethnohistorical literature nor remembered by Aboriginal *Jirrbal* elders as a food source in the recent past. In contrast, the use of *Sundacarpus amara* (black pine) nuts as a food source in the contact period was observed and documented (e.g. Mjöberg 1918) and until recently, *Jirrbal* elder Maisie Barlow still collected and processed black pine nuts (M. Barlow, pers. comm., 2004). Black pine could not be identified with certainty in the Urumbal Pocket plant macrofossil assemblage. However, recent excavations at Mooma Pocket, an archaeological open site on the Atherton Tableland, have demonstrated that black pine nutshells are not too fragile to survive site formation processes (personal observation). Thus, it is possible that since the black pine tree only produces nuts during a short period between October and December, the Urumbal Pocket site was occupied at other times of the seasonal cycle and pine nuts were not processed or used there.

Spatial distribution of plant remains

Distribution of plant remains per square

The numbers of individual plant specimens excavated from each square at Urumbal Pocket and the total weight of all plant remains per square are presented in Table 6.2. It shows that square Z3 and square V8 have the highest numbers of excavated plant remains.

Table 6.2 Total numbers and total weight (g) of plant specimens excavated from each square.

Square	NISP (Number of Identified Specimens)	Total weight (g)
A2	1,350	77.3
Z3	3,209	140.6
V5	1,064	50.2
V8	2,079	94.3
S2	1,145	47.9
O2	302	12.4
Total	9,149	422.7

Source: Author's data.

With almost 95% of the specimens in the assemblage being unidentified fragments, it may potentially produce an inaccurate result to use numbers of plant remains to analyse plant distributions at the site. However, as can be seen from Table 6.2, the total weight of plant specimens, per square, corresponds well with the total numbers in each of the squares. Square Z3 and square V8 have the highest numbers of plant specimens, and also have the highest weight. Variability in the distribution of plant materials between the excavation squares may reflect a combination of human activities at the site such as cooking, trampling and cleaning up at the site before reuse. These activities may also explain the reversal of two radiocarbon dates in square V8 and square S2. However, only two date reversals in deposits that are relatively shallow in nature strongly suggests that the deposits are generally not very disturbed.

Distribution of plant remains in composite spits

The reason for grouping stone artefacts from 2.5 cm spits to 5 cm spits in squares Z3, V8, and S2 into one single unit was provided in Chapter 5. The total weight of plant remains per (composite) spit per square form the basis for the distribution analysis of plant remains at Urumbal Pocket (Table 6.3).

Table 6.3 Total weight (g) of plant remains per composite spit, per square at Urumbal Pocket.

Composite spit	A2	Z3	V5	V8	S2	02
1	19.4	18.7	3.9	37.3	5.2	0.5
2	7.3	23.7	12.5	39.4	8.1	1.5
3	21.5	37.6	8.4	11.3	10.0	3.8
4	17.4	31.5	13.2	3.4	3.6	2.9
5	8.2	13.1	4.3	2.5	3.6	2.8
6	2.0	5.9	3.9	0.4	10.3	0.5
7	0.8	8.0	3.5	0.0	5.1	0.4
8	0.4	2.0	0.3	0.0	0.8	0.0
9	0.2	0.1	0.2	0.0	1.2	0.0
10	0.1	0.0	0.0	0.0	0.0	0.0
Total weight (g)	77.3	140.6	50.2	94.3	47.9	12.4

Source: Author's data.

It was suggested that the concentration of a large number of stone artefacts in the flat section on the spur is likely to represent a central activity zone at the site. The number of artefacts in subsurface deposits in squares A2, Z3, and V5 suggested that these squares form part of a 'central activity area' at Urumbal Pocket. The distribution of plant remains in subsurface deposits suggests that plant processing took place in the area represented by squares Z3, A2, and V8 (Fig 6.12). An expansion of the site was also suggested by the distribution of stone artefacts. This is not as pronounced in the plant remains. A distinct increase in the number of stone artefacts per spit began in composite 7 in squares A2, Z3, and V5. A similar pattern was found in the plant remains but began in composite spit 5 and continued up to spit 2. Spit 1 saw a decrease in plant remains except in square A2 and square V8 with only a slight decrease in spit 1. Overall, the distribution of plant remains from all six squares shows no other pattern except that the bulk of the plant remains are from the first five spits, a feature that is discussed below.

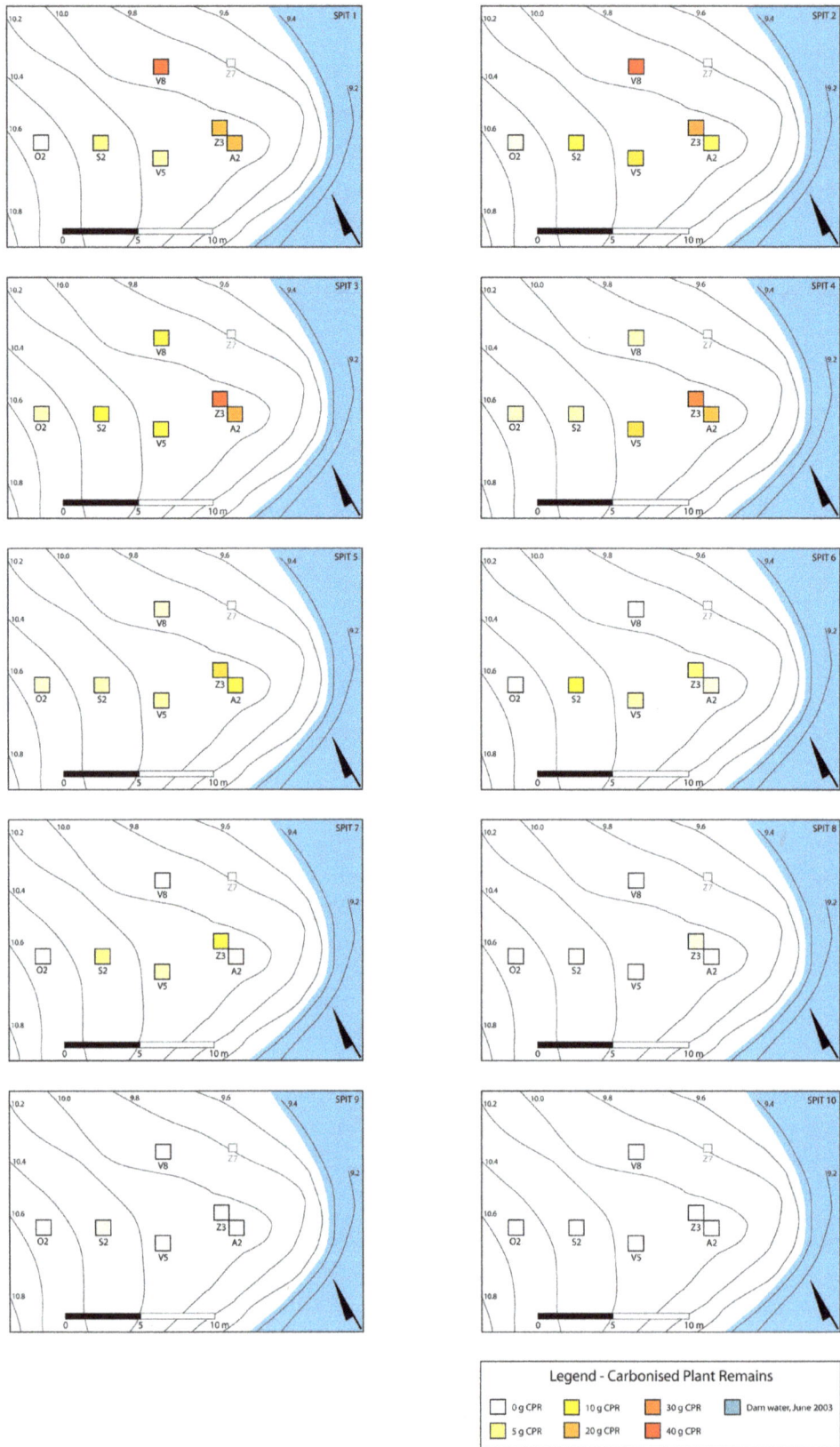

Figure 6.12 Total weights in plant remains recovered from Urumbal Pocket, in composite spits 1–12, per square.

Source: J. de Lange.

Aboriginal plant use through time

In order to analyse the distribution of plant remains through time at Urumbal Pocket, the total weight of plant remains per square and composite spit in the two Analytical Units was analysed.

Table 6.4 Distribution of carbonised plant remains in grams per square and per composite spit in Analytical Units 1 and 2 at Urumbal Pocket.

Square	Analytical Unit 1	Analytical Unit 2
	Weight (g)	
A2	75.8	1.5
Z3	130.5	10.1
V5	49.7	0.5
V8	93.4	0.9
S2	45.1	2.8
O2	12.0	0.4
Total	406.5	16.2

Source: Author's data.

Table 6.4 shows that most of the plant remains were excavated from Analytical Unit 1. Nutshell fragments from Analytical Unit 2 are characteristically smaller in size and lack any clear diagnostic features. They cannot be identified without histological analysis, which was beyond the scope of the analysis. However, the data demonstrate that carbonised nutshells survive in older deposits. Aboriginal people were most likely exploiting rainforest environments and bringing rainforest plant foods to the site before 2,000 years ago; unidentified nutshell fragments were recovered in association with stone artefacts and charcoal in layers radiocarbon dated to ca. 2,500 years old in square Z3 and square A2. The number of plant remains increased dramatically in deposits dated to the last 1,000 years of occupation in squares A2 and Z3, two squares with a well-established and ordered chronology. This pattern is similar to other archaeological sites investigated in the region (Cosgrove et al. 2007; Horsfall 1987) and, therefore, not considered likely to represent site preservation differences at Urumbal Pocket. At Urumbal Pocket, the number of plant remains peak in layers dated to between 800 BP and 400 BP in squares A2 and Z3, a time period also associated with high stone artefact numbers and the presence of rich charcoal deposits. A number of identified endocarp fragments recovered from Urumbal Pocket were dated (refer to Table 4.1) and suggest a minimum age of ca. 1500 BP for Aboriginal people bringing toxic varieties of rainforest nuts to Urumbal Pocket. The evidence suggests that yellow walnut was the most likely plant processed at Urumbal Pocket but it is likely that other varieties (of walnuts or other species) were also used.

Overall, analysing change and continuity in Aboriginal plant use at Urumbal Pocket is difficult due to the fragmented plant macrofossil record. It appears that the species identified have been an important and consistent component of Aboriginal rainforest diet over at least a 1,000-year-long period. Plant remains excavated from layers dated to before 1,500 years ago cannot be identified further than that they originate from nuts similar to those produced by species of Lauraceae, i.e. the yellow and black walnut. It is therefore possible that walnuts were brought to the site before 1500 BP. The identified seed varieties are first encountered in the lower spits of Unit 1, coinciding with other changes in Aboriginal occupation at Urumbal Pocket.

Summary

Analysis of the plant remains excavated from Urumbal Pocket demonstrated that the careful use of ethnographic analogy and the comparison of archaeological plant remains with modern samples are useful in the identification and interpretation of past Aboriginal plant use in the rainforest region.

The plants identified are rainforest species that grow only at certain altitudes, thus the Urumbal Pocket occupants would have had to collect them at locations in the rainforest on their way to the site. The analysis has established that toxic walnuts were being processed at the site, a detoxification process remembered in oral traditions and documented in the ethnohistorical literature as taking several days. This suggests that Aboriginal people stayed at the site for more than one night during each visit, and it is concluded that Aboriginal people continuously collected and processed rainforest walnuts at Urumbal Pocket over approximately the last 1,500 years of occupation.

7

Boignjul

Introduction

Archaeological investigations were carried out at two open sites used by *Jirrbal* people from the Cedar Creek–upper Tully River area in the contact period. The aim of the contact period archaeological investigations was to identify change and continuity in the following trajectories: (i) material culture and technology; (ii) plant subsistence strategies; and (iii) rainforest settlement patterns. Historical documents and oral traditions describe Aboriginal activities at both sites and document contact period Aboriginal rainforest occupation. These historical sources are drawn on to assist with the interpretation of the archaeological record. The focus of this chapter is the investigations of the *Boignjul* open site.

Contact period campsites

Jambilan is an area of rainforest located south of Ravenshoe (Fig. 1.1), which has been described as being a popular weekend and Christmas holiday campsite during the 1920s and 1930s for *Jirrbal* families from Ravenshoe (Duke and Collins 1994). As a young girl in the 1930s, Maisie Barlow remembers staying at *Jambilan* for a few nights on the way to and from Tully Falls and the coastal lowlands:

> We would leave Ravenshoe before Christmas, that's when our parents had time off from work, and walk down to Tully River, crossing the big river near the falls and continue down to Tully over the Cardwell Range and camp near Tully, it was called *Keerea* that bora ground. It was a long way and steep hills to climb. Many people would come from all over the Tablelands, Millaa Millaa, Malanda, Atherton, hundreds of people. We would stop at *Jambilan*, the halfway camp it was called. We camp there for a few days, down the opposite side of the creek away from the ancestor's camp which was on top of the hill (M. Barlow, pers. comm., 2004).

Jambilan is located close to a permanent water source called Charmillan Creek, and according to *Jirrbal* oral tradition and historical documentation, many of the creeks in the study area, and beyond, had an allocated campsite at the time of European contact (Coyyan 1915; M. Barlow, pers. comm., 2004). Archaeological surveys were carried out at *Jambilan* and in surrounding rainforests in an attempt to locate any surviving material culture. A flat area with young rainforest regrowth was identified, but despite reasonable ground surface visibility no archaeological evidence was located aside from several large grinding stones made of basalt found leaning against yellow walnut trees in rainforest. However, the lack of any further surface evidence of material culture resulted in focusing efforts on the location of other sites in the area.

Boignjul

Site location

Duke and Collins (1994) also refer to other Aboriginal campsites in the rainforests south of Ravenshoe that were used in the contact period by *Jirrbal* people. One of these is located within the Wet Tropics World Heritage Area, approximately 15 km south of Ravenshoe and west of Tully Falls Road. Maisie Barlow named the place *Boignjul*, a name used for a small native lizard that she caught sight of during a site visit (Fig. 1.1). She has no recollections of having visited the site in the past. The *Boignjul* open site was relocated by following a transect line that was cleared sometime in the early 1980s during a forest survey (R. Lockyer, pers. comm., 2004). Just inside the rainforest close to, and south of, the corner of two roads, many fragments of broken ceramic plates and glass bottles, together with assorted plastic items, were found scattered on the forest floor. The scatter continued down a relatively steep hill and terminated at a dry creek bed. Based on the manufacturing style and maker's marks on the ceramics, they have been dated to the twentieth century (Godden 2003) and are probably there as a result of local residents dumping rubbish. The dry creek bed continues in a southwesterly direction for approximately 350 m to a clearing, approximately 50 x 20 m in size (Fig. 7.1).

Site description

The clearing is located in a saddle between two hills. A gentle slope borders the site to the west, which terminates at a road called Arthur Baillie Road. Bordering the site to the east is a steep slope, with large rocks eroding out onto the surface of the clearing in the southeast corner.

Figure 7.1 *Boignjul*: a clearing located in a dry creek bed, in a saddle within tropical rainforest.
Source: Photograph by Å. Ferrier.

The south end of the clearing is marked by the emergence of a spring, which has caused some erosion. A tree has fallen over as a result of undercutting, and has exposed a soil profile about 2 m deep. The soil type is common in the area and is identified as Yellow Kandosol (McKenzie et al. 2004:246–247). A small creek continues in a southerly direction from its origin at the spring and joins Charmillan Creek a few hundred metres away. An archaeological site was identified in the clearing when a number of complete bottles of various types, numerous glass shards, and fragments of footwear were found scattered on the forest floor. A closer examination also revealed a small edge-ground basalt stone axe, one basalt grinding stone, one hammer-stone in the form of a river cobble and a small number of flaked stone artefacts. No ceramic was found on the surface, which is the dominant material in the rubbish dump approximately 350 m away. An extensive survey was carried out around the clearing and along the small creek, where a small cobble was located on a bank near a small waterfall. The survey continued along the creek to where it joins Charmillan Creek, but no European or Aboriginal artefacts were found away from the clearing.

Historical background

The late Arthur Baillie, son of the first European settlers in the area south of Ravenshoe, informed Duke and Collins in the 1990s of an Aboriginal campsite located near the house where he grew up (Duke and Collins 1994:67). Arthur Baillie was 12 years old when he moved to Ravenshoe in June 1930. He recounted to Duke and Collins that the scrub came as far as Lawyer and Vine Creeks (north of *Jambilan*) in those days and that there were Aboriginal camps at these creeks, as well as *Boignjul*, slightly further south of Charmillan Creek. Arthur Baillie's first-hand observations were documented by Duke and Collins (1994), who report that a clearing was sometimes used by *Jirrbal* people in the 1930s near the Baillies' property. The documents show that the camp had traditional style *mijas* (huts) thatched with lawyer cane and grass, with a fire inside and a small doorway that could be closed.

European logging activities

The European history in the study area was outlined in Chapter 2 and established that early European settlement in the rainforest region was, in part, to exploit the large stands of red cedar (*Toona ciliata*). Research on the early logging history in the Cedar Creek–upper Tully River area was carried out in order to reconstruct the area's logging history, and provide a historical context for the European material culture items at *Boignjul*. Retired timber-cutter and historical informant Reg Lockyer assisted with the identification of rainforest trees growing on and around *Boignjul*, and provided historical information on the chronology and historical methods of logging in areas south of Ravenshoe.

Logging started in this part of the rainforest region in the mid-1940s and ended in the 1980s with the listing of the Wet Tropics World Heritage Area. Only selected trees were cut, loaded on trucks and taken to mills that were located nearby. Tree stumps show that axes, manual saws, and chain saws were used during different logging phases. Many of the original trees survived for a variety of reasons. The saw mills were limited in what log lengths they could process; small and 'ugly' trees were left, and the marketability of certain timbers were all factors determining what was cut and what was left standing (R. Lockyer, pers. comm., 2004). Evidence for logging around *Boignjul* remains on the gentle slope that borders the clearing to the west, where some tree stumps can be seen. The rainforests south of Arthur Baillie Road were only ever selectively cut and steep terrain deterred the loggers (R. Lockyer, pers. comm., 2004). On the steep hill that borders the clearing in the east, no evidence for logging is visible and the trees are generally bigger and older, with many black and yellow walnut trees, as well as quandongs (Elaeocarpaceae), and other rainforest species. This steep hill terminates at a walking track that leads down to a small waterfall. This walking track is part of a network of rainforest tracks that *Jirrbal* people followed in the past, though most of them no longer exist (Duke and Collins 1994; F. Barlow, pers. comm., 2005).

A significant outcome of Reg Lockyer's visit to *Boignjul* was the identification and age estimation of three large trees that grow on the site today. They are *Sloanea australis*, fast-growing buttressed rainforest trees, estimated to be around 50 to 60 years old. Therefore, it appears that at the time logging began in the 1940s, *Boignjul* was located in a clearing surrounded by rainforest, including walnut trees and other traditional food trees. It has previously been suggested that rainforest nuts, such as walnuts, were collected and cached by Aboriginal people who would sometimes bury them in the ground or stockpile them in camp for later use (Coyyan 1918; Harris 1978; Mjöberg 1918). Reg Lockyer commented on the relative abundance of black and yellow walnuts around *Boignjul*:

> They [Aboriginal people] must have buried some of the walnuts because you would not really get them [walnut trees] growing this far south. Perhaps like the squirrel, they buried them to collect later and did not always remember exactly where they had buried the nuts (R. Lockyer, pers. comm., 2004).

Whether nuts were accidentally left in the ground or deliberately left to encourage certain trees to grow in specific locations to create 'food-patches' in the rainforest is not known. Hynes and Chase (1982) have suggested that on Cape York 'domi-cultures' existed, where dispersion and local abundance of some types of plant foods were altered because people had discarded fruit or seeds at campsites for generations. This behaviour had produced groves of fruit- or seed-bearing trees at particular places, thereby making access more predictable. It appears that the Aboriginal practice of burying nuts in the rainforest, a method probably partly used to avoid having them eaten by white tailed rats and cassowaries, produced patches enriched with food trees. This is suggested by the rainforests near *Boignjul* and *Jambilan*. Once people stopped visiting *Boignjul* and keeping it clear of the encroaching rainforest, the three large rainforest trees presently growing on the site would have germinated quickly, taking advantage of the open and sunny location. As their canopies rapidly closed the gap, no other plants could compete. In 2004, this clearing was still discernible amongst the surrounding rainforests.

Methods

Establishing a chronology of site use

At the time the site was relocated in mid-2004, a pencil sketch was drawn and a selection of the surface artefacts photographed. Photographs of complete bottles were subsequently analysed to try to interpret time periods of occupation. Apart from complete bottles, brown and clear glass shards, shoe remains, and stone artefacts were also identified on the ground surface. A small number of the glass shards had what appeared to be modified edges, i.e. evidence of usewear, whilst others looked as if they had been deliberately retouched along one edge. No plastic or ceramic artefacts were visible on the surface. One question that presented itself at this stage of the research was whether or not the European artefacts on the surface were the remains of a European logging camp on top of a traditional Aboriginal site, or, a place used by Aboriginal people both in the pre-contact and contact periods, or a combination of Aboriginal and European occupation. Historical documents from the study area show that Aboriginal people were paid for labour with clothes and tobacco and that they traded traditional material culture items in exchange for European items (Coyyan 1914; Mjöberg 1913a). Historical information also demonstrates that the area south of Ravenshoe was a popular holiday destination for *Jirrbal* people in the post-contact period. The implications of this history are that the artefacts recovered from *Boignjul* have the potential to provide new information on contact period Aboriginal material culture.

It has been suggested that the time lag between when an object was manufactured and when it became part of the archaeological record is an important constraint on using European artefacts to interpret the chronology of human occupation at archaeological sites (Adams 2003). Some items would have continued in use for a long time, some were repaired and reused (evident in footwear remains, buttons and glass from the site) or were recycled by some person other than the original purchaser or owner. This is particularly so in remote areas, such as far north Queensland's rainforest region in the early to mid-twentieth century, where even today ingenious reuse of old and decrepit items of material culture characterise both European and Indigenous practices. Taking into consideration a time lag between manufacture, use, and discard of the dated historical artefacts, the approximate period of site use reflected in the surface finds is the late 1800s to the 1940s.

Archaeological investigations

The reconstruction of the area's logging history, Aboriginal contact history and the dating of the European artefact assemblage has demonstrated that the surface artefact assemblage was most likely the result of Aboriginal activities. The archaeological record at *Boignjul* therefore has the potential to provide a small but unique window into Aboriginal activities at an open site, set in a rainforest context in the contact period. On this basis it was decided that archaeological excavations at the site be carried out.

Methods

Archaeological investigations were conducted at the site during a four-week period in November to December 2004. The following methods were employed to facilitate investigations into the contact period Aboriginal occupation of the site:

- drawing a plan of the surface artefact distribution using a 2.5 x 2.5 m grid system;
- collecting the surface artefacts and carrying out material culture analyses on the artefact assemblage;
- digging a series of test pits across the site to establish whether or not any cultural material was present in subsurface deposits; and,
- excavating a number of trenches. Their locations selected on the basis of surface artefact concentrations and areas with cultural materials in subsurface deposits, as indicated from test pits.

The forest floor was cleared of leaf litter and other plant material by raking the ground, using plastic rakes, and taking great care not to move any of the surface artefacts. This process uncovered further small artefacts and each was marked with a pink flag to prevent them being trampled or accidentally kicked. Once this task was completed, a grid system was laid out across the clearing using pegs and string line, with the exception of the southeast corner, which was covered in rocks that had rolled down from the steep slope to the east of the site. The grid covered an area of approximately 25 x 15 m made up of 54 2.5 x 2.5 m squares. The 54 squares were plotted on drafting paper, each of their four corners and a central point recorded using an automatic level. Surface artefacts were plotted, with X, Y and Z coordinates for each artefact recorded along with a brief description for each square. All artefacts were then individually bagged and labelled in the field. Soil colour, based on the Munsell soil colour charts (1975), and soil pH were recorded at the surface of each square.

Subsurface test pits

A total of 46 shovel test pits (approximately 50 x 50 cm in size) were excavated across the clearing to test for the presence/absence of cultural materials in subsurface layers (Fig. 7.2). Large trees and roots made this task difficult and, as a result, eight surface squares were not tested. The test pits revealed that the site does not contain deep stratified deposits. Only small amounts of cultural material were recovered in the test pits. These include glass fragments, metal fragments, flaked stone artefacts, carbonised nutshells, and charcoal.

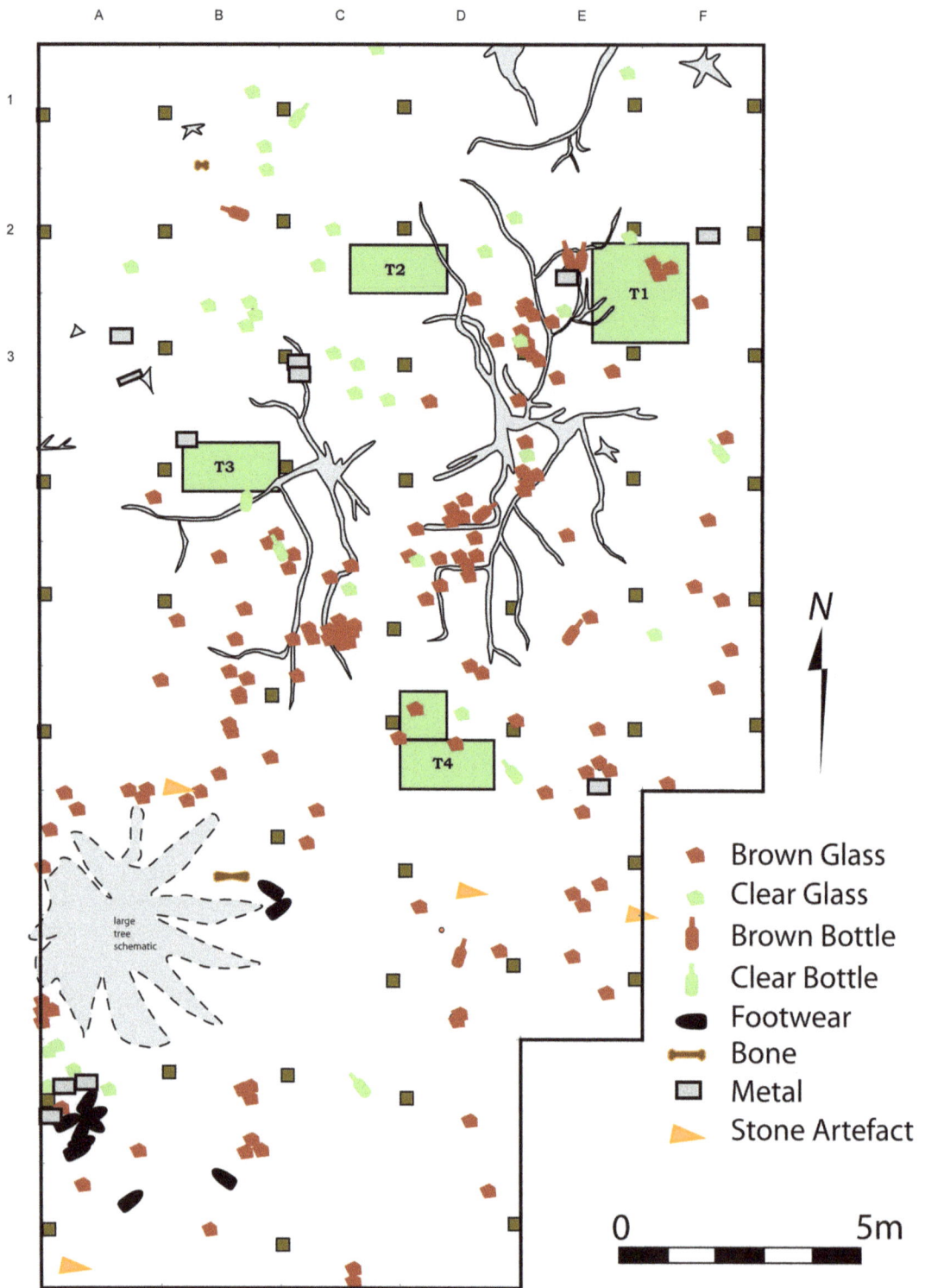

Figure 7.2 Surface plan of the *Boignjul* open archaeological site with surface finds, location of test pits (represented by yellow squares), and excavation trenches T1–T4.

Source: Drawing by Å. Ferrier.

Excavations

The location of the excavation trenches was determined on the basis of the concentration of surface finds and/or a presence of subsurface cultural materials in the test pits. Four trenches (1–4) were excavated in arbitrary spits. All of the excavated sediments were weighed and then dry-sieved through 7 mm, 3 mm, and 1 mm mesh. Cultural items were recovered *in situ*, where possible. They were also collected from the sieves, bagged and labelled on site, and later sorted and analysed. The conditions under which permission to excavate was granted at *Boignjul* restricted the size and number of excavation trenches and wet-sieving was not permitted. Figure 7.2 shows the distribution of surface finds in the clearing and the locations of test pits and excavation trenches.

Trench 1

Trench 1 (Fig. 7.3) is a 2 x 2 m square located in the northeast corner of the clearing. Trench 1 was selected for several reasons. Firstly, it is an area relatively free from tree roots, which would allow for an expansion of the trench. Secondly, surface squares E2-3/F2-3 contained glass fragments, two metal files and metal fragments. In addition, charcoal, burnt animal bone fragments and one piece of flaked glass were recovered from one of the test pits, which suggested that the area could possibly contain subsurface archaeological deposits.

Figure 7.3 Trench 1 showing the top of spit 4 and the 1 x 1 m cell excavated in the southwest corner.
Source: Photograph by Å. Ferrier.

Excavation progressed in 10 cm spits. This decision was based on the absence of stratigraphy in the test pits, and a lack of apparent benefits of excavating in smaller spit sizes. The subsurface deposits in Trench 1 consisted of one relatively uniform dark reddish-brown deposit (5YR ¾) with a pH of 5, the first 10 cm of which was slightly more organic. Cultural material included glass fragments, stone artefacts, charcoal and carbonised nutshells. No artefacts were found below spit 2, about 25 cm below the surface. Charcoal and nutshell were found in very low numbers in spits 3 and 4 before they ceased at around 40 cm below the surface. It was decided to excavate a further 20 cm spit in a 1 x 1 m cell in the southwest corner at the start of spit 4 to rule out any further subsurface archaeological remains. A difference in soil structure was noted at 30 cm below the surface where, although free from tree roots, it became markedly consolidated and difficult to excavate with a trowel. No further cultural material was recovered and further excavations were considered unnecessary. Time constraints did not allow for an extension of Trench 1 and, with very low amounts of cultural material in subsurface deposits, it was decided to open a number of smaller trenches in other parts of the clearing. Figure 7.5 shows the stratigraphic sections in Trench 1.

Figure 7.4 Trench 2 showing the base of spit 4 at a depth of 25 cm.
Source: Photograph by Å. Ferrier.

Trench 2

Trench 2 (Fig. 7.4) is a 2 x 1 m square located in the northwest part of the clearing, adjacent to a large buttressed tree root. The location of Trench 2 was chosen to see if substantial amounts of water had moved across the site. There was some evidence of water moving through the clearing was evident on the forest floor in the form of small rivulets in the leaf litter. It was hypothesised that if the dry creek, in which the archaeological site is located, occasionally floods during the wet season, cultural materials might concentrate against large buttress roots.

BOIGNJUL: TRENCH 1

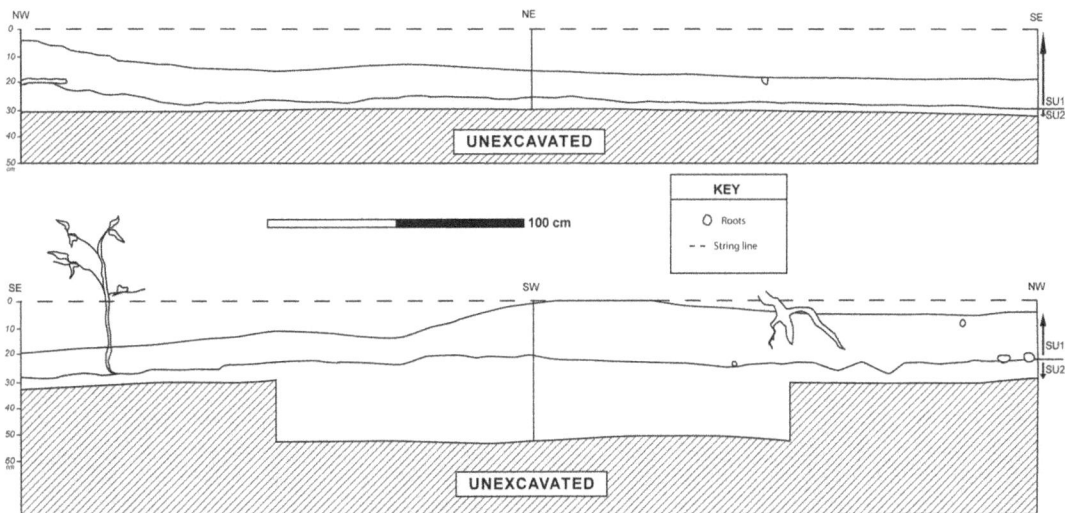

Figure 7.5 Trench 1 stratigraphic sections at *Boignjul*.
Source: Drawing by Å. Ferrier.

BOIGNJUL: TRENCH 2

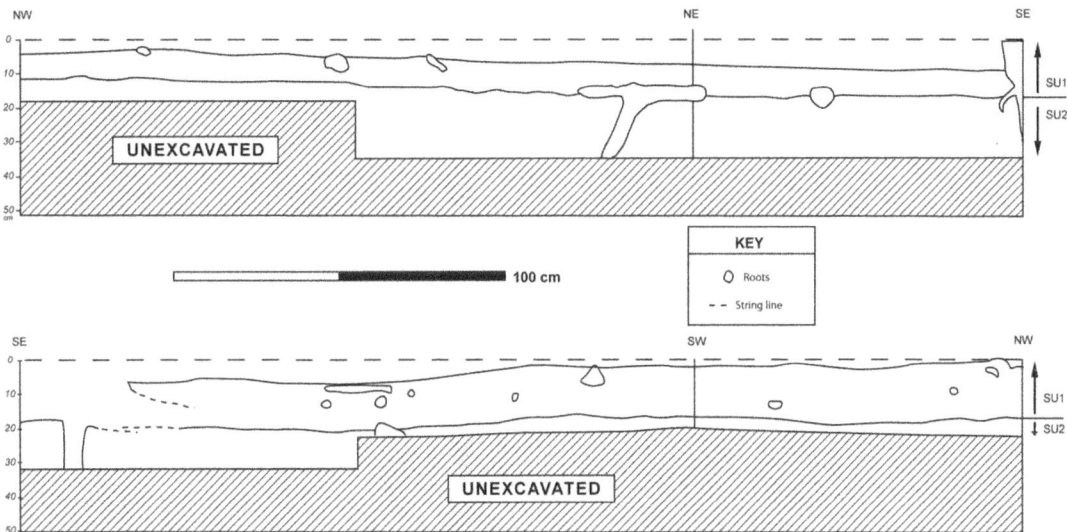

Figure 7.6 Trench 2 stratigraphic sections at *Boignjul*.
Source: Drawing by Å. Ferrier.

Excavation procedures were the same as for Trench 1, however, 5 cm spits were employed due to the presence of numerous large roots, which inhibited excavation. Charcoal, nutshell fragments, and metal fragments were recovered in spits 1 and 2. Spit 3, approximately 15 cm below the surface, contained only charcoal and two nutshell fragments. All cultural material ceased near the base of spit 4 and excavation was stopped. The overall impression of the deposit in Trench 2 is that it is very similar to Trench 1 with the exception of greater root disturbance, as was expected. No evidence of fluvial sorting was found. The subsurface soil containing cultural material is unconsolidated and approximately 20 cm deep, slightly shallower than in Trench 1. Below this layer there is a somewhat more consolidated layer that contains no cultural material. The deposit can be described as a dark reddish-brown (5YR ¾) volcanic rainforest soil with a pH of 5–5.5. Figure 7.6 shows the stratigraphic sections in Trench 2.

Trench 3

Trench 3 (Fig. 7.7) is a 2 x 1 m square located in the northern section of the clearing. The location for Trench 3 was chosen because the area is relatively clear of surface tree roots and is at the northern boundary of the clearing. In addition, charcoal, metal fragments and glass fragments were recovered in nearby test pits 9–10, and 15–16 (Grid reference C2-3/D2-3; Figure 7.2).

Figure 7.7 Trench 3 showing the base of spit 2 at a depth of 20 cm.
Source: Photograph by Å. Ferrier.

Trench 3 was initially excavated in 5 cm spits but because very little cultural material was recovered in spits 1 and 2, spit 3 was excavated in as a 10 cm spit. A change in soil character was encountered towards the base of spit 3 at a depth of 20 cm, where the soil became consolidated and roots were no longer present. The soil was dark red brown in colour (5YR ¾) with an average pH of 5–5.5. Metal fragments, charcoal, glass, ochre, and a penny dated to 1933 were recovered in the top 10 cm of deposit. Figure 7.8 shows the stratigraphic sections in Trench 3.

BOIGNJUL: TRENCH 3

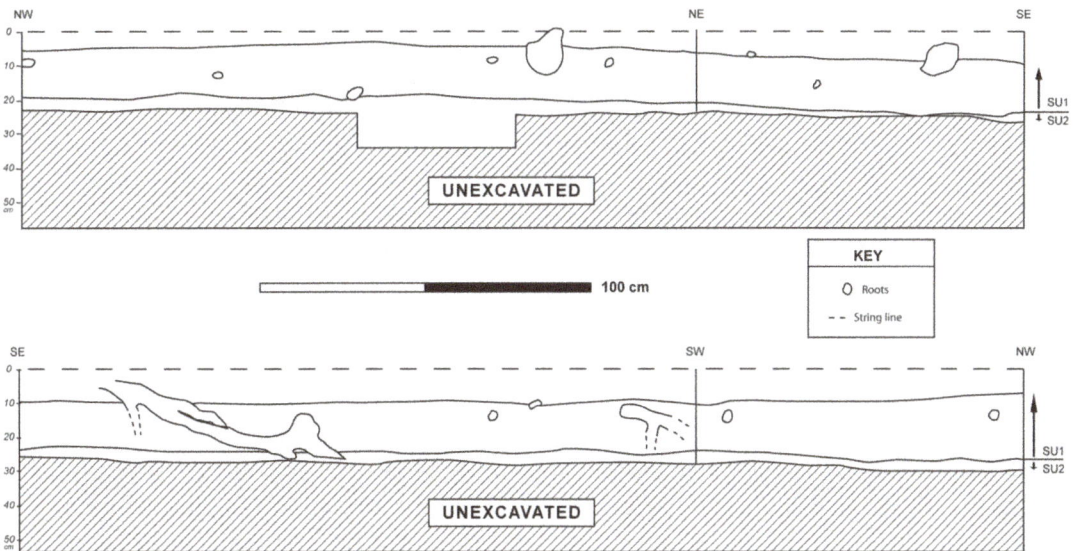

Figure 7.8 Trench 3 stratigraphic sections at *Boignjul.*

Source: Drawing by Å. Ferrier.

Trenches 4 and 5

Trenches 4 and 5 are considered a single unit because Trench 5 was intended to be an extension of Trench 4. Time constraints led to Trench 5 being abandoned after the completion of a single 5 cm spit. No cultural material was encountered in Trench 5.

Figure 7.9 Trench 4 showing the base of spit 2 at a depth of 15 cm.

Source: Photograph by Å. Ferrier.

Trench 4 (Fig. 7.9) is a 2 x 1 m square located, approximately, in the centre of the clearing. The location of Trench 4 was chosen partly because of the lack of trees and surface roots, and because it is closer (than Trenches 1 to 3) to the permanent spring and small creek at the southern end of the clearing. Trench 4 was initially excavated in 5 cm spits. The top two spits were similar to those from previous trenches; an unconsolidated layer of dark red brown rainforest soil (5YR ¾) with a pH of 5, and some evidence for root intrusions. Glass fragments and two coins, a 1904 penny and a 1916 shilling, were recovered in spit 1 (5–10 cm below the surface). Below this layer, the soil became slightly more consolidated. Charcoal was present throughout and two flaked stone artefacts made from rhyolite were recovered from spit 2 (10–15 cm below the surface). Large worms, worm holes, and root channels, approximately 8 mm in diameter, were encountered throughout the deposit. Excavation was stopped at a depth of 30 cm. For unknown reasons, the consolidated layer encountered in Trenches 1 to 3 at an approximate depth of 20 cm was not encountered in Trench 4, and overall it had a less varied stratigraphy than the other Trenches. The stratigraphic sections in Trench 4 are shown in Figure 7.10.

The area between Trench 4 and the creek has many roots on the surface as well as various sized rocks that have rolled down the steep hill. No surface artefacts are present and no excavation took place in this area. The land surface slopes towards the creek and the clearing narrows to 10 m across at its southern boundary. A large tree (*Sloanea australis*) grows in the southwest section of the clearing and effectively ruled out any excavation of the southern section of the clearing. However, in the initial survey of the area surrounding the clearing, a small hammer-stone (on a non-local cobble) was found on the creek bank, which suggests that human activities may have taken place by the creek. A small creek adjacent to the site would have sufficed for leaching toxic nuts.

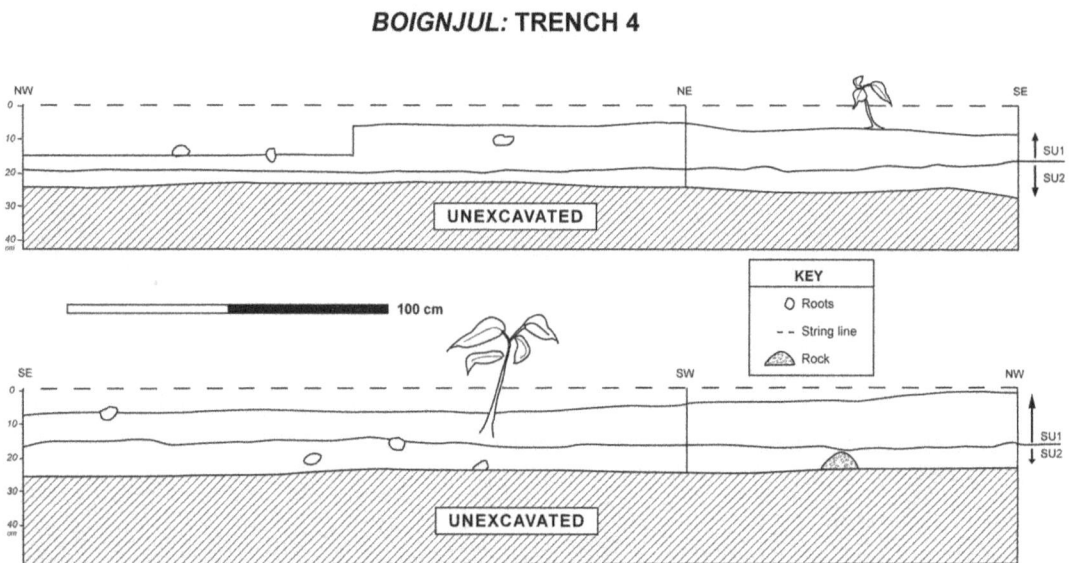

BOIGNJUL: TRENCH 4

Figure 7.10 Trench 4 stratigraphic sections at *Boignjul.*
Source: Drawing by Å. Ferrier.

Summary of the archaeological investigations

After the initial surface survey and the collecting and bagging of all surface artefacts, 46 test pits were excavated to assess the presence/absence of cultural materials in subsurface deposits across the entire clearing. Stone artefacts, carbonised nutshell fragments, glass and metal fragments, and charcoal were recovered from the test pits. A total area of 12 square metres was subsequently excavated, or approximately 4% of the total grid surface. Permission to excavate a slightly larger area was granted but time constraints, heat and tree roots affected progress.

The 46 test pits indicated that low amounts of cultural material are present in subsurface deposits in some areas of the clearing. This was confirmed in the excavations of four trenches located in potential hotspots: Trenches 1 to 4. Trenches 1 to 3 are characterised by an unconsolidated 20–30 cm deep deposit that contained low numbers of stone artefacts, carbonised nutshell fragments, charcoal and European materials. This is underlain by a consolidated deposit, which is free of roots but does contain very small amounts of fragmented charcoal and carbonised nutshells. The consolidated deposit continued to an approximate depth of 40 cm in Trench 1. Trench 4 appeared more organic in its composition and was less consolidated than Trenches 1 to 3. The excavation of four trenches verified the test pit observations, but showed that the subsurface deposits can be broadly divided into two Analytical Units based on soil structure. No European materials or stone artefacts were recovered from Analytical Unit 2.

Material culture analyses

The artefact analyses were designed to make an inventory of the assemblage of surface and excavated artefacts, to investigate the chronology and character of human activities at the site, and to explore human behaviours gleaned from the artefact assemblage to assist in the construction of an occupation history at the *Boignjul* open site. The material culture analyses were framed around a number of questions:

- what is the size and character of the assemblage;
- what types of Aboriginal and/or European activities may be inferred from the material culture evidence;
- what spatial information, including information about taphonomic processes, may be derived from the archaeological record; and,
- does the material culture evidence support the historical records and verify accounts of Aboriginal activity at the site?

Artefact types per material category

All surface and excavated artefacts were grouped into five general categories based on the type of material. These categories are stone, glass, leather, metal, and other, and they provide an overall impression of the artefact assemblage and types present at the site. Table 7.1 shows a summary of artefact types represented in the five raw material categories.

Table 7.1 Artefact types per raw material category represented at *Boignjul*.

Material	Artefact types
Stone	Hammer-stone, grinding stone, axe, flake, core, other stone.
Glass	Complete bottle, broken bottle (base, finish or body or part thereof) unidentified glass fragment, modified glass fragment (with usewear/retouch or flake scars), other glass.
Leather	Part of boot (sole, upper or part thereof), unidentified leather fragment.
Metal	File, nail, matchbox lid, handle, fork, coin, unidentified fragment.
Other	Vulcanite button, bone button, carbonised nutshell, charcoal.

Source: Author's data.

Stone artefacts

The presence of stone artefacts at *Boignjul* unequivocally demonstrates that Aboriginal people visited the site and that some stone-working activities took place there. Stone artefacts collected from within the surface grid are listed in Table 7.2. Raw materials represented correspond with raw materials identified in the Urumbal Pocket lithics assemblage, and with the nearest identified quartz and rhyolite sources (approximately 20 km away). Stone artefacts recovered from the test pits are summarised in Table 7.3.

Table 7.2 Stone artefact types, raw material, and the surface square from which each artefact was collected at *Boignjul*.

Surface square	Artefact type	Raw material
B6	Axe blank	Basalt
A10	Core fragment	Quartz
E8	Hammer-stone	Indeterminate (volcanic raw material)
D7	Notch?	Rhyolite

Source: Author's data.

Table 7.3 Stone artefacts recovered from test pits at *Boignjul*.

Test pit	Surface square	Depth (cm)	Artefact type	Raw material
12	F2	10–20	Angular fragment	Rhyolite
17	F4	0–10	Complete flake	Rhyolite
20	D4	10–20	Complete tool	Rhyolite
21	C4	20–30	Complete flake	Rhyolite
27	C5	10–20	Complete flake	Quartz

Source: Author's data.

A small number of artefacts made of quartz (n=6) and rhyolite (n=1) were also recovered from Analytical Unit 1 across the four excavation trenches. At *Boignjul*, rhyolite and quartz artefacts are found in association with low numbers of glass artefacts on the surface and in subsurface deposits. This may indicate a continued use of lithics in the contact period. However, the overall impression of the first 30 cm of excavated deposit, and the artefacts contained therein, is that it represents a conflation of brief occupation periods including subsurface stone and glass artefact types consistent with types represented in the surface collection.

Basalt axe

A small edge-ground basalt axe, located just outside the surface grid is of interest. Basalt sources can be found near Ravenshoe and cobbles of the type found at *Boignjul* are available in abundance in the Millstream River (personal observation). Both places are about 15 km from *Boignjul*. The axe was sent to usewear and residue analyst Dr Richard Fullagar to identify any residues present and infer a history of use. The results of the analysis show that the axe has numerous fine, irregularly shaped and incised grooves around the butt, some of which are wavy rather than straight (Fig. 7.11).

Figure 7.11 Edge-ground axe collected from the surface at *Boignjul*. Left: Lines incised on butt of the axe and rounded cutting edge (scale=1 cm). Right: Magnified close-up of the usewear and residue, showing the engraved lines in the top left corner and reddish-black residue in the bottom left (scale=mm).
Source: Photograph by R. Frank.

There are approximately 10 grooves present around the butt and some of them overlap. Each groove is around one millimetre in width and the incisions less than one millimetre in depth. Similar grooves are also visible close to the blade of the axe. Usewear analysis suggests that these were probably deliberately incised into the rock to facilitate secure hafting (Fullagar 2007). The grooves look like they were made with a single-point metal implement like a nail, and it was suggested that a fine wire or a wire brush may have been used to create them (Fullagar 2007). The residue analysis shows that globules of a shiny reddish-brown to black residue are very similar to smears on the edges of experimentally constructed stone axes used to cut small trees. As a result, the residue has been interpreted as a resin or other plant exudate mixed with sediment. Several small scars on the axe blade's working edge, which is also quite rounded, indicate that the axe had been used (Fullagar 2007). Usewear and residue analysis on the axe thus demonstrates that at some point in time the axe was a utilitarian object, probably used for tree cutting. It appears that a metal implement was used to improve the hafting of the axe, which in turn suggests that Aboriginal people incorporated European materials in the use and manufacture of some stone implements in the contact period. Perhaps the grooves were created in the process of rehafting a weathered pre-European stone axe with the intention of selling it to European 'artefact collectors' rather than for actual use.

The glass assemblage

Criteria signifying the intentional flaking of bottle glass have been a matter of debate for decades (see, for example, Allen 1969, 2008; Allen and Jones 1980; Williamson 2002). The debate surrounding glass artefacts is mostly about how to distinguish between artefacts made from glass by people and non-artefacts made of glass that exhibit attributes that could be interpreted as intentional flaking. Glass non-artefacts can result from a number of natural processes which create apparent usewear that can easily be mistaken for signs of human agency. Allen and Jones (1980:230–231) have stressed the importance of context in distinguishing between artefacts and non-artefacts on glass. For example, the presence/absence of roads, and large-scale clearing and ploughing should be included as potential agencies of fortuitous glass artefact production (Hewitt 2004:3). In addition, it has been suggested that traditional flaking techniques employed on stone were not necessary for production of useable glass implements and that usewear and residue analysis may be useful in establishing whether a glass fragment has been used or not (Carver 2005; Wolski 2000). Oral testimonies show that glass fragments were used in various scraping and cutting activities in the study area in the contact period:

> The women [1930s] used a piece of glass to slice nuts, and to cut up roots and other plants, it was used for many things because it was sharp, a bit like a knife. The men sharpened their spears with glass, getting ready for the big fight (M. Barlow, pers. comm., 2004).

And:

> When we were kids [1930s], my friends and I used to go to the farm dumps and get bottles for the old Aboriginal men and bring it to them in the camp [Millstream Reserve]. They would break them and use the sharp edge as a scraper and a knife. There were always a lot of broken bottles around their camp (R. Lockyer, pers. comm., 2004).

Complete bottles

Ten complete bottles and one complete jar were collected from the site's surface. Eight came from the northern part of the site. The types of bottles that are represented at the site are shown in Table 7.4. The complete bottles and jar were all machine made. Six of the bottles have a narrow-mouth external-screw finish. This is a type of finish that was patented in 1907 but does not appear in Australian advertisements until after ca. 1920 (Boow 1991:81) and was in widespread use throughout Australia by the 1930s (P. Davies, pers. comm., 2008). In addition, a brown bottle has an embossed date indicating it was made in 1942. The manufacturing dates of the complete bottles therefore range from circa 1920 to 1942.

Table 7.4 Complete bottle types from the *Boignjul* surface collection.

Bottle type	Quantity
Beer/wine	5
Essence of coffee and chicory	1
Jar	1
Medicine bottle	1
Milk bottle	3
Total	11

Source: Author's data.

The function of some of the complete bottles, i.e. essence of coffee and chicory, medicine and sauce, indicate that some of the bottles brought to the site were probably not used as containers to carry water or other liquids.

> When I grow up in the 1940s, most farms had their own dumps and fences and properties didn't really mean anything to the Aborigines in those days. For the most part the settlers were quite unconcerned about seeing a group of Aborigines going through the bottom paddocks or the rubbish dumps (R. Lockyer, pers. comm., 2004).

The presence of complete bottles has been interpreted as evidence of Aboriginal people visiting the clearing, bringing whole bottles to the site, which were probably picked up at rubbish dumps, pubs, etc., as described by Reg Lockyer.

Figure 7.12 Complete bottles from the surface at *Boignjul.*

Top row from left to right: milk bottle (B4/123) and medicine bottle (F4/61). Bottom row from left to right: jar (C5/67) and sauce bottle (C1/5), and a chicory essence bottle (B2/9). Right: beer/wine bottles (D4/52, D8/152) (scale=1 cm).

Source: Photographs by P. Saad.

Glass artefacts

The surface glass assemblage is made up of 178 artefacts. Pieces of brown and clear glass make up most of the surface artefacts collected at the site, the majority of which are brown (n=137). Most of the glass artefacts were located in the northern and central parts of the clearing (Fig. 7.2). A summary of the types and numbers of brown and clear glass artefacts in the surface collection is shown in Table 7.5.

Table 7.5 Types and frequency of brown and clear glass artefacts in the surface collection from *Boignjul.*

Colour	Complete bottle	Jar	Base	Base and body	Finish	Fragment	Total
Brown	6	-	11	1	12	107	137
Clear	4	1	1	1	1	33	41
Total	10	1	12	2	13	140	178

Source: Author's data.

A small number of glass artefacts were also recovered from the test pits and excavation trenches (Table 7.6). As previously mentioned, both the surface and subsurface glass artefacts were found in association with stone artefacts. This strongly suggests that the top 30 cm of excavated deposit and the artefacts contained therein represents a conflation of brief occupation periods.

Table 7.6 Glass fragments recovered from test pits at *Boignjul*.

Test pit	Surface square	Depth (cm)	Artefact type	Glass colour
9	C2	10–20	Bottle finish	Clear
13	F3	0–10	Angular fragment	Brown
14	E3	0–10	Flaked fragment	Brown
19	E3	0–10	Angular fragment	Brown
27	C5	0–10	Flaked fragment	Brown
27	C5	10–20	Window/lantern fragment	Clear
30	F5	0–10	Angular fragment	Brown

Source: Author's data.

The morphology of each glass fragment was described and each fragment was examined under magnification (7–40 X) to see if any type of edge modification such as usewear or deliberate retouch was present. The types of glass artefacts represented in the surface assemblage are summarised in Table 7.7.

Table 7.7 Types of artefacts on brown and clear glass fragments collected from the surface at *Boignjul*.

Artefact type	Clear glass	Brown glass	Number of artefacts
Fragment with usewear	18	19	37
Flaked bottle base	1	6	7
Complete flake	1	3	4
Bipolar core	1	-	1
Core	-	1	1
Notch	-	2	2
Total glass artefacts	21	31	52

Source: Author's data.

Thirty-seven of the glass fragments have what appears to be a continuous series of micro-sized flake scars (Fig. 7.13) similar in appearance to inferred 'scraping implements' made from quartz that were excavated from Urumbal Pocket.

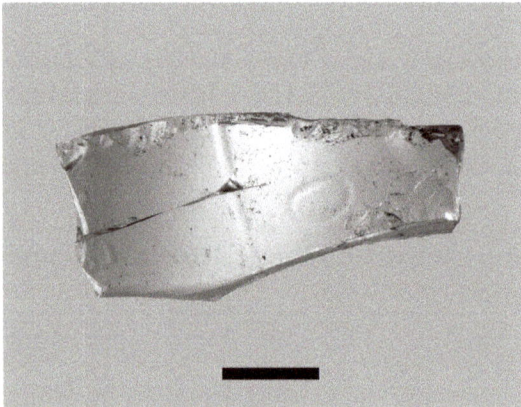

Figure 7.13 Glass fragment (B6/133) from *Boignjul* with micro-sized flake scars along one or more edges (scale=1 cm).
Source: Photograph by P. Saad.

Figure 7.14 Glass fragment (C5/70) from *Boignjul* with apparent retouch modification of one edge (scale=1 cm).
Source: Photograph by P. Saad.

Six of the clear glass fragments appear to have been deliberately retouched along one edge (Fig. 7.14).

Glass fragments with inferred edge modifications (i.e. usewear and/or retouch) are between 3 and 4 mm thick. They have an average maximum dimension of 63 mm but range in size from 48 mm to 78 mm. Glass fragments with the type of modification illustrated in Figures 7.13 and 7.14 are relatively flat and probably originate from the body of complete bottles and/or jars. As post-depositional disturbances have been ruled out as 'creators' of glass artefacts at the site, the glass fragments are interpreted as most likely being the result of human activity.

Flaked glass

Thirteen of the artefacts in the surface glass assemblage from *Boignjul* exhibit modifications, suggesting that reduction technologies used on stone at Urumbal Pocket were applied to glass in the contact period. Seven bottle bases have been flaked: six of brown glass and one of clear glass (Fig. 7.15). Flaked bottle bases have been reported previously from contact sites across Australia (e.g. Allen 1969, 2008; Gibbs and Harrison 2008; Hewitt 2004; Williamson 2002). At *Boignjul*, bottle bases outnumber body and rim fragments, perhaps suggesting preferential transport of bottle bases to the site for reduction. This pattern has been documented elsewhere in Australia (e.g. Allen and Jones 1980; Paterson 2008:98–99). The fact that seven bottle bases exhibit evidence for flaking further supports this suggestion.

Four complete brown glass flakes (non-bipolar) were identified in the surface glass assemblage. These could not be refitted to the flaked bottle bases. One bipolar core of clear glass (Fig. 7.16) was collected from surface square B1, contrasting strongly with the number of bipolar cores in the stone artefact assemblage from Urumbal Pocket. Two glass fragments were classified as possibly being notched tools (Fig. 7.17). Whether or not they were deliberately retouched into notches is unknown.

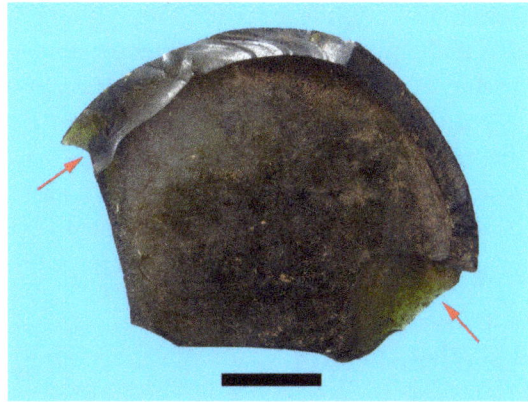

Figure 7.15 Flaked bottle base from *Boignjul*. Arrows indicate locations showing technological attributes (scale=1 cm) (E6/109).
Source: Photograph by P. Saad.

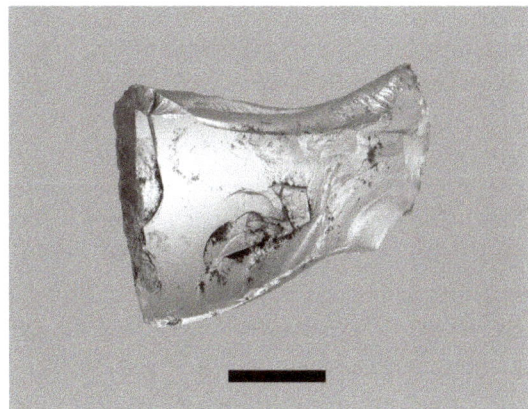

Figure 7.16 Bipolar core on clear glass from *Boignjul* (scale=1 cm) (B1/2).
Source: Photograph by P. Saad.

Figure 7.17 Possible notched tool from *Boignjul* (scale=1 cm) (C1/5).
Source: Photograph by P. Saad.

Assuming an Aboriginal manufacturing origin, the analyses of the surface glass assemblage suggest that traditional flaking technologies on stone continued in limited use in the contact period. Only around 7% of the glass artefacts collected from the surface at *Boignjul* show evidence of the kind of reduction technologies applied to quartz and other lithic raw materials at Urumbal Pocket. The tradition of using bipolar technology on quartz and other raw materials became more or less redundant on glass at *Boignjul*. Thus, it appears that flaking techniques, found in some instances to be unnecessary on quartz in the Urumbal Pocket stone artefact analysis were similarly unnecessary on glass for the production of useable implements.

Leather boots

One complete boot and nine boot fragments were collected from the surface in the southwestern part of the site (Fig. 7.2). Stylistic analyses were carried out by Maya Barker (née Veres), a specialist in the history of footwear. The rounded toes date the footwear to the late 1800s and perhaps into the early 1900s, and suggest that they are the remains of men's lace-up boots (Veres 2010:80, 95). Traces of a reddish-brown colouration remain on the side of one fragment and small holes in the leather are the remains of decorative stitching (Fig. 7.18 top). The boot remains have a machine-stitched upper, a standard practice by the 1880s when Singer sewing machines were common (Veres 2010:107). All of the footwear remains have evidence of repairs being made to their soles, which suggests that they were discarded at the site some time considerably later than their date of manufacture. In this case, the upper has been reattached to the sole with nails not normally used to repair boots and shoes (Fig. 7.18, right). The type of nails used to repair the soles, which are probably packing case nails or hobnails common to the latter half of the nineteenth century, suggests that they were not repaired by a shoemaker (Veres 2010:103). The nails used suggest that the boots were worn by people who repaired the boots themselves and discarded them at the site when they were thought to be beyond further repair. Similar observations on the curation of footwear have been described for a 1930s depression-era camp located near Toowoomba (Barker and Lamb 2009).

Figure 7.18 Footwear collected from the surface at *Boignjul* (scale=1 cm) (221). Left: remains of boot showing nails used to repair boot and decorative stitching in the leather. Right: close-up of nails used to repair boot.
Source: Photograph by P. Saad.

Metal artefacts

The total weight in grams of metal recovered from both test pits and excavations is shown in Table 7.8. The results show that metal recovered from Trench 2 (347.5 g) weighs more than Trenches 1, 3 and 4 and the test pits combined (2,32.1 g). This result is skewed because of the weight of one large metal item (203.3 g) in Trench 2. The item is much corroded but was probably part of some kind of metal container. If the weight of the large metal item is removed from the total weight in Trench 2, the result is that most of the metal recovered in the excavations comes from Trenches 2 and 3.

Table 7.8 The total weight in grams of metal recovered from test pits and excavations.

Location	Test pits	Trench 1	Trench 2	Trench 3	Trench 4	Total weight (g)
Weight	58.2	26.6	347.5	120.9	26.4	579.6

Source: Author's data.

Metal files

Two metal files, one fork, and seven unidentified metal fragments were collected from the surface at *Boignjul*. The files, collected from squares E2 and F2, are both in a corroded condition (Fig. 7.19).

Flat metal files of the type collected from the site were commonly used by timber cutters to sharpen their saws before chainsaws came into use in the 1950s (R. Lockyer, pers. comm., 2004). Metal files at the site may therefore be the result of timber cutters visiting the site after logging began in the 1940s. However, European items were also relatively easy for Aboriginal people to procure. Numerous historical accounts describe how miners' camps were robbed by Aboriginal rainforest people and that raids were carried out on early settlers' homes, particularly during the early period of Aboriginal–European contact. Chapter 3 presented some of the historical accounts that document Europeans encountering deserted Aboriginal rainforest camps in which European items such as metal files and axes were present (Loos 1982). The corroded condition of both files prevents a usewear or residue analysis from being carried out, however they could have been used for sharpening the points of wooden spears and in other woodwork activities. For example, one metal file belonging to a private collector had been modified into a spear point and hafted to a wooden spear (personal observation). Thus, it is quite possible that the two metal files were brought to the site by Aboriginal people.

Figure 7.19 Metal files from *Boignjul* (scale=1 cm) (F2/20, E2/15).

Source: Photograph by P. Saad.

Figure 7.20 Metal handle recovered from test pit 31 at *Boignjul* (scale=1 cm).

Source: Photograph by P. Saad.

Metal handle

Many of the unidentified metal fragments are flat pieces, probably originating from a range of metal containers. A metal handle (Fig. 7.20) recovered from test pit 31 (surface square F6) may have come from a number of containers such as billycans or kerosene tins, both used by Aboriginal people for a range of purposes in the contact period.

Maisie Barlow recalls how metal containers and other metal items were used by *Jirrbal* women in the 1920s and 1930s to boil water and to carry food:

When we set off from town [Ravenshoe] to go to *Jambilan* and down to Tully, the parents carried their tools in dilly bags and kerosene tins and other metal tins. When we stopped and camped at *Jambilan* the ladies would boil water by putting the kerosene tins on fires, to cook all the nuts they had collected on the way there (M. Barlow, pers. comm., 2004).

Nails

Thirty-four complete nails were recovered from test pits and trenches (Fig. 7.21). Small packing case nails suggests that wooden boxes were brought to the site, perhaps used to carry food and other items, and subsequently used as firewood. Some larger types of nails are bent, which possibly suggests that they have been pulled out of timber. Packing case nails were also recycled and used, for example, in repairs to the boots found at the site. Many of the nails are, however, corroded and thus difficult to identify.

Figure 7.21 Complete nails from test pits and trench excavations at *Boignjul* (scale=1 cm).

Source: Photograph by P. Saad.

Figure 7.22 Sew-through bone button collected from surface square B1 at *Boignjul* (scale=1 cm) (B1/3).

Source: Photograph by P. Saad.

Bone artefacts

Bone button

One button was collected from surface square B1 (Fig. 7.22). It is a sew-through button made of bone, utilitarian in design and probably part of a jacket or vest of the kind from the type of clothes illustrated in Figure 7.23. This clothing was commonly in use at the turn of the century and into the twentieth century by Aboriginal people and Europeans alike. Historical documents and oral traditions show that *Jirrbal* people were employed on cattle stations located on the fringe of the rainforest from the late 1800s (Loos 1982; M. Barlow, pers. comm., 2004) and in 1913, Eric Mjöberg commented on the excellent tree climbing skills of Aboriginal men and boys who were working for the timber cutters. By 1920, *Jirrbal* people were working in and around Ravenshoe in a variety of paid employment (M. Barlow, pers. comm., 2004).

Buttons recovered from historical sites in Australia generally show that bone buttons had been replaced by metal, plastic, shell and glass buttons by the mid-nineteenth century (Cameron 1991). One possibility is that the bone button came from hand-me-down work clothes, perhaps given to Aboriginal people as payment for labour.

Figure 7.23 *Jirrbal* people photographed in the early 1920s on South Cedar Creek, near Bellamy's farm.
Source: Culloty 1992:3.

Cow femur

In terms of potential Aboriginal use of this rainforest area in the early contact period, a complete cow femur with cut marks made from an iron implement is an interesting item. Police records from the late 1880s show that the owners of Wooroora Station on Blunder Creek (near the Tully River) were encouraged to supply the local *Jirrbal* people with rations to prevent hostility between the parties (discussed in Chapter 3). From May until November 1889, 33 head of cattle were killed for this purpose, the owners were paid £8 per month by the government in return (Loos 1982:111). While there is no way of knowing whether the cow femur found at *Boignjul* is the remains of one of these cattle, the background to the 1889 food ration resolution is significant in terms of understanding Aboriginal rainforest occupation.

Other faunal remains

Five burnt long-bone fragments were recovered from two test pits in surface square E3 (Table 7.10). They have been identified as the remains of a small to medium-sized animal in the size range of a possum (J. Garvey, pers. comm., 2007).

Table 7.9 Burnt animal bones recovered from test pits in surface square E3 at *Boignjul*.

Test pit	Surface square	Depth(cm)	Description
19	E3	0–10	Two small burnt bone fragments, probably medium-sized animal
19	E3	10–20	Two small burnt bone fragments, probably medium-sized animal
14	E3	0–10	Burnt bone fragment, long-bone from medium-sized animal

Source: Author's data.

Carbonised nutshell fragments and charcoal

The Urumbal Pocket plant analysis demonstrated that carbonised nutshells survive in archaeological sites in the rainforest region. Except for a total absence in the top 10 cm, carbonised nutshells were also present at *Boignjul* in low numbers throughout the deposit (Table 7.10).

Table 7.10 The total weight in grams of nutshell and charcoal recovered from test pits and excavations.

Material	Test pits	Trench 1	Trench 2	Trench 3	Trench 4	Total weight (g)
Nutshell	0.7	15.3	0.94	2.86	9.77	29.57
Charcoal	57.0	187.2	26.5	59.5	147.0	477.2

Source: Author's data.

The absence of carbonised nutshells in the upper 10 cm of deposit may signal an end to the traditional way of processing toxic nuts in ground ovens. The availability of metal containers in the contact period resulted in toxic nuts being boiled in kerosene tins instead of the traditional method of steaming them in a ground oven (M. Barlow, pers. comm., 2005). It is not known what happens to discarded boiled nutshells but they are most likely less preservable than carbonised nutshells, particularly when they come into contact with acidic rainforest soils. Alternatively, the processing of toxic nuts at the site stopped sometime in the contact period and other food items were consumed.

Charcoal from Analytical Unit 1 is mostly fragmented but some larger pieces were also recovered. Excavations in Trench 1 also revealed that carbonised nutshells and charcoal fragments were present in Analytical Unit 2, but no stone or European artefacts were found. The carbonised nutshell assemblage consisted mostly of unidentified flat or slightly concave fragments less than 10 mm in maximum dimension. Four fragments could be identified and belong to the Lauraceae family (yellow or black walnut). Radiocarbon dates on two charred walnut fragments from Analytical Unit 2, i.e. in deposits 30 cm below the surface, suggest that Aboriginal people visited the site occasionally over the last 400 years (437±32 BP = CalBP Wk-18589).

Other material culture items

Vulcanite button

Vulcanite is a hard rubber commonly used to make buttons which was first patented in 1851 (Miller et al. 2000:16), although not commonly used until much later. A button made of vulcanite (Fig. 7.24) was recovered from the 10–20 cm layer in test pit 4, probably originating from a coat (S. Hayes, pers. comm., 2007) perhaps similar to the type worn by *Jirrbal* people in Figure 7.23.

Coins

Two coins were recovered from the 10–20 cm layer in Trench 4 and one from the 0–10 cm layer in Trench 3. Table 7.12 shows their dates and text and they are illustrated in Figure 7.25. The depth at which the two coins in Trench 4 were recovered (120 cm) demonstrates how small surface items like coins became rapidly buried and incorporated into subsurface deposits at the site.

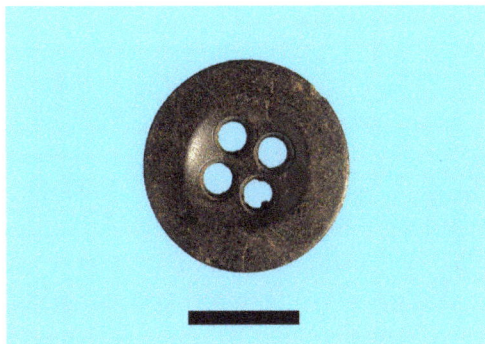

Figure 7.24 Vulcanite button recovered from test pit 4 at *Boignjul*.

Source: Photograph by P. Saad.

Figure 7.25 Coins recovered from the excavations at *Boignjul* (scale=1 cm) (T3/52, T4/68), T4/67).

Source: Photograph by P. Saad.

Table 7.11 Date and text on coins recovered from the excavations at *Boignjul*.

Trench	Depth (cm)	Description	Text
3	0–10	1933 Penny	Commonwealth of Australia
4	10–20	1904 Penny	Commonwealth of Australia
4	10–20	1916 Shilling	'Georgivs V Dig. Bri..in Rex F.D. IND IMP'

Source: Author's data.

Interpreting *Boignjul*'s function through time

Maisie Barlow visited *Boignjul* during the 2004 excavations. Whilst she clearly remembers visiting *Jambilan* and other sites in the area as a young girl, she never previously visited *Boignjul*. She explained the possible reasons behind this:

> Many small family groups would travel separately through the rainforests. They would gather what was needed for a short stay on their way around a series of fixed campsites in the rainforest. Another family could have used this particular location in their travels down to the coast and back again. There were also men's ceremonial sites at secret locations in the rainforest, where the men took the boys to be initiated and teach them about men's business. The women and girls were not allowed to go to them, just like the men were not allowed at *Gumbulumba*, which was a place for *Jirrbal* women only (M. Barlow, pers. comm., 2004).

Aboriginal ceremonial grounds inside rainforests were observed in the early contact period and support Maisie's second interpretation of the site. Whether *Boignjul* functioned as a stop along many of the walking tracks known in the area that Aboriginal people followed in the past, or was a ceremonial site, cannot be deduced from the archaeological record. Radiocarbon dating of carbonised nutshells (Lauraceae) from a soil layer 30 cm below the surface demonstrates that the site was probably occasionally visited by Aboriginal people before European contact. In addition to the small amount of carbonised nutshells, fragments of charcoal were consistently found in the lower layers, perhaps the result of small burn-offs which would have kept the clearing free of the surrounding rainforest vegetation. In fact, charcoal was recovered from every test pit. If the excavated material in Analytical Unit 2 is considered a representative sample of subsurface deposits at the site, Aboriginal pre-contact site visits were of a short-lived nature. The overall impression of the top 30 cm of unconsolidated deposit, i.e. Analytical Unit 1, is that it represents a conflation of brief episodes of occupation in the contact period. Whether or not the flaked stone artefacts found at the site are from the early contact period is not known. It is possible that *Boignjul* and the surrounding rainforest acted as a refuge for Aboriginal people in the early period of conflict and resistance.

The archaeological evidence from *Boignjul* supports Arthur Baillie's account of Aboriginal occupation at the site in the 1930s. Baillie observed traditional-style *mijas* built out of lawyer cane and recounted how the *Jirrbal* people still used traditional items such as lawyer cane baskets and hunted native fauna, such as possums. He recalled how *Jirrbal* people residing and working on farms in Ravenshoe during most of the year would leave town camps on some weekends and at Christmas time and take journeys into the rainforest. This observation is supported by *Jirrbal* oral tradition. Furthermore, he recalled Aboriginal people stripping off their clothes, leaving them hanging in trees and bushes around rainforest camps, providing a fanciful but possible explanation for how two buttons and three coins came to enter the archaeological record at *Boignjul*. The combined evidence points to continuities in some aspects of traditional Aboriginal culture and rainforest occupation in the contact and post-contact periods. At the same time it was a culture in transformation, adapting to changes brought about by European settlement. The archaeological record at *Boignjul* suggests that the site was abandoned sometime in the 1940s.

8

Cedar Creek

Introduction

The Aboriginal campground located at Cedar Creek in Ravenshoe is generally referred to as the 'Golf Links', 'the old golf course' or the 'old peoples' campground' by senior Indigenous and non-Indigenous Ravenshoe residents. It has previously been suggested that the Golf Links property and surrounding land along Cedar Creek is most probably where, in 1913, Swedish scientist Eric Mjöberg documented Aboriginal culture and society and collected ethnographic items (see Chapter 3), a location he referred to as Cedar Creek (Duke and Collins 1994:61). *Jirrbal* elder Lizzie Wood remembers her early childhood years living at the Cedar Creek campground before the campsites and ceremonial ground were turned into a golf course in the early 1920s:

> We were told not to go to the rainforest anymore in those days and had to stay in the old campground, where the old golf course is you know. That's where I was born. We were hungry living there on the old campground. We had no food and weren't allowed to go and get any; they'd [Europeans] shoot at us if we tried to go to the rainforest or go bush. Then they started to give us food and we lived there for a while longer but then they moved us to farms and our parents had to go to work. They moved us around and we never stayed in one place for very long. After that I was sent out to work on a station away from the rainforest (L. Wood, pers. comm., 2004).

Oral traditions have also identified the location of a traditional ceremonial ground at Cedar Creek and its use in the early 1900s. One significant piece of information gleaned from the narrative below is that, for a period after European arrival, the *Jirrbal* people of Cedar Creek and surrounding areas had been settled on their old ceremonial ground:

> I was born in Bill Roger's paddock
> My mother and father …
> They came down from Kirrima Station …
> For *Buyah* ceremony.
> That was very important business.
> Always have that business same place …
> Ceremony ground.
>
> Then we lived in humpy.
> Not in the bush like we should.
> We just lived around the edge of town.
> They settled us on our old ceremony ground …
>
> That Ravenshoe Golf Course,
> Our ceremony ground,
> Our people had to camp there … And they died there.
>
> (Tom Murray in Bird 1999:23)

Based on oral history testimonies and Eric Mjöberg's travel book (1918, 2015), Aboriginal occupation at Cedar Creek at the time of European arrival to the area has been described as 'an Aboriginal settlement site complex that consisted of a large camp as well as a ceremonial meeting and fighting ground' (Duke and Collins 1994:61). In the context of this research project, it was hypothesised that the area may have the archaeological research potential to contribute new information on Aboriginal rainforest occupation and adaptations in the recent past. Information about Aboriginal occupation at Cedar Creek has survived in *Jirrbal* oral traditions and in the ethnohistory. This information is drawn on here to expand on the interpretative possibilities of the archaeological record.

Geographical setting

The Golf Links property is located at the southern edge of the township of Ravenshoe (Fig. 8.1). It comprises approximately 38 hectares of grassland and woodland on a basalt plateau bordered by North Cedar Creek, South Cedar Creek and the Millstream River in the west. It represents a eucalypt 'pocket' once located at the edge of the rainforest, as described by Eric Mjöberg (1913). The topography is relatively flat with some sloping areas falling away to the Millstream River and North and South Cedar Creeks. The Millstream National Park is located west of the property, on the opposite banks of the Millstream River, which forms a natural boundary between the Cainozoic olivine basalt on the property and a Palaeozoic rhyolite in the adjacent National Park (Bird 1999:6). A permanent spring has been identified amongst basaltic rocks in the wooded western section of the property, along the creek line (Bird 1999). Large basalt blocks and steep slopes characterise this area, including one 80–100 m long sharp decline that terminates at Millstream River. Previous vegetation surveys carried out in the context of a cultural heritage investigation estimated that two thirds of the property is today covered with open grasslands, which represent the remains of an old golf course (Bird 1999:7) that was in operation from the early 1920s to the mid-1980s (V. van der Vliet, pers. comm., 2007). The remaining third is covered with open woodland vegetation dominated by one tree species, the rough barked apple (*Angophora floribunda*), and probably represents regrowth of some 30 to 40 years (Winter in Bird 1999:7).

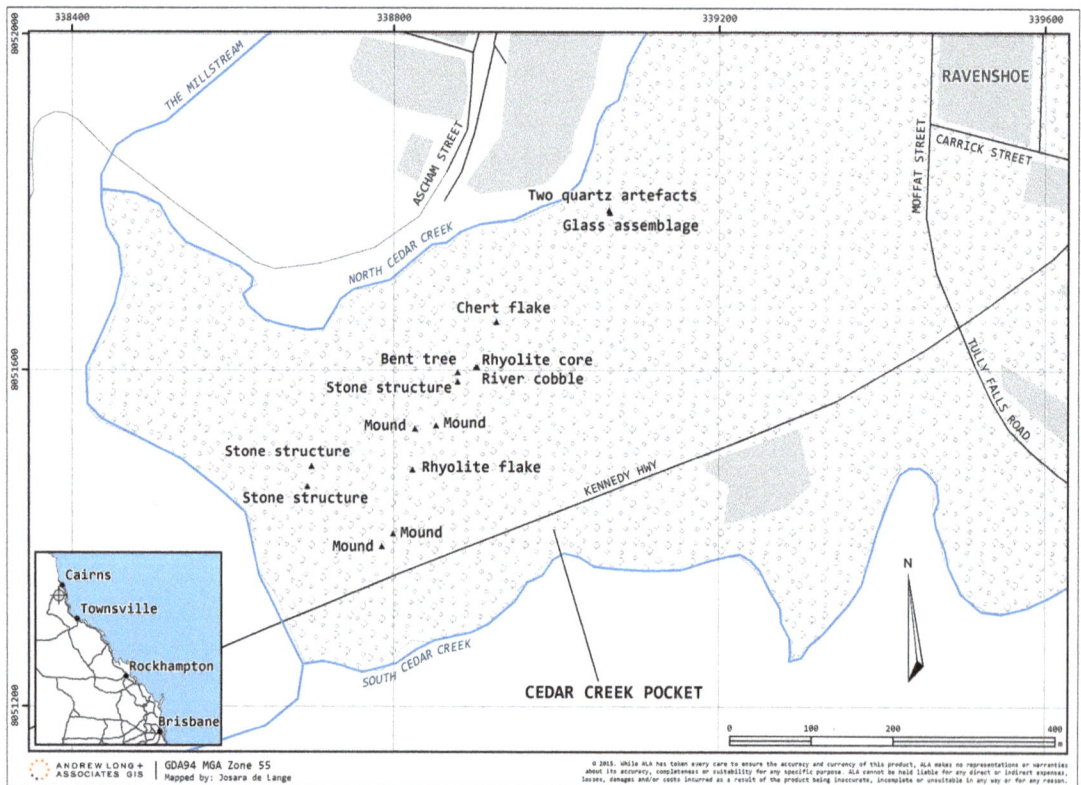

Figure 8.1 Map with the Golf Links property approximately in the centre of the picture (Lot 1 on Plan SP101802). The area highlighted represents a former eucalypt pocket that is bordered by North and South Cedar Creek and the Millstream River to the west (refer to Table 8.2 for archaeological features and finds).

Source: Produced by J. de Lange.

Historical background

Historical documents show that stands of red cedar (*Toona ciliatis*) along the South and North Cedar Creeks had attracted Europeans to this part of the rainforest region by the late 1800s. Selections were available from 1907, and at the time of Eric Mjöberg's visit in 1913, a pub had been erected and a small European settlement was established in the eucalypt pocket (bounded by South Cedar Creek, North Cedar Creek, and the Millstream River). The location of a traditional ceremonial ground in this eucalypt pocket is remembered by *Jirrbal* elders and senior residents in Ravenshoe. According to oral traditions and local history, this is where the *Jirrbal* people of Cedar Creek and upper Tully River hosted the large *buyah* (ceremony or corroboree). This ceremony involved hundreds of people who would walk to Cedar Creek from across the Tablelands and up from the coast at the beginning of the wet season (M. Barlow, pers. comm., 2006). Some of the first European settlers observed this event, when *Jirrbal* people still occupied the pocket in the early 1900s (A. Duke, pers. comm., 2007). The construction of the golf course took place in a portion of the pocket in the early 1920s and in effect ended Aboriginal occupation of traditional campsites and use of the ceremonial ground (M. Barlow, pers. comm., 2004; L. Wood, pers. comm., 2004).

Eric Mjöberg and Cedar Creek

Mjöberg described Cedar Creek as 'a small European settlement established at the edge of the rainforest' (1913a). He provides a description of the landscape that surrounded an Aboriginal camp at Cedar Creek in the summer of 1913:

> From Herberton, located in open forest country, I travelled accompanied by a white gentleman and three natives, with a small horse caravan to Cedar Creek, a place located at the edge of dark rainforests. How far these forests stretch is still unknown, these territories are yet to be explored. A few settlers have set camp at the fringe of the rainforest and are clearing rainforest growing on their land to plant crops. We set camp not far from the edge of the rainforest. Around one hundred metres away was the location of a large native camp. I was very interested in the native black race and discovered many new and interesting facts about the natives in the camps close to Cedar Creek that I had not come across earlier in my travels (Mjöberg 1918:170–171).

Many of Mjöberg's photographs and films from the rainforest were unfortunately destroyed due to the wet tropical conditions, but a small number have survived. Some of these depict Aboriginal people climbing trees at the Cedar Creek campsite (Fig. 8.2), and the campsite is briefly referred to in his diary:

> At Cedar Creek I encountered a traditional wet season native rainforest village used by a large group of native people that inhabit areas around Cedar Creek and Tully River (Mjöberg 1913a).

Figure 8.2 King George's brother demonstrating his tree climbing skills using a rope made from lawyer cane at Cedar Creek.

Source: Courtesy of California Academy of Sciences, Mjöberg collection.

Relatives of living *Jirrbal* elders were born at Cedar Creek (M. Barlow, pers. comm., 2004) and a number of people remember the location and use of the traditional ceremonial ground on what became the Golf Links in the early 1920s. Oral history testimonies recorded in the 1990s with descendants of the first European settlers describe events taking place on the ceremonial ground in the early 1900s:

Aboriginal groups would visit from Millaa Millaa, Malanda and Atherton way and my mother, who was the first white woman in Ravenshoe, wouldn't let the children out as spears were flying and she was afraid they would get hurt. The old ceremonial ground was across Cedar Creek from our house in Ethel Street (E. Condon in Duke and Collins 1994:61).

Evidence gathered in talks with local historians, past and present oral histories and ethnohistorical information, thus indicates that the Golf Links and surrounding area is where Eric Mjöberg observed and documented 'a native village' in 1913.

Previous cultural heritage investigations

Previous investigations on the Golf Links include Duke and Collins' (1994) anthropological cultural mapping study and a cultural heritage assessment by Michelle Bird (1999). Both reports identify the property and surrounds as a place of very high cultural and social significance to the *Jirrbal* people: 'the area represents a cultural landscape which contains several sites and places that are highly significant to the *Jiddabul* [*Jirrbal*] people' (Bird 1999:20). In the current research, the cultural significance of the area has also been identified from oral testimonies given by a number of *Jirrbal* elders, non-Indigenous Ravenshoe residents and the ethnographic record (Mjöberg 1913a, 1913b, 1918, 1925; M. Barlow, pers. comm., 2004; A. Durham, pers. comm., 2004; V. Van der Vliet, pers. comm., 2006; B. White, pers. comm., 2006; L. Wood, pers. comm., 2004). The combined evidence supports the interpretation of the area as a 'site complex' or a 'cultural landscape' consisting of a number of Aboriginal cultural heritage places.

Aboriginal cultural heritage sites previously recorded on the Golf Links include a traditional ceremonial ground, campsites, at least one burial, a 1930s walking track, a track-marker tree, a post-contact food collecting and food-processing site for taro and several unidentified stone arrangements (Bird 1999:20). In addition, the owner of the Golf Links in 2004, Mrs Audrey Durham, provided further information related to Aboriginal activities on South Cedar Creek. She recalled that when her family first moved to Ravenshoe, Aboriginal women used to come down to the creek behind the family house and put their lawyer cane baskets in the creek to leach toxic nuts. The women also erected little huts along the banks of South Cedar Creek (A. Durham, pers. comm., 2004).

European impacts

Bird (1999) reports that, for the majority of the cultural heritage sites on the Golf Links, no tangible archaeological evidence was located. No physical traces of the ceremonial ground, campsites, or burials were visible at the time of the archaeological survey and a number of previously recorded stone arrangements remained unidentified. However, a small number of quartz fragments were located in the golf course zone (Bird 1999:28). This led Bird to suggest that the lack of tangible evidence for Aboriginal occupation on the Golf Links was due to European disturbances combined with a lack of surface visibility at the time of the survey. European modifications of the Golf Links include early twentieth-century small-scale cattle grazing by Bill Roger, the first European owner of the property, and construction of the golf course in the early 1920s that allegedly destroyed the ceremonial ground (Bird 1999; L. Wood, pers. comm., 2004). Motor-cross bike riding continues to take place on the old golf course surface. Aboriginal sites and numerous Aboriginal burials were also destroyed in the construction of a roadhouse and camping ground along South Cedar Creek (Bird 1999; M. Barlow, pers. comm., 2004), opposite the Golf Links and the Kennedy Highway, which runs in an east–west direction through the eucalypt pocket at its southern end (Fig. 8.1). Bird (1999:18) concludes that, in addition to European disturbances in the area, thick grass cover was a major constraint to effective survey coverage. The possibility of subsurface archaeological deposits cannot be ruled out as dense grass cover may have obscured any surviving surface remains (Bird 1999:21).

Archaeological investigations

Survey methods 2004

Two archaeological surveys were conducted on the Golf Links in the context of this project: one on a visit in 2004, and the other covering five days in late 2006. Despite large-scale European disturbances in the area, it was hypothesised that the northern section on the Golf Links (outside the golf course zone) may still contain archaeological evidence. Permission was granted by the property's owner to conduct a surface survey in 2004. The objective of the survey was to see if any archaeological evidence related to Aboriginal occupation was visible on the surface in areas away from the disturbed and grass-covered golf course zone (Fig. 8.1). During the 2004 archaeological survey, two clusters of oval-shaped clearings were identified in the northern section. Glass and stone artefacts were found on the surface nearby. The clusters are approximately 200 m apart. The first consists of five oval-shaped clearings and the second of seven. These clearings vary slightly in size and shape but are, on average, 2 x 3 m in diameter (Fig. 8.3). Compared to the surrounding ground, the surface of the clearings was more compacted and they were interpreted as possibly being the remains of floors where Aboriginal huts had once stood; it was decided to conduct archaeological investigations in one of the clusters.

Figure 8.3 Oval-shaped clearing on the Golf Links identified in the 2004 survey.
Source: Photograph by Å. Ferrier.

Survey methods 2006

In 2004 permission to conduct archaeological excavations in one of the clusters was requested from the landowner. It was not granted, however, probably because the Golf Links was for sale at the time. The Golf Links was bought in late 2005 by a local family, who were prepared to allow excavations to proceed if permission from the traditional owners was granted. The owners had proposed to set aside some 1.8 hectares from future development on the Golf Links, an area containing some of the cultural heritage sites previously identified by Duke and Collins (1994) and Bird (1999). Archaeological excavations in one of the clusters had the potential to provide information about archaeological deposits in locations outside the area that was going to be excluded from development, prior to it commencing. The Jiddibal Aboriginal Corporation, representing the Aboriginal party as defined by the *Queensland Aboriginal Cultural Heritage Act* (2003), allowed for a pedestrian survey and a small test excavation to take place in one of the two clusters, with the aim of establishing their origin and cultural and scientific significance. The second phase of archaeological investigations on the Golf Links was undertaken in November 2006. Due to dense and long grassy vegetation, a burn-off was arranged (Fig. 8.4). This improved ground surface visibility and aided the archaeological surveys and excavations. Three members of the field crew spent two days walking in transect lines across sections of the property that were assumed to be less disturbed than the golf course zone. Visibility after the burn-off was reasonable but smouldering logs, smoke and ash on the ground was blown by wind and stirred by feet, making conditions very uncomfortable. Plastic rakes were used in places where the ash layer was too thick to see the ground surface.

Figure 8.4 Burn-off on the Golf Links property. The flat grassy area in the front of the photo is part of the old golf course and was not surveyed in 2006.
Source: Photograph by Å. Ferrier.

Artefacts and other archaeological features identified during the surveys were flagged and subsequently revisited and recorded. Single surface artefact finds were logged into a handheld GPS and stone structures, mounds and a track-marker tree (bent tree) were photographed and also logged into the GPS. Stone arrangements and other archaeological features were photographed. Stone and glass artefacts were collected and brought back to the laboratory for analysis.

Survey results

Stone structures

A number of previously recorded archaeological features on the Golf Links were relocated and inspected in attempts to distinguish Aboriginal from non-Aboriginal features (Fig. 8.1/GPS points 8–9). Bird (1999) describes 'stone arrangements' near the Millstream River in the western section of the property and two stone arrangements were relocated and inspected during the 2006 survey (Figs. 8.5 and 8.6). This section of the Golf Links is undulating with basalt rocks and with many large boulders on the surface.

A visit to well-preserved World War I sniper pits in an area northwest of Ravenshoe, together with local historians from the Eacham Historical Society, demonstrated that at least one of the stone arrangements on the Golf Links (Fig. 8.6) is similarly orientated and constructed with basalt rocks stacked to create a small shelter (Fig. 8.7).

The Tablelands, including areas near Ravenshoe, was the location for much World War II army training activity (Bird 1999; R. Grant, pers. comm., 2006). Stone pits or shelters were used by the Australian Army and the US Army Air Force in sniper practice, and were commonly built in clusters of seven on two hills opposite one another (R. Grant, pers. comm., 2006). The location of at least two stone arrangements in the high and stony western section on the Golf Links, aiming into the hill opposite the Golf Links in the Millstream National Park across the Millstream River, suggests that sniper practice was carried out in this area (R. Grant, pers. comm., 2006). Thus, the two stone structures revisited in the western section on the Golf Links are interpreted as being the remains of World War II sniper pits, and of non-Aboriginal origin.

Figure 8.5 Stone arrangement (GPS9) located in the western section of the Golf Links.
Source: Photograph by Å. Ferrier.

Figure 8.6 Stone arrangement (GPS8) on the Golf Links with the Millstream River located at the base of a steep hill.
Source: Photograph by Å. Ferrier.

Figure 8.7 World War II sniper pit in a sclerophyll forest area located northwest of Ravenshoe.
Source: Photograph by Å. Ferrier.

Figure 8.8 Mound on the Golf Links property with volcanic stones arranged around it, including a flat grinding stone (arrowed).

Source: Photograph by Å. Ferrier.

Figure 8.9 Bent tree/track-marker tree on the Golf Links.

Source: Photograph by Å. Ferrier.

Figure 8.10 Transect located across one of two clusters of oval-shaped clearings on the Golf Links, November 2006.

Source: Photograph by Å. Ferrier.

A third stone arrangement described by Bird (1999:31) was relocated in the 2006 survey (GPS7), just north of where the old ceremonial ground was once located (Fig. 8.8). It is a roughly rectangular arrangement, 3 x 2 m in size, constructed with volcanic rocks around a small somewhat flat-topped mound that is approximately 40 cm in height. The origin of this arrangement is unknown. Although it might be Aboriginal, it is also possible that it is the remains of a golf tee. Four golf tees located during the survey consisted of square flat-topped mounds but with no associated rocks. All are located on the plateau in the northern section of the property, right on the edge of the old golf course (refer to Table 8.2 for GPS coordinates).

Bent tree/track-marker tree

The stone arrangement in Figure 8.9 is in close proximity to the location of the destroyed ceremonial ground and in the immediate vicinity of a bent tree (Fig. 8.9). Bent trees have previously been observed along rainforest walking tracks and have been described as track-marker trees (Pentecost and Milne 1994).

The age of the tree is unknown but may be part of a 1930s walking track that was used by *Jirrbal* people, then living in the Millstream Reserve, who were allowed to cross the golf course to get into town (Duke and Collins 1994).

Subsurface investigations

The cluster of clearings described above and investigated in 2006, is located in the northern section of the Golf Links and was relocated using GPS coordinates recorded during the 2004 archaeological survey (Fig. 8.1: GPS1). Due to the delay in gaining access to the property for this research project, as well as organising permission from the Jiddibal Aboriginal Corporation to carry out subsurface investigations, a time frame of five days was allocated to complete the excavations and carry out a survey of approximately one third of the property. Six 50 x 50 cm pits were considered a sufficient and manageable size to address the aims of the investigation. The six pits were located 10 m apart along a 50 m transect crossing six clearings (Fig. 8.10). This method resulted in two of the pits being located inside clearings, two between clearings, and two just outside of clearings, thereby testing all possibilities for subsurface archaeological deposits or features within the cluster. The pits were excavated in 10 cm spits. The excavated soil was dry-sieved using 10 and 3 mm mesh. Soil colour was not recorded due to time constraints.

Table 8.1 shows that charcoal weighing a total of 99.8 g was recovered in a layer 20–30 cm below the surface in Pit 1 and 2.3 g of charcoal was recovered in Pit 4. No artefacts or other cultural material were present in Pit 4. The origin of the charcoal is unknown and cannot be interpreted as a result of human activity. Two quartz artefacts were recovered from around 30 cm below the surface in Pit 6. The quartz is similar to the type of quartz that was described in the Urumbal Pocket stone artefact analysis. A concentration of glass artefacts, approximately 20 x 20 m in diameter, was recorded on the surface around Pit 6 (Fig. 8.1: GPS 2), and was collected and bagged separately.

Table 8.1 Summary of subsurface investigations on the Golf Links.

Pit	Location	Depth of finds (cm)	Excavated material
1	Outside clearing	20–30	Charcoal (99.8 g)
2	Inside clearing	20–30	None
3	Middle of clearing	20–30	None
4	Middle of clearing	20–30	Charcoal (2.3 g)
5	Outside clearing	20–30	None
6	Part inside / partly outside clearing	30–40	Quartz artefacts (n=2)

Source: Author's data.

Table 8.2 Summary of the archaeological evidence identified on the Golf Links property in 2006 (GPS datum AGD66 UTM 55K) (see Fig. 8.1).

GPS Point	Description	East	North	Comments
1	Two quartz artefacts	338950	8051614	In subsurface deposit in Pit 6
2	Glass assemblage	338951	8051611	Glass fragments (n=65) and one chert flake
3	River cobble	338787	8051427	Isolated surface find
4	Rhyolite core	338789	8051427	Isolated surface find
5	Chert flake	338812	8051481	Isolated surface find
6	Rhyolite flake	338709	8051305	Isolated surface find
7	Stone structure	338765	8051410	Square stone structure and earth mound
8	Stone structure	338583	8051309	Circular structure. WW 2 relic?
9	Stone structure	338578	8051285	WW 2 sniper pit
10	Bent tree	338765	8051421	Track-marker tree
11	Mound	338738	8051358	Probable golf tee
12	Mound	338712	8051354	Probable golf tee
13	Mound	338685	8051229	Probable golf tee
14	Mound	338671	8051214	Probable golf tee

Source: Author's data.

Table 8.2 is a summary of the archaeological evidence identified on the Golf Links during the 2006 investigations. It shows the UTM East and North values recorded for 14 GPS points followed by a brief description of the archaeological feature or artefact represented by each point. Figure 8.1 illustrates where each of the archaeological features and artefact finds were identified on the Golf Links.

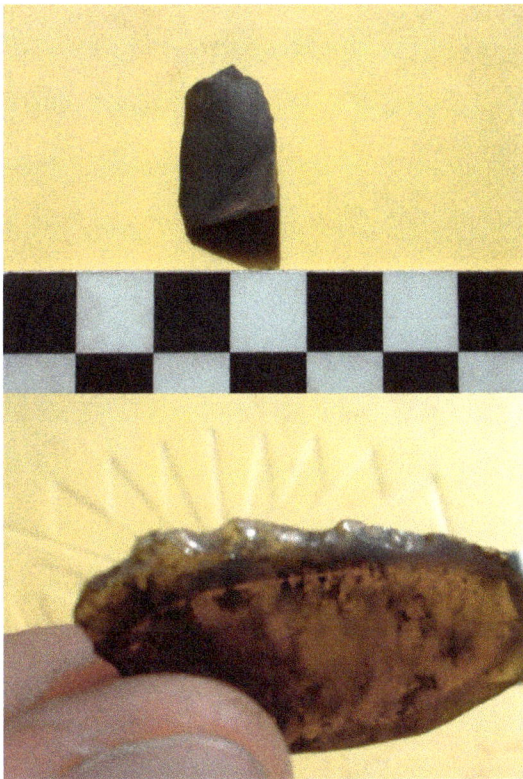

Figure 8.11 Artefacts found on the Golf Links during the 2004 archaeological survey. Top: proximal flake made of chert (scale=cm). Bottom: scraper made on the base of a small brown bottle/jar (scale=cm).

Source: Photographs by Å. Ferrier.

Figure 8.12 An area with good quality white quartz in the Evelyn area, located in open sclerophyll forest some 20 km northwest of Ravenshoe, November 2006.

Source: Photograph by Å. Ferrier.

The material culture record

Artefacts recorded in the 2004 survey

During the 2004 survey, unmodified glass fragments, flaked glass artefacts, glass fragments with potential usewear evidence and glass cores were identified on the surface of a slightly raised plateau-like area north of the golf course zone. In addition, two artefacts made of chert were located. Artefacts were photographed and recorded but not collected. Figure 8.11 illustrates two of the artefacts found in 2004 near the cluster discussed above.

Surface and excavated artefacts recorded in 2006

Six stone artefacts were found, with most collected from the surface. The attributes recorded for each artefact are the same as those in the Urumbal Pocket stone artefact assemblage. The 65 glass artefacts were analysed for indications of Aboriginal use using the definitions described in the *Boignjul* glass assemblage.

Lithics analysis

The raw materials represented in the flaked stone artefact assemblage are quartz, chert, and rhyolite. No outcrops or exposures of these raw materials are present in the immediate vicinity of the Golf Links. Rhyolite sources are available relatively closely, in the open and drier areas to the west of Cedar Creek (approximately 10 km away), whilst chert sources are located further away, to the northwest of the study area (see Chapter 5). The nearest known source of good quality white quartz, represented in the two artefacts excavated from Pit 6, is at a place called Evelyn, located in open sclerophyll forest approximately 15 km northwest of Ravenshoe (Fig. 8.12).

In addition to flaked stone artefacts, one worked cobble was identified on the Golf Links (Fig. 8.13). It is made of an unknown volcanic material and was found on the ground in the central part of the survey area (Fig. 8.1: GPS 3). This type of cobble is found in abundance in the Millstream River, which borders the eucalypt pocket to the west.

Figure 8.13 Worked cobble identified on the Golf Links, November 2006 (scale=10 cm).
Source: Photograph by Å. Ferrier.

Two complete flakes, one proximal flake, one single platform core, and two worked cobbles were identified in the artefact assemblage. They were all collected from the surface in the northern section of the property, which is slightly higher in elevation than the golf course zone (Fig. 8.1). This is in the same area that the stone and glass artefacts, illustrated in Figure 8.11, were found in 2004. In addition, during a site visit in heavy rain, stone artefacts made from a variety of raw materials, including chert, slate, quartz and crystal quartz, were observed eroding out from a road cutting adjacent to the Kennedy Highway (personal observation 2004).

Not much can be inferred from such a small number of artefacts in terms of artefact manufacture or usage. However, the presence of stone artefacts corroborates the oral traditions about Aboriginal use of this eucalypt pocket before Europeans arrived in the area. None of the flaked stone artefacts collected on the Golf Links show any evidence of use. Usewear on the two cobbles suggests that they may have been used as hammer stones, one of them possibly in some sort of grinding activity. Flaking technologies used in stone artefact manufacture on the Golf Links include freehand percussion technology, where a hammer stone or other hard object is used to strike flakes off another stone (Holdaway and Stern 2004:11). This technique was used to detach the chert and rhyolite flakes represented in the Golf Links assemblage. The bipolar technique is also present on quartz in the Golf Links stone assemblage.

The glass assemblage

A glass assemblage made up of 65 artefacts was collected from the ground surface in an area approximately 20 x 20 m in diameter around Pit 6 (Fig. 8.1: GPS2.) The presence of glass artefacts in the northern section on the Golf Links suggests that Aboriginal people were in this area in the contact period. The glass artefacts are brown (n=42), clear (n=14) and green (n=9) in colour. Information on sources of glass in the study area and on the use of glass in Aboriginal artefact manufacture in the contact period was discussed in Chapter 6. Table 8.3 shows the types and numbers of brown, clear and green glass artefacts represented in the surface collection.

Table 8.3 Types and numbers of glass artefacts in the surface collection.

Glass colour	Base	Finish	Fragment	Total
Brown	5	2	35	42
Clear	1	1	12	14
Green	0	0	9	9
Total	6	3	56	65

Source: Author's data.

One artefact of a European origin that can be dated is a bottle base with a maker's mark consisting of a large clover and the letters MBVC (Manufacturer Bottle Company of Victoria). This has a minimum date of 1903 (Boow 1991). The presence of glass artefacts may demonstrate Aboriginal use of the eucalypt pocket after European contact, which corroborates Mjöberg's descriptions of Aboriginal people living at Cedar Creek in 1913. The glass assemblage from the Golf Links is similar in appearance to the glass assemblage from the *Boignjul* open site in that it mostly consists of relatively flat pieces of glass from the body of bottles. Artefacts average 48 mm in maximum dimension and range in thickness between 2 and 6.5 mm.

The edges on each glass artefact from the Golf Links were examined under magnification (7–40X) in an effort to distinguish between edge modification as a result of human activity, and post-depositional damage. The result was that 25 of the glass artefacts showed a continuous series of crushing (i.e. micro-sized) flake scars along one or more edges. Three artefacts appeared to have been deliberately retouched along one edge. A lack of post-depositional disturbance at the *Boignjul* open site, combined with Arthur Baillie's description of Aboriginal activities in the clearing, led to the suggestion that evidence of usewear was present on some of the surface glass artefacts. European disturbance of the Golf Links, which include early cattle grazing, construction of the golf course, and recent ploughing could easily have created the edge modifications present on some of the glass artefacts from the Golf Links. Although the northern section of the Golf Links is assumed to be less disturbed by European activities, the impact from the construction of the golf course in this section of the property is unknown. For example, four probable golf tees were identified at the edge of the golf course and soil has been dumped in places, probably from levelling out of the golf course surface (personal observation).

Usewear analysis

To verify the interpretation that Aboriginal people may have used some of the glass artefacts, two of them were analysed for usewear by Richard Fullagar (2007). The study of a bottle base fragment (Fig. 8.14) showed that continuous flaking along one edge most likely represents deliberate retouch. The edge showed slight to moderate rounding and early stages of polish had started to form. The opposite surface has some small bending initiated scars and abundant striations, and it was suggested that the base was used as a scraper on a light to medium density (low silica) wood (Fullagar 2007).

A second analysed artefact is a clear glass fragment, probably originating from a jar or a bottle (Fig. 8.15). One edge has been continuously flaked, which most likely represents deliberate retouch (Fullagar 2007). The retouched edge is very steep at about 90 degrees but shows little or no rounding. Its suggested use was a scraping activity, but it could not be determined what material had been worked (Fullagar 2007).

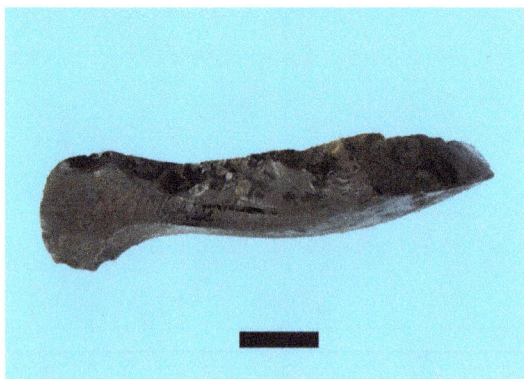

Figure 8.14 Scraper on a brown bottle base (scale=1 cm) (CKGC77).

Source: Photograph by P. Saad.

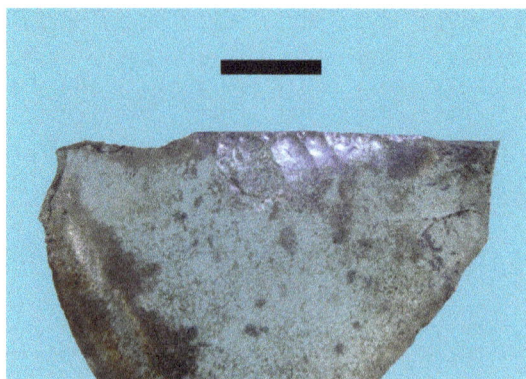

Figure 8.15 Clear glass fragment with deliberate retouch along one edge (scale=1 cm) (CKGC99).

Source: Photograph by P. Saad.

Based on these results, it is possible that a further 17 glass artefacts in the assemblage have been used. The majority (n=13) of these have one modified edge, three have two opposing edges, and one has three modified edges. In addition, five of the glass artefacts were classified as notches and one bipolar core on brown glass was also identified.

Summary

Archaeological excavations did not establish the origin of the two clusters of oval-shaped clearings on the Golf Links. The possibility that they are the remains of Aboriginal huts cannot be conclusively ruled out but appears unlikely. It has been established that stone used in artefact manufacture on the Golf Links comes from raw material sources located at least 10 km to the west. Stone could have been traded or exchanged at the time of ceremonial gatherings or collected during hunting and gathering expeditions in areas west of Cedar Creek. This area is within the traditional territory of the *Jirrbal* people and dominated by open woodlands. The historical records demonstrate that the proximity of this grassy eucalypt pocket to rainforest and open woodlands made it ideally placed for an Aboriginal campsite and associated ceremonial ground. It has been established that at Cedar Creek Aboriginal groups would come together and participate in elaborate ceremonies in the wet season, with the local *Jirrbal* people hosting these events. Traditional rainforest foods were processed at the site, and probably partly facilitated these large ceremonial gatherings. However, the extent and nature of Aboriginal activities that took place at Cedar Creek in either the recent or more distant past is difficult to infer from the archaeological record.

9

Research Outcomes

Introduction

The main objective of the research presented was to investigate long-term Aboriginal culture change and continuity in a small but unique area of northeast Queensland's rainforest region. It is recognised that the relatively small amount of archaeological research conducted to date in the Wet Tropics Bioregion is an obvious shortcoming in an investigation of long-term change and continuity. Nevertheless, the research provides a valuable contribution to the discipline by furthering the knowledge of pre- and post-contact Aboriginal rainforest occupation in a previously unexplored part of Australia's Wet Tropics Bioregion. The present aim is to draw together the threads of evidence compiled from the analyses of the archaeological and historical datasets to explore long-term Aboriginal behavioural modifications and responses to change, including the effects of European arrival on traditional Aboriginal rainforest culture and society.

Pre-European Aboriginal rainforest use

Palaeoenvironmental research in the rainforest region has demonstrated that the period approximately between 8500 BP and 3500 BP witnessed a dramatic expansion of complex rainforest on the Tablelands, replacing the eucalypt woodlands that dominated the landscape during the late Pleistocene period (Haberle 2005). From this, it has been interpreted that early Aboriginal visits to Urumbal Pocket, approximately 8,000 years ago, and the rainforests on the Evelyn Tableland, coincided with changes in the climate and environment. Historical maps and documents demonstrate that at the time of European arrival, eucalypt pockets were present on the Tablelands within dense rainforest (e.g. Mjöberg 1913a). Observations by early European explorers and miners traversing the rainforest demonstrate that such pockets were used by Aboriginal rainforest people for prolonged periods during the wet season as campsites and places where large inter-tribal ceremonial gatherings took place (e.g. Coyyan 1918). Whether some of these open forest pockets like Urumbal Pocket are remnants of the eucalypt woodlands that dominated the region prior to 8,500 years ago and were maintained by Aboriginal people over a long time, is currently being investigated but appears likely. What has become clear from the analyses of the archaeological and historical records is that there is a long-term association between eucalypt pockets in rainforest and Aboriginal rainforest occupation and use.

The majority of the cultural materials excavated from the Urumbal Pocket open site represent approximately the last 1,500 years of Aboriginal activities at the site. Earlier use of the site (8000–1500 BP) is represented by much smaller quantities of cultural material. The lithics analysis demonstrated that the Urumbal Pocket occupants mostly worked good-quality white quartz, which is present throughout the deposit. This same pattern has been reported from other excavated sites in the rainforest region (Cosgrove et al. 2007; Horsfall 1987, 1996). The research has demonstrated that the use of bipolar technology on quartz and other raw materials continued through time, and that bipolar cores were sometimes used as scrapers in wood-working activities. The lithics analysis also shows that the occupants used a variety of non-local lithic materials, some of which would have been available in the drier savannah region to the west, and others on the coast. The presence of these non-local raw materials has been interpreted as a sign of seasonal group mobility. It is most likely a reflection of Aboriginal rainforest people accessing raw materials (and other resources) from different environments within their own tribal country, as well as trading with neighbouring groups.

The identification and dating of toxic plant species at Urumbal Pocket indicates a minimum calibrated age of around 1500 BP for the processing of yellow walnuts (*Beilschmiedia bancroftii*). Nutshell fragments from deposits older than 1500 BP are characteristically smaller and lack any clear diagnostic features. However, their presence at Urumbal Pocket demonstrates that Aboriginal people were exploiting rainforest environments and bringing rainforest plant foods to the site before 1500 BP. Unidentified nutshell fragments recovered in association with stone artefacts and charcoal in layers radiocarbon dated to approximately 2,500 years old support this suggestion.

Late Holocene change

The archaeological record from Urumbal Pocket indicates a change in the way the site was used by Aboriginal people in the late Holocene period: from a relatively small-scale use of the site to a relatively sudden increase in occupation that peaked in the last 1,000 years. Major increases in cultural material are present in the deposit dated to within the last 1,000 years, including the appearance of incised slate grinding stones used to process toxic nuts. This archaeological evidence points to significant changes in the way Aboriginal people were exploiting the rainforest environment and its resources during the late Holocene. Plant remains peak in layers dated to between 800 BP and 400 BP, a time period associated with high stone artefact numbers and the presence of rich charcoal deposits. Based on this evidence, it has been interpreted that each visit to the site during the late Holocene period would have lasted a few days to allow for the processing of toxic nuts, assuming that the occupants used the same toxic nut processing techniques as historically recorded and that they did the whole processing cycle on site.

The apparent intensified use of Urumbal Pocket in the late Holocene period is a pattern that is seen in archaeological sites investigated across the rainforest region (Brayshaw 1990; Cosgrove et al. 2007; Horsfall 1987). This change in the way people used the rainforest region in the late Holocene period has been linked to climatic instability, with the onset of ENSO events around 5,000 years ago (Cosgrove et al. 2007; Ferrier and Cosgrove 2012; Turney and Hobbs 2006). It has been postulated that with extended periods of environmental pressure, Aboriginal people living on or near the fringe of the rainforest were undertaking, perhaps out of necessity, journeys into the rainforest more frequently, to access predictable resources like rainforest tree nuts. This interpretation is supported in the archaeological record of two other archaeological sites investigated in the study area: *Murubun* and Goddard Creek (Cosgrove et al. 2007). The archaeological record from all three sites suggest a change from the exploitation of a semi-dry landscape bordering the rainforest region to the west, to a more intensified use of rainforest resources in the late Holocene.

The archaeological record from Urumbal Pocket confirms that plant food species, identified from the historical literature and recorded in oral history testimonies as food staples, were an important and consistent component of the Aboriginal rainforest diet for what appears to be at least a 1,000-year period. Analyses of the historical sources suggest that at the time of Aboriginal–European contact on the Evelyn Tableland in the early 1880s, a variety of rainforest tree nuts provided a reliable staple food source during the wet season. The historical records show that rainforest tree nuts provided the means for large inter-tribal ceremonial gatherings to be held during the wet season, when large quantities were consumed (Coyyan 1918). Thus the late Holocene strategy of exploiting rainforest tree nuts may have played a significant role in the development of the unique and complex Aboriginal rainforest culture observed and documented at first contact.

A culture in transition—vanishing and enduring traditions

Analysis of the archaeological record from the *Boignjul* open site, located in a small saddle inside rainforest, demonstrated that pre-European Aboriginal rainforest occupation also took place in smaller rainforest clearings. Such clearings were described by some of the early European explorers, who often referred to them as 'bora-grounds', i.e. locations where ceremonial gatherings or 'corroborees' took place (e.g. Jack 1922). The archaeological investigations at *Boignjul* showed that pre-European use of the site occurred during short-lived visits. Perhaps it was a location where rainforest foods would have been collected as indicated by the surrounding rainforest vegetation or, as Maisie Barlow suggested, a place where men carried out their ceremonies away from women and children. From the combined archaeological and historical evidence, it is argued that these types of rainforest sites were most likely part of a network of tracks connecting clearings inside and on the edges of the rainforest.

The archaeological and documentary records show that glass and metal quickly replaced quartz and other stone materials as these European items gradually became more easily attainable (Coyyan 1915). The archaeological evidence from each of the three sites investigated shows that bipolar technology continued to be used in the early contact period. However, it became more or less redundant with the adoption of bottle glass as a preferred raw material later in the contact period. This may reflect changes in pre-European Aboriginal rainforest traditions related to the production of bipolar cores, or simply that glass was preferred over stone, and bipolar technology became redundant as a result. In 1913, Mjöberg documented that grinding stones and nut-cracking stones were still being used in the processing of toxic walnuts at Cedar Creek. This shows that *Jirrbal* people continued to use some task-specific stone tools, perhaps because the function they played was superior, or they were preferred to any European items available to them. Analyses of glass fragments from the surface at *Boignjul* also demonstrated that traditional stone artefact technologies (except bipolar technology) were being applied to glass in the contact period.

Loos (1982) has suggested that traditional campsites in remote rainforest areas on the Atherton-Evelyn Tablelands would have provided a refuge for Aboriginal people in the early contact period, as a way of escaping conflict with the native police troopers and the fast encroachment of Europeans on traditional Aboriginal lands. Historical documents describing traditional Aboriginal rainforest campsites on the Tablelands in the early contact period demonstrate that European items, including European foods such as corn, as well as more durable materials such as iron axes and metal files, were commonly lying around the camps (Coyyan 1915; Loos 1982). The observation of European materials in remote rainforest locations on the upper Tully River, as well as in other remote areas of the rainforest region, adds further support to this suggestion (Cosgrove 1999; Horsfall 1987). The archaeological investigations at *Boignjul* showed that the site may have functioned as a refuge for Aboriginal people in the early contact period. Flaked bottle bases, a bipolar core on glass, two metal files and sundry metal fragments that cannot be dated may be the remains of early contact period site use. Whether *Boignjul* and the surrounding rainforest functioned as a rainforest refuge zone in the early contact period cannot be conclusively confirmed from the archaeological record, but local historical documents show that the rainforest environment in the study area provided safety from Europeans. Communications between police constables and Aboriginal rainforest people reveal that as a result of prolonged periods of rainforest confinement, people were starving and forced to steal food from European settlers. New government legislation in the early twentieth century resolved this 'food problem'. This resulted in *Jirrbal* people taking up residence in allocated campsites on the fringe of European settlements, such as at Cedar Creek, where they were provided with European foods. In terms of understanding pre-European Aboriginal rainforest occupation, one significant observation gleaned from the historical documents is that rainforest confinement could not be sustained by Aboriginal rainforest people over any longer periods of time. This, in turn, supports the suggestion that seasonal mobility and continued access to a variety of rainforest and non-rainforest resources were vital components of Aboriginal rainforest occupation.

Despite Cedar Creek being described as 'an Aboriginal semi-sedentary settlement the size of a small village' (Mjöberg 1913a), and a location remembered as a pre- and post-contact campsite and ceremonial ground (L. Wood, pers. comm., 2004), archaeological surveys and excavations produced little archaeological evidence attesting to the scale of Aboriginal activity that took place there. Only a small number of stone and glass artefacts were found, and may be compared to the stone and glass technologies identified at Urumbal Pocket and *Boignjul*. The archaeological investigations at Cedar Creek pocket highlight the issue of site preservation in the rainforest region; in particular, the extent to which European settlement has impacted upon traditional Aboriginal campsites and ceremonial grounds that were once located in the eucalypt pockets within the rainforest environment. Analyses of the historical evidence associated with Aboriginal occupation at the Cedar Creek site, however, provides important historical information on Aboriginal rainforest settlement patterns during the transitional contact period. Eric Mjöberg documented that the people he observed living in traditional huts along South Cedar Creek at the edge of the rainforest in 1913 still used some of their organic traditional material culture items and had retained the tradition of toxic nut processing. Mjöberg's diary entries from 1913, oral history testimonies and newspaper clippings from around the same time, also show that the *Jirrbal* people of Cedar Creek and the upper Tully River were, at least to some extent, allowed to hunt and forage in the rainforest and adjacent woodlands, and to host and attend ceremonial gatherings in neighbouring countries. Thus, some *Jirrbal* people stayed in their traditional country and continued to occupy traditional campsites during the transitional contact period.

Mjöberg documented some of the traditional material cultural items that were no longer used by the Cedar Creek people, including most traditional stone implements described by Coyyan on the upper Tully River in the 1880s. Mjöberg predominantly collected the organic component of pre-European material culture and, in his published travel account of 1918, suggested that many traditional organic material culture items were still used by the *Jirrbal* people in 1913. However, the analysis of his diary shows that some of the material culture items in his collection were purchased from European settlers near townships like Ravenshoe, and that Europeans provided him with information about their traditional use. Material culture items no longer made and/or used by the *Jirrbal* people were sometimes commissioned by Mjöberg, and on a number of occasions his young Aboriginal male guides made him reproductions (Mjöberg 1913a). During his rainforest journeys, he sometimes encountered groups of *Jirrbal* people who were allowed to live in their traditional campsites whilst working for the new European landowners. Some of the young boys and men worked and lived with the land surveyors and loggers in undisturbed rainforest, whilst the old people lived in allocated campsites at the town's edge. The combined evidence points to continuities in some aspects of traditional *Jirrbal* culture, society and rainforest occupation. At the same time, *Jirrbal* people were modifying their behaviours and adapting to the many changes brought about by European settlement.

An escape from everyday life

Analyses of the historical evidence shows that later in the post-contact period, i.e. the 1930s, *Jirrbal* people who resided and worked in and around Ravenshoe (Cedar Creek), sometimes undertook weekend visits to traditional rainforest campsites south of Ravenshoe and travelled down to the coast along traditional rainforest tracks during the extended Christmas break (M. Barlow, pers. comm., 2004). During these rainforest visits, some of the traditional activities carried out included the construction of thatched *mijas*, the gathering and cooking of traditional foods such as rainforest tree nuts, and participating in ceremonial gatherings (M. Barlow, pers. comm., 2004).

Thus for the *Jirrbal* people, the rainforests south of Cedar Creek and along the upper Tully River became a refuge from everyday life in the post-contact period. The archaeological record from *Boignjul* supports the historical record in that traditional activities were carried out at campsites away from town and farm camps in the rainforest south of Ravenshoe. The archaeological record suggests that these occasional visits to traditional rainforest sites stopped sometime in the 1940s, which is supported by the historical evidence. From this time, logging activities expanded into these previously undisturbed rainforest areas. These activities, combined with the employment of Aboriginal people as young as 12, who were sent away from their traditional land and families, ended the traditional life ways *Jirrbal* people had transformed after contact.

Conclusion

The archaeological record from the Urumbal Pocket open site on the upper Tully River suggests a major change in the ways Aboriginal people used this location sometime in the last 1,000 to 1,500 years; perhaps from a life spent mostly on the rainforest fringe, to a more permanent life in the rainforest region. This change in the way Aboriginal people used the rainforest environment and its resources in the late Holocene period has been interpreted as a long-term outcome of extended periods of regional climatic instability. The lithics analyses showed that no stone artefacts typical of the so-called Australian small tool tradition were recovered from the three sites investigated. Nor have they been recorded from archaeological sites investigated elsewhere in the rainforest region. It appears that the significant changes evident in Aboriginal societies outside of the rainforest region did not necessarily influence the life ways of Aboriginal rainforest people, at least none that appear in the archaeological record. The research provides further evidence of variability in Australian Aboriginal societies during the mid- to late Holocene period. It highlights the importance of archaeological investigations and explanations at a regional scale, and that changes within particular sites or regions are viewed as largely independent.

The research has demonstrated that late Holocene Aboriginal rainforest settlement patterns and group mobility on the Evelyn Tableland was dependent on subsistence adaptation and resource distribution, but that other factors played a role in facilitating and maintaining what was a predominantly rainforest existence. The association between people and eucalypt pockets is significant in terms of understanding long-term Aboriginal rainforest occupation, including during the contact period. Their presence in the rainforest facilitated the pre-European development of large 'villages' that were used by Aboriginal people during the wet season, and later as a more permanent base in the contact period. Furthermore, the maintenance of tracks through the rainforest connecting smaller clearings allowed people to take journeys into the rainforest, to collect food and other items, and preserve social network systems. The metamorphic artefacts excavated from Urumbal Pocket may be evidence for the late Holocene development of interactions between groups occupying different areas of the rainforest region. Analyses of the historical evidence showed that *Jirrbal* culture and society on the Evelyn Tableland underwent many transformations in the transitional contact period, to accommodate the new and dominant European culture imposed upon them. However, the combined archaeological and historical evidence from traditional campsites that continued to be used in the contact period, demonstrates that *Jirrbal* rainforest culture and society transformed rather than ceased in the contact period; *Jirrbal* people continued to adapt to changes brought about by European settlement throughout the contact period.

The combined evidence, therefore, suggests that the complex nature of Aboriginal rainforest occupation first documented by Europeans in the region relied on seasonal mobility connected to food resource availability, combined with long-term maintenance of eucalypt pockets, tracks and smaller clearings within the rainforest. Although speculative, the common occurrence of cycad plants (*Cycas* spp.) in areas adjacent to the rainforest region may point to prior knowledge in toxic food processing techniques. Future archaeological research on sites located along the rainforest fringe, and on the specific source locations of stone raw materials, may provide further evidence on the long-term use of two proximate but very different environments. Investigation into the notion of Aboriginal rainforest people developing some type of domi-culture, as suggested by Hynes and Chase (1982) on Cape York, might also lead to an improved understanding of Aboriginal rainforest food plant regimes, and the ways in which the rainforest environment was used and managed by Aboriginal rainforest people in the past.

A long-term approach to the archaeology of contact has only been applied in a handful of studies in Australia (e.g. Clarke 1994; Colley 2000; Williamson 1998). These studies have demonstrated that the application of a temporal and interdisciplinary framework can produce useful new perspectives in the interpretation of archaeological records. Applying this archaeological framework in investigations of long-term Aboriginal culture change and continuity also highlights the dynamic nature of Aboriginal culture and society, and the adaptive and flexible nature of Aboriginal people, before and after European arrival. The research presented supports previous findings. Analyses of archaeological data, which has allowed access to the products of actual human behaviour at open sites, combined with the historical data, have shown that change and continuity can be traced through time in cultural trajectories identified from archaeological records in north Queensland's tropical rainforest region. The task now is to clarify local and regional sequences, patterns and developments through fine-grained analyses of archaeological sites and material culture records, and continue to construct longitudinal histories of Aboriginal Australia.

Reference List

Adams, W.H. 2003. Dating historical sites: The importance of understanding time lag in the acquisition, curation, use, and disposal of artifacts. *Historical Archaeology* 37(2):38–64.

Allen, J. 1969. Archaeology and the history of Port Essington. Unpublished PhD thesis, The Australian National University, Canberra.

Allen, J. 2008. *Port Essington: The historical archaeology of a North Australian nineteenth-century military outpost*. Studies in Australasian Historical Archaeology Vol 1. Sydney: Sydney University Press.

Allen, J. and Jones, R. 1980. Oyster Cove: Archaeological traces of the last Tasmanians and notes on the criteria for the authentication of flaked glass artefacts. *Papers and Proceedings of the Royal Society of Tasmania* 114:225–233.

Anderberg, L. 1994. *Atlas of Seeds and Small Fruits of Northwest-European Plant Species*. Stockholm: Swedish Museum of Natural History.

An Act to make Provision for the Better Protection and Care of the Aboriginal and Half-Caste Inhabitants of the Colony, and to make more Effectual Provision for Restricting the Sale and Distribution of Opium, Queensland, 1897.

Asmussen, B. 2008. Anything more than a picnic? Re-considering arguments for ceremonial *Macrozamia* use in mid-Holocene Australia. *Archaeology in Oceania* 43:93–103.

Attwood, B. 1989. *The Making of the Aborigines*. North Sydney, NSW: Allen & Unwin.

Barker, B. 1991. Nara Inlet 1: Coastal resource use and the Holocene marine transgression in the Whitsunday Islands, central Queensland. *Archaeology in Oceania* 26:102–109.

Barker, B. and Lamb, L. 2009. The archaeology of poverty and human dignity: Charity and the work ethic in a 1930s Depression era itinerant's camp on the Toowoomba Range escarpment, Queensland. *Archaeologies* 5(2):263–279.

Barlow, M. 2001. *Jirrbal Rainforest Dreamtime Stories*. Broome: Magabala Books Aboriginal Corporation.

Beale, E. 1977. *Kennedy of Cape York*. Adelaide: Rigby.

Beasley, J. 2006. *Plants of Tropical North Queensland*. Kuranda: Footloose Publications.

Beaton, J. 1985. Evidence for a coastal occupation time-lag at Princess Charlotte Bay (North Queensland) and implications for coastal colonisation and population growth theories for Aboriginal Australia. *Archaeology in Oceania* 20:1–20.

Beck, W.A., Clarke, A. and Head, L. (eds) 1989. *Plants in Australian Archaeology*. Tempus Vol. 1. St Lucia, QLD: University of Queensland.

Berry, D. 1999. The Early Days of Ravenshoe. A selection of articles compiled from older newspapers. Unpublished research paper, Ravenshoe Historical Society.

Binford, L. 1979. Organization and formation processes: Looking at curated technologies. *Journal of Anthropological Research* 35(3):225–273.

Binford, L. 1980. Willow smoke and dogs' tails: Hunter-gatherer settlement systems and archaeological site formation. *American Antiquity* 45(1):4–20.

Bird, C.F.M. and Frankel, D. 1991a. Problems in constructing a prehistoric regional sequence: Holocene southeast Australia. *World Archaeology* 23(2):179–192.

Bird, C.F.M. and Frankel, D. 1991b. Chronology and explanation in western Victoria and south-east Australia. *Archaeology in Oceania* 26:1–16.

Bird, M. 1999. Cultural heritage assessment of a proposed park residential estate development site, Ravenshoe, North Queensland. Unpublished cultural heritage assessment report, Aitkenvale, Queensland.

Bird, C. and Frankel, D. 2005. *An archaeology of Gariwerd. From Pleistocene to Holocene in western Victoria.* Tempus Vol. 8. St. Lucia, QLD: University of Queensland.

Birmingham, J. 1992. *Wybalenna: The Archaeology of Cultural Accommodation in Nineteenth Century Tasmania. A report of the historical archaeological investigation of the Aboriginal establishment on Flinders Island.* Sydney: The Australian Society for Historical Archaeology.

Birmingham, J. 2000. Resistance, creolization or optimal foraging at Killalpaninna Mission, South Australia. In R. Torrence and A. Clarke (eds), *The Archaeology of Difference: Negotiating cross-cultural engagement in Oceania*, One World Archaeology 38, pp.360–405, London: Routledge.

Birtles, T.G. 1997a. Aboriginal use and rainforest clearing on the Atherton Tablelands before 1920. In J. Dargavel (ed.), *Australia's Ever-Changing Forests III*: Proceedings of the Third National Conference on Australian forest history. Canberra: ANU Centre for Resource and Environmental Studies.

Birtles, T.G. 1997b. First contact: Colonial European preconceptions of tropical Queensland rainforest and its people. *Journal of Historical Geography* 23(4):393–417.

Boow, J. 1991. *Early Australian Commercial Glass: Manufacturing Processes.* Sydney: Department of Planning and Heritage Council of New South Wales.

Bottoms, T. 1999. *Djabugay Country: An Aboriginal History of Tropical North Queensland.* St. Leonards, NSW: Allen & Unwin.

Bourke, P., Brockwell, S., Faulkner, P. and Meehan, B. 2007. Climate variability in the mid to late Holocene Arnhem Land Region, North Australia: Archaeological archives of environmental and cultural change. *Archaeology in Oceania* 42(3):91–101.

Brayshaw, H. 1990. *Well Beaten Paths: Aborigines of the Herbert/Burdekin District, North Queensland: An ethnographic and archaeological study.* Townsville: Department of History, James Cook University of North Queensland.

Brock, J. 2005. *Native Plants of Northern Australia.* Chatswood, NSW: Reeds Books.

Brockwell, S., Marwick, B., Bourke, P., Faulkner, P., Willan, R., 2013. Late Holocene climate change and human behavioural variability in the coastal wet-dry tropics of northern Australia: Evidence from a pilot study of oxygen isotopes in marine bivalve shells from archaeological sites. *Australian Archaeology* 76:21–33.

Brown, S., Avery, S. and Goulding, M. 2002. Recent Investigations at the Ebenezer Mission cemetery In R. Harrison and C. Williamson (eds), *After Captain Cook: The Archaeology of the Recent Indigenous Past in Australia*, Sydney University Archaeological Methods Series 8, pp.147–170, Sydney, NSW: Archaeological Computing Laboratory, University of Sydney.

Bultitude, R.J., Garrad, P.D., Donchak, P.T.J., Domagala, J., Champion, D.C., Rees, I.D., Mackinzie, D.E., Wellman, P., Knutson, J., Fanning, C.M., Fordham, B.G., Grimes, K.G., Oversby, B.S., Rienks, I.P., Stevenson, P.J., Pain, C.F., Wilford, J.R., Rigby, J.F. and Woodbury, M.J. 1997. Cairns Region. In J.H.C. Bain and J.J. Draper (eds), *North Queensland Geology*. AGSO Bulletin 240 / Queensland Geology 9. Canberra: Commonwealth Department of Primary Industries and Energy.

Cameron, F. 1991. *Analysis of Buttons, Clothing Hardware and Textiles of the Nineteenth Century Chinese Goldminers of Central Otago.* Otago, New Zealand: Archaeological Laboratory, University of Otago Archaeological Laboratory.

Campbell, J.B. 1982. New radiocarbon results for North Queensland Prehistory. *Australian Archaeology* 14:62–66.

Campbell, W.W. 1923. Theodolite Traverse of the Tully River. Field notes, Cwl. 555 and 6, Department of Natural Resources and Mines, Queensland Government.

Carver, G. 2005. Post-Contact Archaeology at Nuccaleena, South Australia: An investigation of glass tool use by Indigenous Australians. Unpublished MA thesis, Department of Archaeology, Flinders University, Adelaide.

Clarke, A. 1994. Winds of change: An archaeology of contact in the Groote Eylandt archipelago, Northern Australia. Unpublished PhD thesis, The Australian National University, Canberra.

Clarke, A. 2000. Cross-cultural engagements, Groote Eylandt. In R. Torrence and A. Clarke (eds), *The Archaeology of Difference: Negotiating cross-cultural engagement in Oceania*, One World Archaeology 38, pp.142–181, London: Routledge.

Clarke, A. and Paterson, A. 2003. Case studies in the archaeology of cross-cultural interaction. *Archaeology in Oceania* 38(2). Special guest edited journal volume.

Clarke, D. and Chapman, B. 1978. *Analytical Archaeology.* Second edition. London: Methuen and Co. Ltd.

Clarkson, C. and Lamb, L. (eds), 2005. *Lithics 'Down Under': Australian Perspectives on Lithic Reduction, Use and Classification.* Oxford: Archaeopress.

Colley, S. 2000. The colonial impact? Contact archaeology and indigenous sites in southern New South Wales. In R. Torrence and A. Clarke (eds), *The Archaeology of Difference: Negotiating cross-cultural engagement in Oceania*, One World Archaeology 38, pp.278–299, London: Routledge.

Colley, S. and Bickford, A. 1995. 'Real Aborigines' and 'Real Archaeology': Aboriginal places and Australian historical archaeology. *World Archaeological Bulletin* 7:5–21.

Colliver, S. and Woolston, F. 1966. Some stone artefacts from North Queensland rainforests. *Occasional Papers in Anthropology* 1:104–125.

Colliver, S. and Woolston, F. 1980. The rainforest sword and shield in Queensland. *Occasional Papers in Anthropology* 10:63–94.

Cooper, W. and Cooper, W.T. 2004. *Fruits of the Australian Tropical Rainforest.* Melbourne: Nokomis Editions Pty Ltd.

Cosgrove, R. 1979. Ground-edge artefacts from the rainforest area, northeast Queensland: A preliminary review. Unpublished report to the Australian Institute of Aboriginal Studies.

Cosgrove, R. 1984. A stylist and use-wear study of the Ooyurka. Unpublished MA thesis, James Cook University, Townsville.

Cosgrove, R. 1996. Origin and development of Australian Aboriginal tropical rainforest culture: A reconsideration. *Antiquity* 70:900–912.

Cosgrove, R. 1997. Rainforest Archaeology Project Report No. 1 with appendix 1: Williamson, C. Unpublished report on artefacts identified at Top Camp, an Aboriginal Historic Site, North Queensland, Archaeological Survey of the Russell and Johnstone Rivers. Townsville: Material Culture Unit, James Cook University.

Cosgrove, R. 1999. Rainforest Archaeology Project Report No. 2. Archaeological Survey of the Russell and Johnstone Rivers. Unpublished report to the Australian Institute of Aboriginal and Torres Strait Islander Studies. Bundoora: La Trobe University.

Cosgrove, R. 2005. Coping with noxious nuts. *Natural Australia* 28(6):46–53.

Cosgrove, R. and Field, J. 2004. Unpublished interim report to the Environmental Protection Agency, Queensland. Bundoora: La Trobe University.

Cosgrove, R., Field, J. and Ferrier, Å. 2007. The archaeology of Australia's tropical rainforests. *Palaeogeography, Palaeoclimatology, Palaeoecology* 251:150–173.

Cosgrove, R. and Raymont, E. 2002. Jiyer Cave revisited: Preliminary results from northeast Queensland rainforest. *Australian Archaeology* 54:29–36.

Courtney, K. and McNiven I.J. 1998. Clay tobacco pipes from Aboriginal middens on Fraser Island, Queensland. *Australian Archaeology* 47:44–53.

Coutts, P., Witter, D. and Parsons, D. 1977. Impacts of European settlement on Aboriginal Society in Western Victoria. *Records of the Victoria Archaeological Survey* 4:21–47.

Coyyan, 1915. Aboriginese. [sic] *The Cairns Post*, 22.1.15, pp.2–3.

Coyyan, 1918. The Aboriginals Parts I–X. *The Northern Herald*, January–May 1918.

Craig, J.A. 1947. Culpa Lands, Parishes of Ramleh, Bankton, Ismailia and Timsah, County of Cardwell, North Qld District.

Culloty, D. 1992. (ed.), *More than Memories: Stories Told to a Group of Year 5 Students by the Senior Residents of Ravenshoe District.* Priority Country Area Program, Education Department, Queensland.

Cusick, J.G. (ed.) 1998. *Studies in Culture Contact: Interaction, Culture Change and Archaeology.* Carbondale, ILL: Centre for Archaeological Investigations Southern Illinois University.

David, B. and Chant, D. 1995. Rock art and regionalisation in North Queensland prehistory. *Memoirs of the Queensland Museum* 37(2):357–528.

Dickson, F. 1977. Quartz flaking. In R.V.S. Wright (ed.), *Stone Tools as Cultural Markers: Change, Evolution and Complexity*, pp. 97–103. Canberra: Australian Institute of Aboriginal Studies.

Dixon, R.M.W. 1972. *The Dyirbal language of North Queensland.* Cambridge: Cambridge University Press.

Dixon, R.M.W. 1991. *Words of our Country: Stories, place names and vocabulary in Yidinji, the Aboriginal language of the Cairns-Yarrabah Region.* St Lucia, QLD: Queensland University Press.

Dixon, R.M.W. and Koch, G. 1995. *Dyirbal Song Poetry: The oral literature of an Australian rainforest people.* St Lucia, QLD: University of Queensland Press.

Duke, A. and Collins, S. 1994. Jirrbal Heritage and History Project Cultural Mapping. Unpublished report prepared for Jiddabul Aboriginal Corporation, Restricted Edition.

Duke, A. and Collins, S. 1999. Cultural Heritage Assessment (Indigenous) of Potential High Impact Areas of the Koombooloomba Ecotourism Project. Unpublished report to Girringun Elders and Reference Group (Aboriginal Corporation).

Evans, R., Saunders, K. and Cronin, K. 1988. *Race Relations in Colonial Queensland: A history of exclusion, exploitation and extermination.* Second edition. Brisbane: University of Queensland Press.

Ferrier, Å. 1999. A study of contact period Aboriginal material culture from the rainforest region of Northeast Queensland. Unpublished Honours thesis, Department of Archaeology, La Trobe University, Bundoora.

Ferrier, Å. 2002. The Mjöberg collection and contact period Aboriginal material culture from northeast Queensland's rainforest region. In R. Harrison and C. Williamson (eds), *After Captain Cook: The archaeology of the recent Indigenous past in Australia*, Sydney University Archaeological Methods Series 8, pp.17–36, Sydney, NSW: Archaeological Computing Laboratory, University of Sydney.

Ferrier, Å. 2006. Dr Eric Mjöberg's 1913 scientific exploration of North Queensland's rainforest region. *Memoirs of the Queensland Museum, Cultural Heritage Series* 4(1):1–27.

Ferrier, Å. and Cosgrove, R. 2012. Aboriginal exploitation of toxic nuts as a late-Holocene subsistence strategy in Australia's tropical rainforests. In S.G. Haberle and B. David (eds), *Peopled Landscapes. Archaeological and Biogeographic Approaches to Landscapes,* Terra Australis 34, pp.103–120, Canberra: ANU E Press.

Field, J., Cosgrove, R., Fullagar, R. and Lance, B. 2009. Survival of starch residues on grinding stones in private collections: A study of morahs from the tropical rainforests of NE Queensland. In M. Haslam, G. Robertson, A. Crowther, S. Nugent and L. Kirkwood (eds), *Archaeological Science Under A Microscope: Studies in Residue and DNA Analysis in Honour of Thomas H. Loy,* Terra Australis 30, pp.228–238, Canberra: ANU E Press.

Fink, D., Hotchkis, M., Hua, Q., Jacobsen, G., Smith, A.M., Zoppi, U., Child, D., Mifsud, C., Gaast, H. van Der., Williams, A. and Williams, M. 2004. The ANTARES AMS facility at ANSTO. Nuclear Instruments and Methods in Physics Research Section B: Interactions with Materials and Atoms. Proceedings of the Ninth International Conference on Accelerator Mass Spectrometry 223–224:109–115.

Flenniken, J. F. 1981. Replicative Systems Analysis: A model applied to the vein quartz artifacts from the Hoko River site. *Reports of Investigations 59*. Pullman, WA: Washington State University, Laboratory of Anthropology.

Flenniken, J. and White, J.P. 1985. Australian flaked stone tools: A technological perspective. *Records of the Australian Museum* 36:131–151.

Flood, J. 1992. *Archaeology of the Dreamtime: The story of prehistoric Australia and its people.* Pymble, NSW: Angus and Robertson.

Frankel, D. 1991. *Remains to be Seen: Archaeological insights into Australian prehistory.* Melbourne, VIC: Longman Cheshire Pty Ltd.

Frankel, D. 1993. Pleistocene chronological structures and explanations: A challenge. In M.A. Smith, M. Spriggs and , B. Fankhauser (eds), *Sahul in Review: Pleistocene archaeology in Australia, New Guinea and Island Melanesia*, Occasional Papers in Prehistory 24, pp.24–33, Canberra: The Australian National University, Department of Prehistory, Research School of Pacific Studies.

Frawley, K.J. 1990. An ancient assemblage: The Australian rainforests in European conceptions of nature. *Continuum* 3(1):137–167.

Frederick, U. 1999. At the centre of it all: Constructing contact through the rock art of Watarrka National Park, central Australia. *Archaeology in Oceania* 34(3):132–144.

Fullagar, R. 2007, Artefact report. Unpublished artefact report on stone and glass artefact residue and usewear analyses for Åsa Ferrier. Wollongong.

Fullagar, R. and Head, L. 2000. Archaeology and native title in Australia: national and local perspectives. In I. Lilley (ed.) *Native title and the Transformation of Archaeology in the Postcolonial World*, Oceania Monograph 50, pp.24–34, Sydney: University of Sydney.

Genever, G. 2006. *Failure of Justice: The story of the Irvinebank massacre.* Malanda, QLD: Eacham Historical Society.

Gibbs, M. and Harrison, R. 2008. Dynamics of dispersion revisited? Archaeological context and the study of Aboriginal knapped glass artefacts in Australia. *Australian Archaeology* 67:61–68.

Godden, G.A. 2003. *Encyclopaedia of British Pottery and Porcelain Marks.* London: Ebury Publishing.

Gould, R. 1980. *Living Archaeology.* Cambridge: Cambridge University Press.

Haberle, S. 2005. A 23,000-year pollen record from Lake Euramoo, Wet Tropics of NE Queensland, Australia. *Quaternary Research* 64(3):343–356.

Haberle, S. and David, B. 2004. Climates of change: human dimensions of Holocene environmental change in low latitudes of the PEPII transect. *Quaternary International* 118/119:165–179.

Harris, D.R. 1975. Traditional patterns of plant-food procurement in the Cape York Peninsula and Torres Strait Islands. Unpublished report on fieldwork carried out Aug–Nov 1974.

Harris, D. 1978. Adaptation to a tropical rain-forest environment: Aboriginal subsistence in northeastern Queensland. In N.G. Blurton Jones and V. Reynolds (eds), *Human Behaviour and Adaptation*, pp.113–134, London: Taylor & Francis.

Harris, D. 1987. Aboriginal subsistence in a tropical rain forest environment: Food procurement, cannibalism, and population regulation in northeastern Australia. In M. Harris and E.B. Ross (eds), *Food Evolution: Toward a theory of human food habits*, pp.357–385, Philadelphia, PA: Temple University Press.

Harrison, R. 2000. Challenging the authenticity of antiquity: Contact archaeology and native title in Australia. In I. Lilley (ed.) *Native title and the Transformation of Archaeology in the Postcolonial World*, Oceania Monograph 50, pp.35–53, Sydney: University of Sydney.

Harrison, R. and Williamson, C. (eds), 2002. *After Captain Cook: The archaeology of the recent Indigenous past in Australia*, Sydney University Archaeological Methods Series 8, Sydney, NSW: Archaeological Computing Laboratory, University of Sydney.

Harrison, R. 2004. *Shared Landscapes: Archaeologies of attachment to the pastoral industry in New South Wales*. Sydney: University of New South Wales Press.

Harrison, R. 2005. Contact archaeology and native title. *Australian Aboriginal Studies* 1:16–29.

Harrison, R. and Williamson, C. (eds), 2002. *After Captain Cook: The Archaeology of the Recent Indigenous Past in Australia*, Sydney University Archaeological Methods Series 8, Archaeological Computing Laboratory, University of Sydney, Sydney.

Head, L. and Fullagar, R. 1997. Hunter-gatherer archaeology and pastoral contact: perspectives from the northwest northern Territory, Australia. *World Archaeology* 28(3):418–428.

Henderson, R.A. and Stephenson, P.J. 1980. *The Geology and Geophysics of Northeastern Australia*. Brisbane: Geological Society of Australia, Queensland Division.

Herberton Advertiser, 1888. Report from the police commissioner of Herberton, 17 June 1888, Herberton, Queensland.

Herberton Advertiser, 1889. Report from the police commissioner of Herberton, 18 January 1889, Herberton, Queensland.

Hewitt, G. 2004. Koey Ngurtain: Analysis of the glass and metal artefacts. Unpublished report describing and analysing metal and glass artefacts recovered by Dr B. David from cultural sites on Koey Ngurtain, an island in the Torres Strait.

Hilbert, D.W., Graham, A. and Hopkins, M.S. 2007. Glacial and interglacial refugia within a long-term rainforest refugium: The Wet Tropics Bioregion of NE Queensland, Australia. *Palaeogeography, Palaeoclimatology, Palaeoecology* 251:104–118.

Hill, R. and Baird, A. 2003. Kuku-Yalanji rainforest Aboriginal people and carbohydrate resource management in the wet tropics of Queensland, Australia. *Human Ecology: An Interdisciplinary Journal* 31:1–26.

Hiscock, P. 1986. Technological change in the Hunter River valley and the interpretation of late Holocene change in Australia. *Archaeology in Oceania* 21(1):40–50.

Hiscock, P. 1996. Mobility and technology in the Kakadu coastal wetlands. *Bulletin of the Indo-Pacific Prehistory Association* 15:151–157.

Hiscock, P. and Attenbrow, V. 1998. Early Holocene backed artefacts from Australia. *Archaeology in Oceania* 33(2):49–62.

Hiscock, P. and Kershaw, A.P. 1992. Palaeoenvironments and prehistory of Australia's tropical Top End. In J. Dodson (ed.), *The Naive Lands: Prehistory and environmental change in Australia and the Southwest Pacific*, pp. 43–75, Melbourne: Longman Cheshire.

Holdaway, S., Fanning, P.C., Jones, M., Shiner, J., Witter, D.C., and Nicholls, G. 2002. Variability in the chronology of late Holocene Aboriginal occupation on the arid margin of southeastern Australia. *Journal of Archaeological Science* 29:351–363.

Holdaway, S. and Porch, N. 1995. Cyclical patterns in the Pleistocene human occupation of southwest Tasmania. *Archaeology in Oceania* 30:74–82.

Holdaway, S. and Stern, N. 2004. *A Record in Stone: The study of Australia's flaked stone artefacts*. Canberra: Museum Victoria and Aboriginal Studies Press.

Hopkins, M.S., Ash, J., Graham, A.W., Head, J. and Hewitt, R.K. 1993. Charcoal evidence of the spatial extent of the Eucalyptus woodland expansions and rainforest contractions in north Queensland during the late Pleistocene. *Journal of Biogeography* 20:357–372.

Horsfall, N. 1987. Living in rainforest: The prehistoric occupation of North Queensland's humid tropics. Unpublished PhD thesis, James Cook University, Townsville.

Horsfall, N. 1988. Tully-Millstream Hydro-Electric Scheme Feasibility Study: Environmental issues and planning responses. Brisbane: Queensland Electricity Commission.

Horsfall, N. 1990. People and the rainforest: An archaeological perspective. In L.J. Webb and J. Kikkawa (eds), *Australian Tropical Rainforests: Science-Values-Meaning*, pp. 33–39, Melbourne, VIC: CSIRO.

Horsfall, N. 1996. *Holocene occupation of the tropical rainforests of North Queensland*, Tempus 4:174–190.

Hynes, R.A. and Chase A.K. 1982. Plants, sites and domiculture: Aboriginal influence upon plant communities in Cape York Peninsula. *Archaeology in Oceania* 17:38–50.

Jack, R.L. 1998 [1922]. *Northmost Australia: three centuries of exploration, discovery, and adventure in and around the Cape York Peninsula, Queensland: with a study of the narratives of all explorers by sea and land in the light of modern charting.* Carlisle, WA: Hesperian Press.

Jenkinson, A. 2007. Unpublished report on AMS analysis of burnt endocarp fragments for Richard Cosgrove. Sydney: Australian Nuclear Science and Technology Organisation (ANSTO).

Kamminga, J. 1978. Journey into the Microcosms: A functional analysis of certain classes of prehistoric Australian stone tools. Unpublished PhD thesis, Department of Anthropology, University of Sydney, Sydney.

Keepax, C. 1977. Contamination of archaeological deposits by seeds of modern origin with particular reference to the use of flotation machines. *Journal of Archaeological Science* 4:221–229.

Kent, S. 1987. *Method and Theory for Activity Area Research.* New York: Columbia University Press.

Kershaw, A.P. 1976. A late Pleistocene and Holocene pollen diagram from Lynch's Crater, northeastern Queensland, Australia. *New Phytologist* 77:469–498.

Kershaw, A.P. 1986. The last two glacial-interglacial cycles from northeastern Australia: Implications for climate change and Aboriginal burning. *Nature* 322:47–49.

Kershaw, A.P. 1994. Pleistocene vegetation of the humid tropics of northeastern Queensland, Australia. *Palaeogeography, Palaeoclimatology, Palaeoecology* 109:399–412.

Kronestedt, T. 1989. Fjärran forskningsfärder med rikt entomologiskt utbyte, Särtryck ur *Naturen berätter*, pp.57–66, Stockholm: Naturhistoriska Riksmuseet.

Lampert, R.J. 1971. *Burrill Lake and Currarong: coastal sites in southern New South Wales*, Terra Australis 1. Canberra: Department of Prehistory, Research School of Pacific Studies, The Australian National University.

Lightfoot, K.G. 1995. Culture contact studies: Redefining the relationship between prehistoric and historical archaeology. *American Antiquity* 60(2):199–218.

Lilley, I. (ed.) 2000. *Native title and the Transformation of Archaeology in the Postcolonial World*, Oceania Monograph 50. Sydney: University of Sydney.

Loos, N. 1982. *Invasion and Resistance: Aboriginal-European Relations on the North Queensland Frontier 1861–1897.* Canberra: Australian National University Press.

Lourandos, H. 1977. Aboriginal spatial organisation and population: Southwestern Victoria reconsidered. *Archaeology and Physical Anthropology in Oceania* 12:202–225.

Lourandos, H. 1983. Intensification: A Late Pleistocene-Holocene archaeological sequence from southwestern Victoria. *Archaeology in Oceania* 18:81–94.

Lourandos, H. 1985. Intensification and Australian prehistory. In T.D. Price and J.A. Brown (eds), *Prehistoric Hunter-Gatherers: The emergence of cultural complexity*, pp. 385–423, London: Academic Press.

Lourandos, H. 1997. *Continent of Hunter-Gatherers.* Cambridge: Cambridge University Press.

Lourandos, H. and David, B. 1998. Comparing long-term archaeological and environmental trends: North Queensland, arid and semi-arid Australia. *The Artefact* 21:105–114.

Lourandos, H. and Ross, A. 1994. The great 'intensification debate': Its history and place in Australian archaeology. *Australian Archaeology* 39:54–63.

Lumholtz, C. 1980 [1889]. *Among Cannibals: Account of four years travels in Australia and of camp life with the Aborigines of Queensland.* Canberra: Australian National University Press.

Lydon, J. 2002. 'This civilising experiment': Photography at Corranderk Aboriginal Station during the 1860s. In R. Harrison and C. Williamson (eds), *After Captain Cook: The archaeology of the recent Indigenous past in Australia*, Sydney University Archaeological Methods Series 8, pp.59–74, Sydney, NSW: Archaeological Computing Laboratory, University of Sydney.

May, S. 2010. *Collecting Cultures: Myth, politics and collaboration in the 1948 Arnhem Land Expedition.* Lanham, MD: AltaMira Press.

May, S.K., Taçon, P.S.C., Wesley, D. and Travers, M. 2010. Painting history: Indigenous observations and depictions of the 'other' in Northwestern Arnhem Land, Australia. Australian Archaeology 71:57–65.

McBryde, I. 1978. Wil-im-ee Moor-ring: Or, where do axes come from? *Mankind* 11:354–382.

McDonald, J. 2000. Archaeology, rock art, ethnicity and native title. In I. Lilley (ed.) *Native title and the Transformation of Archaeology in the Postcolonial World*, Oceania Monograph 50, pp.54–64, Sydney: University of Sydney.

McKenzie, N., Jacquier, D., Isbell, R. and Brown, K. 2004. *Australian Soils and Landscapes: An illustrated compendium.* Melbourne: CSIRO.

McKnight, C.C. 1976. *The voyage to Marege: Macassan trepangers in northern Australia.* Melbourne: Melbourne University Press.

Meehan, B. and Jones, R. (eds), 1988. *Archaeology with Ethnography: An Australian perspective.* Canberra: The Australian National University.

Meston, A. 1889. *Report of the Government Scientific Expedition to Bellenden-Ker Range upon the flora and fauna of that part of the colony.* Brisbane: Government Printer.

Miller, G., Samford, P., Shlasko, E. and Madsen, A. 2000. Telling time for archaeologists. *Northeast Historical Archaeology* 29:1–22.

Minnis, P.E. 1981. Seeds in archaeological sites: Sources and some interpretive problem. *American Antiquity* 48(1):143–152.

Mjöberg, E. 1913a. The unpublished diaries from the second Australia expedition. Eric Mjöberg collection, Accession numbers 26851, 26852 and 26858, Box 5, California Academy of Sciences, San Francisco, CA.

Mjöberg, E. 1913b. Dr Mjöberg's biological expedition to Australia. *Ymer 33*:365–366.

Mjöberg, E. 1914. Travel account from Dr E. Mjöberg to the Royal Academy of Sciences, Stockholm.

Mjöberg, E. 1915. *Bland Vilda Djur och Människor i Australien (Amongst Wild Animals and People in Australia).* Stockholm: Albert Bonniers Boktryckeri.

Mjöberg, E. 1918. *Bland Stenåldersmänniskor i Queenslands Vildmarker (Among Stone Age People in the Queensland Wilderness).* Stockholm: Albert Bonniers Boktryckeri.

Mjöberg, E. 1923. Vom Phalluskult in Nordaustralien. *Archiv für Anthropologie* 19(4):86–88.

Mjöberg, E. 1925. Beiträge zur kenntnis der Eingeborenen von Nord-Queensland, *Archiv für Anthropologie* 20(9):108–135.

Mjöberg, E. 2012. *Among Wild Animals and People in Australia.* Translated by M. Luotsinen. and K. Akerman. The Western Australian Explorer's Diaries Project. Carlisle, WA: Hesperian Press.

Mjöberg, E. 2015. *Amongst Stone Age People in the Queensland Wilderness.* Translated by S.M. Fryer. Å. Ferrier and R. Ritchie (eds). Carlisle, WA: Hesperian Press.

Morris, B. 1989. *Domesticating Resistance: The Dhan-Gadi Aborigines and the Australian state*. Oxford: Berg.

Moss, P. and Kershaw, A.P. 2000. The last glacial cycle from the humid tropics of northeastern Australia: Comparison of a terrestrial and a marine record. *Palaeogeography, Palaeoclimatology, Palaeoecology* 155:155–176.

Moss, P. and Kershaw, A.P. 2007. A late Quaternary marine palynological record (Oxygen isotope stages 1–7) for the humid tropics of northeastern Australia based on ODP Site 820. *Palaeogeography, Palaeoclimatology, Palaeoecology* 251:4–22.

Mulligan, J. 1876 *The Queenslander,* 3 June 1876, Letter to the Editor.

Mulligan, J.V. 1877. Expedition in search of gold and other minerals in the Palmer districts, by Mulligan and party. *Votes and Proceedings of the Legislative Assembly* 3:395–417. Brisbane.

Mulligan, J. 1885a *The Queenslander,* 28 March 1885, Letter to the Editor.

Mulligan, J. 1885b *The Queenslander,* 4 April 1885, Letter to the Editor.

Mulligan, J. 1885c *The Queenslander,* 15 April 1885, Letter to the Editor.

Mulvaney, D.J. and Kamminga, J. 1999. *Prehistory of Australia*. St Leonards, NSW: Allen & Unwin.

Munsell Color, 1975. Munsell Color (Firm), Baltimore, MD.

Murray, T. 1996. Creating a post-Mabo archaeology of Australia. In B. Attwood (ed.), *In the Age of Mabo: History, Aborigines and Australia*, pp.73–87, St Leonards, NSW: Allen & Unwin.

Murray, T. 1996a. Contact archaeology: Shared histories? Shared identities? In S. Hunt and J. Lydon (eds), *Sites: Nailing the Debate: archaeology and interpretation in museums*, pp.200–213, Sydney: Historic Houses Trust of New South Wales.

Murray, T. 2000. 'Digging with documents': Understanding intention and outcome in northwest Tasmania 1825–1835. In A. Anderson and T. Murray (eds), *Australian Archaeologist. Collected Papers in Honour of Jim Allen*, pp.145–160, Canberra: Coombs Academic Publishing.

Murray, T. 2002. Epilogue: An archaeology of indigenous/non-indigenous Australia from 1788. In R. Harrison and C. Williamson (eds), *After Captain Cook: The archaeology of the recent Indigenous past in Australia*, Sydney University Archaeological Methods Series 8, pp.214–223, Sydney, NSW: Archaeological Computing Laboratory, University of Sydney.

Murray, T. 2004. The archaeology of contact in settler societies. In T. Murray (ed.), *The Archaeology of Contact in Settler Societies*, pp.1–16. Cambridge: Cambridge University Press.

Nix, H.A. 1991. Biogeography: Patterns and process. In H.A. Nix and M.A. Switzer (eds), *Rainforest Animals: Atlas of vertebrates endemic to Australia's wet tropics*. Kowari 1. Canberra: Australian National Parks and Wildlife Service.

North Cedar Creek Settlers Group, 1908. Minutes of meetings between first settlers at Cedar Creek, John Oxley Library, Box 8617, Brisbane.

Nott, J., Thomas, M.F. and Price, D.M. 2001. Alluvial fans, landslides and Late Quaternary climatic change in the wet tropics of northeast Queensland. *Australian Journal of Earth Sciences* 48(6):875–882.

O'Connor, S. 1992. The timing and nature of prehistoric island use in northern Australia. *Archaeology in Oceania* 27:49–60.

Palmerston, C. 1883. From Mourilyan Harbour to Herberton. *The Queenslander* September 22, 1883 pp.477–588.

Palmerston, C. 1885-1886. From Herberton to the Barron Falls, North Queensland. *Transactions and Proceedings of the Royal Geographic Society of Australia* 4: 231–44.

Palmerston, C. 1887. The diary of a northern pioneer. *The Queensland Figaro,* February 12, 1887, 265–266, 291, 346, 351, 385, 443, 467, 491, 545–546, 596, 651.

Parry, W.J. and Kelly, R.L. 1987. Expedient core technology and sedentism. In J.K. Johnson and C.A. Morrow (eds), *The Organization of Core Technology*, pp.285–304. Boulder, CO: Westview Press.

Paterson, A. 2008. *The Lost Legions: Culture Contact in Colonial Australia*. Lanham, MD: Altamira Press.

Pedley, H. 1992. *Aboriginal Life in the Rainforest: by the Aboriginal people of Jumbun*. Brisbane, QLD: Department of Education, Queensland.

Pedley, H. 1993. Plant detoxification in the rainforest: The processing of poisonous plant foods by the Jirrbal-Girramay people. Unpublished MA thesis, Material Culture Unit, James Cook University, Townsville.

Pentecost, P. and Milne, S. 1994. Relocation of Aboriginal rainforest walking tracks and cultural sites on Girramay tribal lands, North Queensland. Unpublished report to Camu and Jumbun Aboriginal Communities, the Wet Tropics Management Authority and the Aboriginal and Torres Strait Islander Commission.

Philips, J. Gumbulumba, n.d. What you'd like to know about Ravenshoe. Ravenshoe, QLD: The Ravenshoe Writer's Club.

Police Department, Nigger Creek Station 1898. Letter book 1898–1904, file A/38047, 7.7.1898 [44]. Ravenshoe Historical Society.

Police Department, Herberton Station 1914. Letter book 1913–1915, file A/38015, 30.12.1914. Ravenshoe Historical Society.

Porter, J. 2003. Blackfellows Waterhole. The Study of an Aboriginal contact period site in Western Victoria. Unpublished Honours thesis, La Trobe University, Bundoora.

Ravenshoe Writer's Group 1999. What you would like to know about Ravenshoe. Ravenshoe: Ravenshoe Historical Society.

Reynolds, H. 1972. *Aborigines and Settlers*. Stanmore, NSW: Cassell.

Reynolds, H. 1990. *The Other Side of the Frontier: Aboriginal resistance to the European invasion of Australia*. Ringwood, VIC: Penguin.

Rhodes, D. 1986. The Lake Condah Aboriginal mission dormitory: An archaeological and historical investigation. Unpublished MA thesis, La Trobe University, Bundoora.

Riches, L. 2002. Legislating the past: Native title and the history of Aboriginal Australia. In R. Harrison and C. Williamson (eds), *After Captain Cook: The archaeology of the recent Indigenous past in Australia*, Sydney University Archaeological Methods Series 8, pp.105–115, Sydney, NSW: Archaeological Computing Laboratory, University of Sydney.

Ritchie, R. 1989. *Seeing the Rainforests in Nineteenth Century Australia*. Paddington, NSW: Rainforest Publishing.

Rogers, J.D. and Wilson, S.M. (eds) 1993. *Ethnohistory and Archaeology: Approaches to postcontact change in the Americas*. New York: Plenum Press.

Ross, A. 1981. Holocene environments and prehistoric site patterning in the Victorian Mallee. *Archaeology in Oceania* 16:145–155.

Roth, W.E. 1898. Some ethnological notes on the Atherton Blacks. Scientific report to the under secretary, Brisbane.

Roth, W.E. 1900. On the natives of the (lower) Tully River. Scientific report to the under secretary, Brisbane.

Roth, W.E. 1901–10. *North Queensland ethnography*, Bulletins 1–8. Brisbane: Department of Home Secretary, Queensland.

Rowland, M. 1999. Holocene environmental variability: Have its impacts been underestimated in Australian pre-History? *The Artefact* 22:11–48.

Savage, P. 1989. *Christie Palmerston, Explorer*. Townsville: Department of History and Politics, James Cook University.

Smith, A. (ed.), 2001. *Red Gold to Ravenshoe*. Ravenshoe: Ravenshoe Historical Society.

Smith, M. 1993. Biogeography, human ecology and prehistory in the sandridge deserts. *Archaeology in Oceania* 37:35–50.

Stevens, J. 2004. Instruments of a thousand uses: A comparative study of edge-ground axe assemblages from tropical rainforest environments in far north Queensland. Unpublished Honours thesis, Archaeology Program, La Trobe University, Bundoora.

Svenskt Biografiskt Lexikon, 1984. Stockholm: Svenska Vetenskaps-akademin.

Taçon, P.S.C., South, B. and Hopper, S.B. 2003. Depicting cross-cultural interaction: Figurative designs in wood, earth, and stone from south-east Australia. *Archaeology in Oceania* 38(2):89–102.

The Moreton Bay Courier 1849. The late Mr Kennedy Expedition. Brisbane, Qld. Saturday 31 March 1849:4. Available from: trove.nla.gov.au./ndp/del/article/3711172?searchTerm=%22Edmund%20Kennedy%22.

Tibby, J. and Haberle, S. 2007. A late glacial to present diatom record from Lake Euramoo, wet tropics of Queensland, Australia. *Palaeogeography, Palaeoclimatology, Palaeoecology* 251:46–56.

Tindale, N.B. 1974. *Aboriginal Tribes of Australia*. Berkeley: University of California Press.

Tindale, N. and Birdsell, J.B. 1941. Results of the Harvard-Adelaide Universities Anthropological Expedition, 1938–1939: Tasmanoid Tribes in North Queensland. *Records of the South Australian Museum* 7:1–9.

Toohey, E. 2001. *From Bullock Team to Puffing Billy: The settling of the Atherton Tableland and its Hinterland*. Rockhampton: Central Queensland University Press.

Torrence, R. and Clarke, A. (eds), 2000. *The Archaeology of Difference: Negotiating cross-cultural engagement in Oceania*. London: Routledge.

Tracey, J.G. 1982. *The Vegetation of the Humid Tropical Region of North Queensland*. Melbourne: CSIRO.

Tracey, J.G. and Webb, L.J. 1975. *Vegetation of the Humid Tropical Region of North Queensland*. Melbourne: CSIRO.

Traveller's Club, 1912. *Årsbok för*. Stockholm: Nyman & Schultz Bokförlag.

Trigger, B. 1983. American archaeology as native history: A review essay. *William and Mary Quarterly* 40:413–452.

Troy, J. 1993. *King Plates: A history of Aboriginal gorgets*. Canberra: Aboriginal Studies Press.

Tuechler, A. 2010. Toxic plant food processing in north-east Queensland's rainforest region. A study in cost-benefit ratio. Unpublished Honours thesis, Archaeology Program, La Trobe University, Bundoora.

Tuechler, A., Ferrier, Å. and Cosgrove, R. 2014. Transforming the inedible to the edible: An analysis of the nutritional returns from Aboriginal nut processing in Queensland's Wet Tropics. *Australian Archaeology* 79:26–33.

Tully, E. 1881. Report to the Undersecretary for Lands, Legislative assembly, WA.

Turney, C.S.M. and Hobbs, D.R. 2006. ENSO influence on Holocene Aboriginal populations in Queensland, Australia. *Journal of Archaeological Science* 33:1744–1748.

Turney, C.S.M., Kershaw, A.P., Moss, P., Bird, M.I., Fifield, L.K., Cresswell, R.G., Santos, G.M., di Tada, M.L., Hausladen, P.A. and Zhou, Y. 2001. Redating the onset of burning at Lynch's Crater (North Queensland): Implications for human settlement in Australia. *Journal of Quaternary Science* 16(8):767–771.

Ulm, S. 2004. Themes in the archaeology of mid-to-late Holocene Australia. In T Murray (ed.), *Archaeology from Australia*, pp.187–201, Melbourne: Australian Scholarly Publishing.

Ulm, S. and Hall, J. 1996. Radiocarbon and cultural chronologies in southeast Queensland prehistory. In S. Ulm, I. Lilley and A. Ross (eds), *Australian Archaeology '95: Proceedings of the 1995 Australian Archaeological Association Annual Conference*, Tempus 6, pp.45–62, St Lucia, QLD: Anthropology Museum, University of Queensland.

Veres, M.S. 2010. Colonial Footprints: An archaeological Analysis of Leather Footwear from Colonial Australia. Unpublished PhD thesis, La Trobe University, Melbourne.

Veth, P. 1995. Marginal returns and fringe benefits: Characterising the prehistory of the lowland deserts of Australia (A reply to Smith). *Australian Archaeology* 40:32–38.

Veth, P. 1996. *Islands in the Interior: The Dynamics of Prehistoric Adaptations within the Arid Zone of Australia.* Archaeological Series 3. Ann Arbor, MICH: International Monographs in Prehistory.

Veth, P. 2000. The contemporary voice of archaeology and its relevance to native title. In I. Lilley (ed.) *Native title and the Transformation of Archaeology in the Postcolonial World*, Oceania Monograph 50, pp.78–87, Sydney: University of Sydney.

Walker, M., Johnsen, S., Olander Rasmussen, Sune., Popp, T., Steffensen, J-P., Gibbard, P., Hoek, W., Lowe, J., Andrews, J., Björck, S., Cwynar L.C., Hughen, K., Kershaw, P., Kromer, B., Litt, T., Lowe, D.J., Nakagawa, T., Newnham, R. and Schwander, J. 2009. Formal definition and dating of the GSSP (Global Stratotype Section and Point) for the base of the Holocene using the Greenland NGRIP ice core, and selected auxiliary records. *Journal of Quaternary Science* 24(1):3–17.

Webb, L.J. 1959. A physiognomic classification of Australian rainforests. *Journal of Ecology* 47:551–570.

Wet Tropics 2012. Queensland Government Department of National Parks, Sport, and Racing. Available from:
www.nprsr.qld.gov.au/world-heritage-areas/wet-tropics/ [14 May 2012].

Wet Tropics Management Authority (nd). National Heritage Listing. The National Heritage List, Cultural Values. Available from: www.wettropics.gov.au/national-heritage-listing.

White, P. 1968. Fabricators, outilsècaillès or scalar cores? *Mankind* 6:658–666.

Williams, A.N. 2013. A new population curve for prehistoric Australia. *Proceedings of the Royal Society B: Biological Sciences* 280, 20130486.

Williamson, C. 1998. Late Holocene Australia and the writing of Aboriginal history. In T. Murray (ed.), *Archaeology of Aboriginal Australia: A reader*, pp.141–148. St Leonards, NSW: Allen & Unwin.

Williamson, C. 2002. Finding meaning in the patterns: The analysis of material culture from a contact site in Tasmania. In R. Harrison and C. Williamson (eds), *After Captain Cook: The archaeology of the recent Indigenous past in Australia*, pp.75–104, Sydney University Archaeological Methods Series 8. Sydney, NSW: Archaeological Computing Laboratory, University of Sydney.

Williamson, C. 2004. Contact archaeology and Aboriginal history. In T. Murray (ed.), *The Archaeology of Contact in Settler Societies*, pp.176–200. Cambridge: Cambridge University Press.

Witter, D. 1992. Regions and Resources. Unpublished PhD thesis, Department of Prehistory, Research School of Pacific Studies, The Australian National University, Canberra.

Wolski, N. 2000. Brushing against the grain: Excavating for Aboriginal-European interaction on the colonial frontier in Western Victoria, Australia. Unpublished PhD thesis, The University of Melbourne, Melbourne.

Wolski, N. and Loy, T.H. 1999. On the invisibility of contact: Residue analyses on Aboriginal glass artefacts from western Victoria. *The Artefact* 22:65–73.

Woolston, F.P. and Colliver F.S. 1973. Some Stone Artifacts from North Queensland Rain Forests. Melbourne: Melbourne Museum.

Wright, R.V.S. 1971. *Prehistory in the Cape York Peninsula*. Canberra: Australian National University Press.